Tad Michael Malpass
April 21, 1991

Dave Barry's GREATEST HITS

Dave Barry's GREATEST HITS

CROWN PUBLISHERS, INC., NEW YORK

Individual columns in this book first appeared in the *Miami Herald* and are used with permission of the *Miami Herald.*

Publisher's Note: Many of the products and services mentioned in these pieces are trademarks of their respective companies. Every effort has been made to identify these trademarks by initial capitalization. Should there be an omission in this respect, we shall be pleased to make the necessary corrections in future printings.

Published by Crown Publishers, Inc.,
225 Park Avenue South, New York, New York 10003
and represented in Canada by the Canadian MANDA Group

CROWN is a trademark of Crown Publishers, Inc.

Manufactured in the United States of America

Library of Congress Cataloging-in-Publication Data

Barry, Dave.
  Dave Barry's greatest hits.
  I. Title.
PN4874.B328A25 1988   814'.54   88-3822
ISBN 0-517-56944-2

10 9 8 7 6 5 4 3 2 1
First Edition

TO
BETH & GENE

CONTENTS

Dave Barry's GREATEST HITS

WHY HUMOR IS FUNNY

AS A PROFESSIONAL HUMORIST, I OFTEN GET LET-
ters from readers who are interested in the basic nature of
humor. "What kind of a sick, perverted, disgusting person
are you," these letters typically ask, "that you make jokes
about setting fire to a goat?"

And that, of course, is the wonderful thing about
humor. What may seem depressing or even tragic to one
person may seem like an absolute scream to another person,
especially if he has had between four and seven beers. But
most people agree on what is funny, and most people like to
be around a person with a great sense of humor, provided
he also has reasonable hygiene habits. This is why people so
often ask me: "Dave, I'd like to be popular, too. How can I
get a sense of humor like yours, only with less of a depen-
dence on jokes that are primarily excuses to use the word
'booger'?"

This is not an easy question. Ever since prehistoric times,
wise men have tried to understand what exactly makes people laugh. That's why they were called wise men. All the
other prehistoric people were out puncturing each other
with spears, and the wise men were back in the cave saying:
"How about: Here's my wife, please take her right now. No.
How about: Would you like to take something? My wife is
available. No. How about . . ."

Mankind didn't develop a logical system of humor until

1

thousands of years later when Aristotle discovered, while shaving, the famous Humor Syllogism, which states, "If A is equal to B, and B is equal to C, then it would not be particularly amusing if the three of them went around poking each other in the eyes and going 'Nyuk nyuk nyuk.' At least *I* don't think it would be."

By the Elizabethan era, humor had become extremely popular. The works of Shakespeare, for example, are filled with scenes that English teachers always claim are real thigh-slappers, although when you actually decode them, it turns out they mostly depend on the use of the Elizabethan word for "booger." In America today, of course, our humor is much more sophisticated, ranging all the way from television shows featuring outtakes of situation comedies where the actors can't get the words right to television shows featuring outtakes of *commercials* where the actors can't get the words right. Also we have Woody Allen, whose humor has become so sophisticated that nobody gets it anymore except Mia Farrow. All those who think Mia Farrow should go back to making movies where the devil gets her pregnant and Woody Allen should go back to dressing up as a human sperm, please raise your hands. Thank you.

If you want to develop a sense of humor of your own, you need to learn some jokes. Notice I do not say "puns." Puns are little "plays on words" that a certain breed of person loves to spring on you and then look at you in a certain self-satisfied way to indicate that he thinks that *you* must think that he is by far the cleverest person on Earth now that Benjamin Franklin is dead, when in fact what you are thinking is that if this person ever ends up in a lifeboat, the other passengers will hurl him overboard by the end of the first day even if they have plenty of food and water.

So what you want is *real* jokes. The best source for these is the authoritative *Encyclopedia Britannica* article entitled "Humor and Wit," which is in volume 99 (Humidity—Ivory Coast). This is where Carson gets all his material. It's a regular treasure trove of fun. Here's a real corker from right at the beginning:

"A masochist is a person who likes a cold shower in the morning, so he takes a hot one."

Whoooeee! That is one authoritative joke! Tell that one at a dull party, and just watch as the other guests suddenly come to life and remember important dental appointments!

But it is not enough merely to know a lot of great jokes. You also have to be able to tell them properly. Here are some tips:

1. When you tell vicious racist jokes, you should first announce that you were a liberal back when it was legal to be one.

2. Men have a certain body part that women do not have, and men always think jokes about it are a stone riot, but if you tell such a joke to a woman, she will look at you as though you are a Baggie filled with mouse remains. I don't know why this is, but it never fails. So you want to avoid this particular type of joke in coeducational social settings such as Windsor Castle.

3. If, after you tell a joke, somebody attempts to tell you one back, you should keep assuring him that you haven't heard it, and then, when he gets to the punchline, no matter how funny it is, you should react as though he just told you the relative humidity and say: "Yeah, I heard that."

4. Never attend a large dinner party with my former mother-in-law, because she will shout across the table at you: "Tell the one about the man who's seeking the truth and he finally gets all the way to Tibet and the wise man tells him that a wet bird doesn't fly at night," and then she'll *insist* that you tell it, and then she'll tell you you told it wrong, and you might have to kill her with a fork.

SNEWS

READERS ARE SOMETIMES CRITICAL OF ME BE-
cause just about everything I write about is an irresponsible
lie. But now I'm going to write a column in which everything
is true. See how you like it.

Our first true item comes from a news release from the
J I Case company. For the benefit of those of you who have
real jobs and are not involved in the news business, I should
first explain that a *news release* is an article that has been typed
up by a public-relations professional hired by a client who
wants to get certain information published, which is then
mailed out to several thousand newspapers, almost all of
which throw it away without reading it. If you ever commit a
really horrible crime and you want to keep it out of the
papers, you should have a public-relations professional issue
a news release about it.

You ask: "Wouldn't it be more efficient if the public-
relations professionals simply threw the releases away themselves?" Frankly, that is the kind of ignorant question that
makes us journalists want to forget about trying to inform
the public and instead just sit around awarding journalism
prizes to each other. But I'll tell you the answer: Because this
is America. Because two hundred years ago, a band of brave
men got extremely cold at Valley Forge so that the press
would have the freedom to throw away its own releases without prior censorship, that's why.

Anyway, this release from the J I Case company opens with this statement: "J I Case and Burlington, Iowa, the loader/backhoe capital of the world, today jointly celebrated the production of the 175,000th Case loader/backhoe." The release said they had a nice ceremony attended by the mayor of Burlington, a person named Wayne W. Hogberg, so I called him up to confirm the story. He works at the post office.

"Does Burlington really call itself the loader/backhoe capital of the world?" I asked. Newsmen are paid to ask the hard questions. "Oh yes," replied Mayor Hogberg. "We definitely lay claim to that. We use it whenever we have the opportunity. As a mayor I sort of rub it in with any other mayors I have occasion to meet." I bet that really steams the other mayors, don't you? I bet they are consumed with jealousy, when mayors get together.

Our second completely true news item was sent to me by Mr. H. Boyce Connell Jr. of Atlanta, Georgia, where he is involved in a law firm. One thing I like about the South is, folks there care about tradition. If somebody gets handed a name like "H. Boyce," he hangs on to it, puts it on his legal stationery, even passes it on to his son, rather than do what a lesser person would do, such as get it changed or kill himself.

What H. Boyce sent was a copy of a decision handed down by the Georgia Court of Appeals in the case of Apostol-Athanasiou vs. White. It seems the former had hired the latter to mow her lawn. What happened next, in the words of the court, is that "White allegedly slipped on some dog feces concealed in the tall grass, and his left foot was severely cut as it slid under the lawnmower." I am not going to tell you how this case came out, because you'll want to find out for yourself in the event that it is released as a major motion picture, but I will say, by way of a hint, that in the court's opinion "neither party had actual knowledge of the specific deposit of dog feces on which White apparently slipped."

Our next item comes from a release sent out by the

Vodka Information Bureau, in New York City. The Vodka Information Bureau has learned that a whopping 42 percent of the women surveyed consider themselves "primary decision makers" in deciding what brand of vodka to buy. This raises in my mind, as I am sure it does in yours, a number of questions, primarily: What, exactly, do we mean by the verb "to whop"? So I looked it up in the *Oxford English Dictionary*, and there I found—remember, this is the column where we are not making things up—these helpful examples:

• "In less time than you can think whop comes a big black thing down, as big as the stone of a cheese-press."

• "Mother would whop me if I came home without the basket."

So I called my mother, who said, and I quote, "I always make the vodka-buying decision as follows: the largest bottle for the smallest amount of money." So I called the Vodka Information Bureau and told them what my mother said, and they said, sure, you can buy the cheapest vodka if you don't mind getting a lot of impurities, but if you want a nice clean vodka, you want a brand such as is manufactured by the company that sponsors the Vodka Information Bureau.

Finally, and sadly, we have received word of the death, at age 85, of Sir Seewoosagur Ramgoolam, who of course was governor general of the island nation of Mauritius from 1968 to 1982. Mauritius has an area of 720 square miles and was once the home of the dodo bird, which is now extinct. It is hard, at a time of such tragedy—I refer to the demise of Sir Seewoosagur Ramgoolam—to find words to express our feelings, but I think that I speak for all of us when I say that a cheese-press is "an apparatus for pressing the curds in cheese-making."

PUBLIC-SPIRITED CITIZENS SUCH AS YOU

I LOVE JOKES. THE WORSE THE BETTER. AMONG the happiest moments of my life were those at summer camp when I was 11, lying in my bunk at night just after the counselor, Mr. Newton, had gone off to play cards with the other counselors, which meant that Eugene was going to tell the joke whose punchline is: "Ding dong, dammit! Ding DONG!" Maybe you know this joke. It involves marital infidelity and a closet. By the second week of camp, Eugene had developed a half-hour version, and campers were creeping over from the other cabins to hear it.

So there we'd all be, listening in the dark with lunatic grins of anticipation on our faces, barely able to restrain ourselves, until finally Eugene would reach the punchline. "Ding dong, dammit," he'd say, and we'd start vibrating like tuning forks, and then Eugene would say "Ding DONG," and we'd dive down into the depths of our sleeping bags, out of control, howling and snorting, thinking nobody could hear us, although of course in the peaceful stillness of the forest night we must have sounded like water buffalo giving birth over a public-address system.

Mr. Newton would slam his cards down and come storming over, and he'd tell us that he was really sick of this, night after night, and if he heard one more sound out of us we'd have to clean the latrine the next day. This was a serious threat, because it was the kind of highly odorous summer-

7

camp latrine where you wondered how it could possibly be so disgusting when nobody ever had the courage to use it. Evidently somewhere along the line it had reached Critical Latrine Mass and developed a life-style of its own.

After making this threat, Mr. Newton would stalk off back to his cards, and there would be silence for maybe a minute, and then there would be this tiny whisper from Eugene's direction, so faint that only a trained ear could discern it:

"Ding," said the whisper, "DONG."

And of course this resulted in a situation where, never mind having to clean the latrine, never mind that Mr. Newton was now standing in the middle of the cabin clutching a weighty flashlight and threatening to break everybody's heads, the only thing any of us could think about was whether we would ever be able to draw breath again.

And so we had a terrific summer, and all because of one idiot joke, which, although I would not tell it in public except under the influence of sodium pentothal, still does a better job of cheering me up than any major religion. I'd like to meet the person who made that joke up, but of course that's always one of the big mysteries about jokes: Nobody knows who makes them up. They're just *there*, floating around and lowering the productivity of offices and factories everywhere. And they've been there throughout human history. Archaeologists found this joke in an Egyptian tomb:

HE: Did you hear about the Sumerian?

SHE: No. What about the Sumerian?

HE: He was extremely stupid. Ha ha!

SHE: No, I had not heard about him.

This, of course, is a primitive version of the modern "ethnic joke," which still carries the same basic message, although it has become much more sophisticated over the years thanks to the introduction of such innovations as the light bulb. But who introduced them?

Other mysteries about jokes are: How come you can

remember extremely complex jokes involving a minister, a priest, and a rabbi, but you can't remember your mother's birthday? How do jokes travel so fast, and so far? (The Apollo 7 astronauts found traces of a joke on the moon!) Also: Does Queen Elizabeth ever hear any jokes? Who tells them to her? What about the pope?

To answer these and other questions, I think we should set up a research project wherein we scientifically track the progress of a specified joke, similar to the way the flight patterns of birds are tracked by scientists called ornithologists, who attach metal wires and rubber bands to the birds' beaks and make them come back every week for appointments. No! Hold it! My mistake! I'm thinking of "orthodontists." What ornithologists do is attach bands of metal to a bird's leg, then toss it gently off the roof of a tall building and watch it splat into the pavement below at upwards of 100 miles an hour. People try to tell the ornithologists that the metal bands they're using are too heavy, but they just laugh. Recently they dropped a common wood warbler to which they had attached a 1983 Chevette.

But the theory is sound, and I was thinking maybe we could come up with some kind of similar system for tracking a joke. What I propose to do is inject a brand-new joke into the population at certain known places and times. This joke will have a distinguishing characteristic, so that as it spreads around the country, public-spirited citizens such as yourself can act as spotters. As soon as you hear this joke, I want you to report it via postal card to: The Joke Tracking Center, P.O. Box 011509, Miami, FL 33101.

Please include a summary of the joke, where and when you heard it, who told it to you, and any other helpful background information such as whether you were drinking liquor right out of the bottle at the time.

Obviously, I cannot reveal the joke here, but its distinguishing characteristic is that it answers the question: "Why is Walter Mondale nicknamed 'Fritz'?" Everybody got that? I have tested this joke on a carefully selected panel of lowlifes, all sworn to secrecy, and they assure me that it is in very poor taste and should spread like wildfire.

So let's all Simonize our watches and keep a sharp ear out for this joke. I'm very serious about this. Trained personnel are standing by now at the Joke Tracking Center. So report those sightings! Together, we have a chance here to obtain scientific findings of great significance, and possibly a large federal grant. Remember: This chain has never been broken.

THE SNAKE

THE WAY I PICTURE IT, ADULTHOOD IS A BIG, sleek jungle snake, swimming just around the bend in the River of Life. It swallows you subtly, an inch at a time, so you barely notice the signs: You start reading the labels on things *before* you eat them, rather than to pass the time *while* you eat them; you find yourself listening to talk radio because the hit songs they play on the rock stations (can this really be *you*, thinking this?) all begin to *sound the same.* Before you know it, you have monogrammed towels in your bathroom, and all your furniture is nice. And suddenly you realize it's too late, that you'd rather sit around on your furniture and talk about the warning signs of colon cancer with other grown-ups than, for example, find out what happens when you set one of those plastic milk jugs on fire. And if your *kid* sets a milk jug on fire, you yell at him, "Somebody could get *hurt*," and really mean it, from inside the snake.

I mention all this to explain how I came to buy, at age 38, an electric guitar. I had one once before, from 1965 through 1969 when I was in college. It was a Fender Jazz-master, and I played lead guitar in a band called The Federal Duck, which is the kind of name that was popular in the sixties as a result of controlled substances being in wide-spread use. Back then, there were no restrictions, in terms of talent, on who could make an album, so we made one, and it sounds like a group of people who have been given powerful but unfamiliar instruments as a therapy for a degenerative nerve disease.

We mainly played songs like "Gloria," which was great for sixties bands, because it had only three chords; it had a solo that was so simple it could be learned in minutes, even by a nonmusical person or an advanced fish; and it had great lyrics.

My band career ended late in my senior year when John Cooper and I threw my amplifier out the dormitory window. We did not act in haste. First we checked to make sure the amplifier would fit through the frame, using the belt from my bathrobe to measure, then we picked up the amplifier and backed up to my bedroom door. Then we rushed forward shouting "The WHO! The WHO!" and we launched my amplifier perfectly, as though we had been doing it all our lives, clean through the window and down onto the sidewalk, where a small but appreciative crowd had gathered. I would like to be able to say that this was a symbolic act, an effort on my part to break cleanly away from one stage in my life and move on to another, but the truth is, Cooper and I really just wanted to find out what it would sound like. It sounded OK.

Unlike The Who, I couldn't afford a new amplifier, and playing an unamplified electric guitar is like strumming on a picnic table, so I sold my Jazzmaster and got a cheap acoustic guitar, which I diddled around on for 16 years. It was fine for "Kum By Yah," but ill-suited for "My Baby Does the Hanky Panky." So there's been this void in my life, which I've tried to fill by having a career, but I see now I was kidding myself.

So recently, *Ms* magazine sent me a check for $800 for an article I wrote about sex. This seemed like such a bizarre way to get hold of $800 that I figured I should do something special with it, so I thought about it, and what came to mind is—this is the scary part of the story, coming up now—*a new sofa*. Our primary living-room sofa looks like a buffalo that has been dead for some time, and I thought: "Maybe we should get a nicer sofa." Which is when I felt the snake of adulthood slithering around my leg.

So I said to my wife: "I am going to take this money and buy an electric guitar." And she said—I believe I married her in anticipation of this moment—"Fine."

I have never been so happy. My amplifier has a knob called overdrive, which, if you turn it all the way up to 10, makes it so that all you have to do is touch a string to make a noise that would destroy a greenhouse. My wife and son and dog spend more time back in the bedroom these days. Out in the living room, I put the Paul Butterfield Blues Band on the stereo, and when they do "Got My Mojo Workin'," I play the guitar solo at the same time Mike Bloomfield does. I am not as accurate as he is in terms of hitting the desired notes, but you can hear me better because I have "overdrive."

I bet I know what you're thinking: You're thinking my electric guitar is a Midlife Crisis Object that I bought in the Midlife Crisis Store filled with middle-aged guys who wear jogging shoes and claim they love Bruce Springsteen but really think he's merely adequate. And you may be right. I don't care if you are. To me, my guitar is a wonderful thing. It's a Gibson, with the classic old electric-guitar shape. It looks like a modernistic oar, which you could use, in a pinch, to row against the current in the River of Life, or at least stay even with it for a while.

WE NEED TO DO SOMETHING ABOUT THIS NA-
tional tendency to try to make new things look like they are
old.

First off, we should enact an "e" tax. Government agents
would roam the country looking for stores whose names contained any word that ended in an unnecessary "e," such as
"shoppe" or "olde," and the owners of these stores would be
taxed at a flat rate of $50,000 per year per "e." We should
also consider an additional $50,000 "ye" tax, so that the
owner of a store called "Ye Olde Shoppe" would have to fork
over $150,000 a year. In extreme cases, such as "Ye Olde
Barne Shoppe," the owner would simply be taken outside
and shot.

We also need some kind of law about the number of
inappropriate objects you can hang on walls in restaurants. I
am especially concerned here about the restaurants that have
sprung up in shopping complexes everywhere to provide
young urban professionals with a place to go for margaritas
and potato skins. You know the restaurants I mean: they
always have names like Flanagan's, Hanrahan's, O'Toole's,
or O'Reilley's, as if the owner were a genial red-faced Irish
bartender, when in fact it is probably 14 absentee proctologists in need of tax shelter.

You have probably noticed that inevitably the walls in
these places are covered with objects we do not ordinarily

attach to walls, such as barber poles, traffic lights, washboards, street signs, and farm implements. This decor scheme is presumably intended to create an atmosphere of relaxed old-fashioned funkiness, but in fact it creates an atmosphere of great weirdness. It is as if a young urban professional with telekinetic powers, the kind Sissy Spacek exhibited in the movie *Carrie,* got really tanked up on margaritas one night and decided to embed an entire flea market in the wall.

I think it's too much. I think we need to pass a law stating that the only objects that may be hung on restaurant walls are those that God intended to be hung on restaurant walls, such as pictures, mirrors, and the heads of deceased animals. Any restaurant caught violating this law would have to get rid of its phony Irish-bartender name and adopt a name that clearly reflected its actual ownership. ("Say, let's go get some potato skins at Fourteen Absentee Proctologists in Need of Tax Shelter.")

And I suppose it goes without saying that anybody caught manufacturing "collectible" plates, mugs, or figurines of any kind should be shipped directly to Devil's Island.

Now I know what you're thinking. You're thinking: "Dave, I hear what you're saying, but wouldn't laws such as these constitute unwarranted government interference in the private sector?"

The answer is: Yes, they would. But unwarranted government interference in the private sector is a small price to pay if it draws the government away from its efforts to revitalize decaying urban areas. The government inevitably tries to do this by installing 60 billion new red bricks and several dozen vaguely old-fashioned streetlights in an effort to create a look I would call "Sort of Colonial or Something."

The government did this to a town right near where I used to live, West Chester, Pennsylvania. This is a nice little old town, with a lot of nice little old houses, but about 10 years ago some of the downtown merchants started getting really upset because they were losing business to the "shopping malls," a phrase the merchants always say in the same tone of voice you might use to say "Nazi Germany." Now, as a consumer, I would argue that the reason most of us were going to the shopping malls was that the downtown stores tended to have window displays that had not been changed since the Truman administration, featuring crepe paper faded to the color of old oatmeal, accented by the occasional dead insect. And the actual merchandise in these stores was not the kind you would go out of your way to purchase or even accept as gifts. We are talking, for example, about clothing so dowdy that it could not be used even to clean up after a pet.

What I am saying is that the problem with the downtown West Chester stores, from this consumer's point of view, was that they didn't have much that anybody would want to buy. From the merchants' point of view, however, the problem was that the entire downtown needed to be Revitalized, and they nagged the local government for years until finally it applied for a federal grant of God knows how many million dollars, which was used to rip up the streets for several years, so as to discourage the few remaining West Chester shoppers. When they finally got it all together again, the new revitalized West Chester consisted of mostly the same old stores, only in front of them were (surprise!) red brick sidewalks garnished with vaguely old-fashioned streetlights. The whole effect was definitely Sort Of Colonial or Something, and some shoppers even stopped by to take a look at it on their way to the mall.

I gather this process has been repeated in a great many towns around the country, and it seems to me that it's a tremendous waste of federal time and effort that could otherwise be spent getting rid of the extra "e." I urge those of you who agree with me to write letters to your congresspersons, unless you use that stationery with the "old-fashioned" ragged edges, in which case I urge you to go to your local Flanagan's and impale yourself on one of the farm implements.

A BOY AND HIS HOBBY

RECENTLY, I BEGAN TO FEEL THIS VOID IN MY life, even after meals, and I said to myself: "Dave, all you do with your spare time is sit around and drink beer. You need a hobby." So I got a hobby. I make beer.

I never could get into the traditional hobbies, like religion or stamp collecting. I mean, the way you collect stamps is: Every week or so the Postal Service dreams up a new stamp to mark National Peat Bog Awareness Month, or whatever, and you rush down and clog the Post Office lines to buy a batch of these stamps, but instead of putting them to a useful purpose such as mailing toxic spiders to the Publisher's Clearing House, you take them home and just sort of *have* them. Am I right? Have I left any moments of drama out of this action sequence? And then the *biggest* thrill, as I understand it, the real *payoff*, comes when you get lucky and collect a stamp on which the Postal Service has made a *mistake*, such as instead of "Peat Bog" it prints "Beat Pog," which causes stamp collectors to just about wet their polyester pants, right?

So for many years I had no hobby. When I would fill out questionnaires and they would ask what my hobbies were, I would put "narcotics," which was of course a totally false humorous joke. And then one day my editor took me to a store where they sell beer-making equipment. Other writers, they have editors who inspire them to new heights

17

of literary achievement, but the two major contributions my editor has made to my artistic development are (1) teaching me to juggle and (2) taking me to his beer-making store where a person named Craig gave me free samples until he could get hold of my Visa card.

But I'm glad I got into beer-making, because the beer sold here in the United States is sweet and watery and lacking in taste and overcarbonated and just generally the lamest, wimpiest beer in the entire known world. All the other nations are drinking Ray Charles beer, and we are drinking Barry Manilow. This is why American TV beer commercials are so ludicrously masculine. It's a classic case of overcompensation. You may have seen, for example, the Budweiser or Miller commercial where some big hairy men are standing around on the side of a river when a barge breaks loose and starts drifting out of control. Now *real* men, men who drink *real* beer, would have enough confidence in their own masculinity to say: "Don't worry; it's probably insured."

But the men in the commercial feel this compulsion to go racing off on a tugboat and capture the barge with big hairy ropes, after which they make excited masculine hand gestures at each other to indicate they have done a task requiring absolute *gallons* of testosterone. Then they go to a bar where they drink Miller or Budweiser and continue to reassure themselves that they are truly a collection of major stud horses, which is why you don't see any women around. The women have grown weary of listening to the men say: "Hey! We sure rescued THAT barge, didn't we?!" And: "You think it's easy, to rescue a barge? Well, it's NOT!" and, much later at night: "Hey! Let's go let the barge loose again!" So the women have all gone off in search of men who make their own beer.

Some of you may be reluctant to make your own beer because you've heard stories to the effect that it's difficult to make, or it's illegal, or it makes you go blind. Let me assure you that these are falsehoods, especially the part about making you go bleof nisdc dsdf,sdfkQ$$%"%.

18

Ha ha! Just a little tasteless humor there, designed to elicit angry letters from liberals. The truth is, homemade beer is perfectly safe, unless the bottle explodes. We'll have more on that if space permits. Also it's completely legal to make beer at home. In fact, as I read the current federal tax laws—I use a strobe light—if you make your own beer, you can take a tax credit of up to $4,000, provided you claim you spent it on insulation!

And it's very easy to make your own beer: You just mix your ingredients and stride briskly away. (You may of course vary this recipe to suit your own personal taste.) Your two main ingredients are (1) a can of beer ingredients that you get from Craig or an equivalent person, and (2) yeast. Yeast is a wonderful little plant or animal that, despite the fact that it has only one cell, has figured out how to convert sugar to alcohol. This was a far greater accomplishment than anything we can attribute to giant complex multicelled organisms such as, for example, the Secretary of Transportation.

After the little yeasts are done converting your ingredients into beer, they die horrible deaths by the millions. You shouldn't feel bad about this. Bear in mind this is *yeast* we're talking about, and there's plenty more available, out on the enormous yeast ranches of the Southwest. For now, your job is to siphon your beer into bottles. This is the tricky part, because what can happen is the phone rings and you get involved in a lengthy conversation during which your son, who is 4½, gets hold of the hose and spews premature beer, called "wort," all over the kitchen and himself, and you become the target of an investigation by child welfare authorities because yours is the only child who comes to preschool smelling like a fraternity carpet.

But that's the only real drawback I have found, and the beer tastes delicious, except of course on those rare occasions when it explodes. Which leads us to another advantage: If you make your own beer, you no longer need to worry about running out if we have a nuclear war of sufficient severity to close the commercial breweries.

DAZE OF WINE AND ROSES

I HAVE NEVER GOTTEN INTO WINE. I'M A BEER man. What I like about beer is you basically just drink it, then you order another one. You don't sniff at it, or hold it up to the light and slosh it around, and above all you don't drone on and on about it, the way people do with wine. Your beer drinker tends to be a straightforward, decent, friendly, down-to-earth person who enjoys talking about the importance of relief pitching, whereas your serious wine fancier tends to be an insufferable snot.

I realize I am generalizing here, but, as is often the case when I generalize, I don't care.

Nevertheless, I decided recently to try to learn more about the wine community. Specifically, I engaged the services of a rental tuxedo and attended the Grand Finale of the First Annual French Wine Sommelier Contest in America, which was held at the famous Waldorf-Astoria hotel in New York. For the benefit of those of you with plastic slip-covers, I should explain that a "sommelier" is a wine steward, the dignified person who comes up to you at expensive restaurants, hands you the wine list, and says "Excellent choice, sir," when you point to French writing that, translated, says "Sales Tax Included."

Several hundred wine-oriented people were on hand for the sommelier competition. First we mingled and drank champagne, then we sat down to eat dinner and watch the competition. I found it immensely entertaining, especially after the champagne, because for one thing many of the speakers were actual French persons who spoke with comical accents, which I suspect they practiced in their hotel rooms ("Zees epeetomizes zee hrole av zee sommelier sroo-out eestory . . . ," etc.) Also we in the audience got to drink just gallons of wine. At least I did. My policy with wine is very similar to my policy with beer, which is just pretty much drink it and look around for more. The people at my table, on the other hand, leaned more toward the slosh-and-sniff approach, where you don't so much *drink* the wine as you frown and then make a thoughtful remark about it such as you might make about a job applicant ("I find it ambitious, but somewhat strident." Or: "It's lucid, yes, but almost Episcopalian in its predictability.") As it happened, I was sitting next to a French person named Mary, and I asked her if people in France carry on this way about wine. "No," she said, "they just drink it. They're more used to it."

There were 12 sommeliers from around the country in the contest; they got there by winning regional competitions, and earlier in the day they had taken a written exam with questions like: "Which of the following appellations belong to the Savoie region? (a) Crepy; (b) Seyssel; (c) Arbois; (d) Etoile; (e) Ripple." (I'm just kidding about the Ripple, of course. The Savoie region would not use Ripple as an insecticide.)

The first event of the evening competition was a blind tasting, where the sommeliers had to identify a mystery wine. We in the audience got to try it, too. It was a wine that I would describe as yellow in color, and everybody at my table agreed it was awful. "Much too woody," said one person. "Heavily oxidized," said another. "Bat urine," I offered. The others felt this was a tad harsh. I was the only one who finished my glass.

Next we got a nonmystery wine, red in color, with a French name, and I thought it was swell, gulped it right down, but one of the wine writers at my table got upset

because it was a 1979, and the program said we were supposed to get a 1978. If you can imagine. So we got some
1978, and it was swell, too. "They're both credible," said the
wine writer, "but there's a great difference in character." I
was the only one who laughed, although I think Mary sort of
wanted to.

The highlight of the evening was the Harmony of Wine
and Food event, where the sommelier contestants were given
a menu where the actual nature of the food was disguised
via French words ("Crochets sur le Pont en Voiture," etc.),
and they had to select a wine for each of the five courses.
This is where a sommelier has to be really good, because if
he is going to talk an actual paying customer into spending
as much money on wine for one meal as it would cost to
purchase a half-dozen state legislators for a year, he has to
say something more than, "A lotta people like this here char-
donnay."

Well, these sommeliers were good. They were *into* the
Harmony of Wine and Food, and they expressesd firm views.
They would say things like: "I felt the (name of French wine)
would have the richness to deal with the foie gras," or "My
feeling about Roquefort is that. . . ." I thought it was fabu-
lous entertainment, and at least two people at my table asked
how I came to be invited.

Anyway, as the Harmony event dragged on, a major
issue developed concerning the salad. The salad was Lamb's-
Lettuce with—you are going to be shocked when I tell you
this—Walnut Vinaigrette. A lot of people in the audience
felt that this was a major screw-up, or "gaffe," on the part of
the contest organizers, because of course vinaigrette is just
going to fight any wine you try to marry it with. "I strongly
disagree with the salad dressing," is how one wine writer at
my table put it, and I could tell she meant it.

So the contestants were all really battling the vinaigrette
problem, and you could just feel a current of unrest in the
room. Things finally came to a head, or "tete," when contes-
tant Mark Hightower came right out and said that if the rules

hadn't prevented him, he wouldn't have chosen any wine at all with the salad. "Ideally," he said, "I would have liked to have recommended an Evian mineral water." Well, the room just erupted in spontaneous applause, very similar to what you hear at Democratic Party dinners when somebody mentions the Poor.

Anyway, the winning sommelier, who gets a trip to Paris, was Joshua Wesson, who works at a restaurant named Huberts in New York. I knew he'd win, because he began his Harmony of Wine and Food presentation by saying: "Whenever I see oysters on a menu, I am reminded of a quote. . . ." Nobody's ever going to try buying a moderately priced wine from a man who is reminded of a quote by oysters.

It turns out however, that Wesson is actually an OK guy who just happens to have a God-given ability to lay it on with a trowel and get along with the French. I talked to him briefly afterwards, and he didn't seem to take himself too seriously at all. I realize many people think I make things up, so let me assure you ahead of time that this is the actual, complete transcript of the interview:

ME: So. What do you think?

WESSON: I feel good. My arm felt good, my curve ball was popping. I felt I could help the ball team.

ME: What about the vinaigrette?

WESSON: It was definitely the turning point. One can look at vinaigrette from many angles. It's like electricity.

I swear that's what he said, and furthermore at the time it made a lot of sense.

RANDOMLY AMONGST THE BLOBS

WITHOUT MY EYEGLASSES, I HAVE A GREAT DEAL of trouble distinguishing between house fires and beer signs. I wear the kind of glasses that they never show in those eyeglasses advertisements where the lenses are obviously fake because they don't distort the attractive model's face at all. My lenses make the entire middle of my head appear smaller. When professional photographers take my picture, they always suggest that I take my glasses off, because otherwise the picture shows this head with the normal top and bottom, but in the middle there's this little perfect miniature human head, maybe the size of an orange, staring out from behind my glasses.

People like photographers and dentists and barbers are always asking me to take my glasses off, and I hate it because it makes me stupid and paranoid. I worry that the dentist and his aides are creeping up on me with acetylene torches, or have sneaked out of the room and left me chatting away at the dental spittoon. So I use a sonar technique originally developed by bats, wherein I fire off a constant stream of idiot conversational remarks designed to draw replies so I can keep track of which blobs in the room represent people. This makes it very hard to work on my teeth.

Swimming at the beach is the worst. If I go into the ocean with my glasses off, which is the traditional way to go into the ocean, I cannot frolic in the surf like a normal person because (a) I usually can't see the waves until they knock me over and drag me along the bottom and fill my mouth with sand, and (b) the current always carries me down the beach, away from my wife and towel and glasses. When I emerge from the water, all I can see is this enormous white blur (the beach?) covered with darkish blobs (people?), and I run the risk of plopping down next to a blob that I think is my wife and throwing my arm over it in an affectionate manner, only to discover that it is actually horseshoe crabs mating, or a girlfriend of an enormous violent jealous weight-lifter, or, God help me, the violent weightlifter himself.

So what I do in these circumstances is wander randomly amongst the blobs, making quiet semidesperate noises designed not to bother any civilians, yet to draw the attention of whatever blob might be my wife. "Well, here I am!" I say, trying to appear as casual as possible. "Yes, here I am! Dave Barry! Ha ha! Help!" And so forth. I'm not sure I'm all that unobtrusive on account of my mouth is full of sand.

Mostly these days when I go to the beach I just stay out of the water altogether. I sit on the shore and play cretin, sand-digging games with my three-year-old son, and I watch the lifeguards, who sit way up on the beach with their 20–20 vision and blow their whistles at swimmers I couldn't see even with the aid of a radio telescope, off the coast of France somewhere.

At least I no longer have to worry about necking on dates, the way I did in high school. That was awful. See, you have to take your glasses off when you neck, lest you cause facial injury to the other necker. So I'd be sitting on the sofa with a girl, watching a late movie on television, and I'd figure the time was right, and I'd very casually remove my glasses, rendering myself batlike, and lean toward the blob representing the girl and plant a sensuous kiss on the side of her head owing to the fact that she was still watching the movie. Now what? Do I try again, on the theory that she has been aroused by being kissed on the side of the head? Or is she angry? Is she still watching television? Is she still on the sofa?

There was no way to tell. The world was a blur. So I'd have to very casually grope around for my glasses and put them back on for a little reconnaissance, but by the time I found them likely as not the potential co-necker had fallen asleep.

I suppose I could wear contact lenses, but people who wear contact lenses are always weeping and blinking, and their eyes turn red, as though their mothers had just died. You want to go up to them on the street and say "There, there," and maybe give them money. Also, you never hear of anybody who wears them successfully for more than maybe three weeks. People are always saying, "I really liked them, but my hair started to fall out," or, "I had this girlfriend, Denise, and one of her contacts slid up under her eyelid and went into her bloodstream and got stuck in her brain and now she never finishes her sentences."

I guess I should be grateful that I can see at all, and I am. I just felt like wallowing in self-pity for a while, is all. I promise I won't do it again. Those of you with worse afflictions than mine, such as migraine headaches or pregnancy, are welcome to write me long, descriptive letters. I promise to look them over, although not necessarily with my glasses on.

VALUABLE PRESIDENTIAL FREEBIES!

MY WIFE RECENTLY GOT TWO OFFERS IN THE mail, one from Ed McMahon and one from President Reagan. Ed's offer is that if my wife will stick some little stickers on a card and send it back, he'll give her $2 million. I figure there has to be a catch. Maybe there's some kind of espionage chemical on the back of the sticker so that when you lick it your nasal passages swell up and explode and you can't collect your two million. Because otherwise it just seems too easy, you know?

President Reagan's offer looks better. He's offering my wife the opportunity to be on a special Presidential Task Force. Apparently this is a limited offer being made only to a select group consisting of all current and former Republicans, living or dead, in the world. My wife used to be a Republican before she quit voting altogether, except for when there are judicial candidates with humorous names.

According to the colorful brochure my wife got, her primary task as a member of the Presidential Task Force is to send in $120. President Reagan is going to use this money to prevent the government from falling into the hands of the Democrats, who, according to the brochure, are all disease-ridden vermin. As tokens of the president's gratitude, my wife will receive a number of Valuable Gifts, including (I swear I am not making this up):

• A "Medal of Merit" in a "handsome case," in recognition for highly meritorious service to the nation in the form of coming up with the 120 beans.

- A lapel pin, which the brochure says will "signify your special relationship with President Reagan."
- An embossed Presidential Task Force Membership Card, which "reveals your toll-free, members-only, Washington hotline number; your direct line to important developments in the United States Senate; your superfast way to contact President Reagan and every Republican in the United States Senate."

Except for the time that our dog was throwing up what appeared to be squirrel parts in the living room, I can't honestly think of any occasion in recent years when we needed to get hold of President Reagan and every Republican in the senate on short notice. Nevertheless, I think the embossed Task Force card hotline number could come in mighty handy.

Let's say my wife and I are at the department store and we're trying to get waited on by a small clot of sales personnel who are clearly annoyed that some idiot has gone and left the doors open again, thus permitting members of the public to get into the store and actually try to purchase things, if you can imagine, right in the middle of a very important sales personnel discussion about hair design.

Ordinarily what my wife and I do in these situations is stand around in an obvious manner for several minutes, after which we ask politely several times to be waited on, after which we escalate to rude remarks, after which we discharge small arms in the direction of the ceiling, after which we give up and go home. But if my wife were a Task Force member, the sales personnel would notice her lapel pin and say to each other in hushed tones: "That pin signifies that she has a special relationship with President Reagan! We had best make an exception in her case, and permit her to make a purchase!" For they would know that if they didn't, my wife would be on the horn pronto, contacting President Reagan and all the senate Republicans, and heaven only knows what kind of strong corrective action they would take, except that it would probably involve the shipment of missiles to camel-oriented nations.

So all in all I think the president has made my wife a fine offer. Not only does she get the valuable Free Gifts, but she gets to keep the government in Republican hands and thus save the Republic and ensure a brighter future for the entire Free World for generations to come. Of course we must weigh this against the fact that $120 will buy you enough beer to last nearly two weeks in mild weather.

SO I GOT THIS LETTER, WHICH SAID I HAD BEEN
selected by a "merchandise distribution organization" to receive some merchandise. The way the letter sounded, these
people just woke up one day and said, "Hey! We have some
merchandise! Let's form an organization and *distribute* it!"
The letter said I could receive as much as $1,000 in cash, but
I was not so naive as to think I would get that. I figure I'd
have a better shot at the Disney World vacation, or the 24-
karat gold bracelet with the rubies and diamonds, or maybe
even—you never can tell—the *five function LCD watch.*

So I made an appointment to go get the merchandise,
and they told me that, while I was there, they would tell me
about a new Leisure Concept, and I had to bring my spouse.
This is a normal legal precaution they take to avoid a situation where you sign a contract, and when you get home your
spouse finds out and stabs you to death with a potato peeler,
which could void the contract.

So we went to the appointed place and sat for a while in
a room filled with other couples, and every now and then a
person would come in, call out a name, and lead a couple
off, and the rest of us would wonder what was going to
happen to them. I thought maybe it would be like a fraternity initiation, in which they'd shove us into a darkened room
where sales representatives would taunt us and poke us with

sharp sticks, then give us our merchandise. But it turns out they don't let you off that easy.

Finally, our name was called by a person named Joe. Joe is the kind of person who cannot begin a sentence without saying, "Let me be honest with you," and cannot end one without grasping your forearm to let you know he is your best personal friend in the world. When Joe was born, the obstetrician examined him briefly and told the nurse: "Do not sign *anything* this baby gives you."

Joe told us his organization didn't invite just any old set of spouses out there to offer this new Leisure Concept to. He said they had already spent somewhere between $400 and $700 on us—not that we should feel obligated or anything!—to check us out thoroughly to make sure we were not convicted felons, because he knew that nice people like us certainly didn't want to be part of any Leisure Concept that allowed convicted felons to join, right? (Grasp.) So my wife asked exactly how they could check on something like that, which made Joe very nervous. I think it suddenly occurred to him that we might actually *be* convicted felons, because he launched into a murky speech about "extenuating circumstances," the gist of which seemed to be that when he said they didn't allow convicted felons, he didn't mean *us*.

Next we found out how you can get AIDS from hotel bedsheets. The way this came up is, Joe asked us where we liked to stay during vacations, and we said, hotels. So Joe went over the pluses and minuses of hotels for us, and the only plus he could think of was that hotels have maid service, but even then, being honest, he had to admit that you never know who has been sleeping on those sheets, and you have to worry when you read all these newspaper stories about AIDS. You know? (Grasp.) This was when we realized that, whatever Joe's Leisure Concept was, it didn't have maid service.

So finally Joe let it slip out that his Leisure Concept was "resorts." As he explained it, basically, we were supposed to give them $11,000 plus annual dues, and then we could spend our Leisure Time at these resorts, which Joe's company had already built some of and plans to build lots more of. To help illustrate their resort in Virginia, for example, they had a nice picture of the dome of the U.S. Capitol, although when we asked Joe about it, he admitted that the Capitol was not, to be honest, technically on the resort property per se.

My wife, a picky shopper, said that yes, these were certainly very attractive photographs but generally before she spends $11,000 on resorts she likes to see at least one in person. So Joe told us they had one right outside, which he showed us. What it was, to be honest with you, was a campground. It was one of those modern ones with swimming pools and miniature golf and video games, the kind that's popular with people whose idea of getting close to nature is turn the air conditioning in their recreational vechicles down to medium. My reaction was that I would spend my Leisure Time there only if this were one of the demands made by people who had kidnapped my son.

So we went back inside, and Joe lunged at us with a Special Offer, good only that day: For only $8,000, we could join his resorts! Plus annual dues! Plus we could stay at affiliated resorts! For a small fee! There are thousands of them! They litter the nation! Plus we could get discounts at condominiums! Waikiki Beach! Air fares! A castle in Germany! Rental cars! *Several* castles in Germany! Snorkeling! Roy Orbison's Greatest Hits! But we had to act today! Right now! For various reasons! Did we have any questions?!!

My major question was, essentially, did they think we had the same Scholastic Aptitude Test scores as mayonnaise. My wife's questions were: What are you talking about? What resorts? What condominiums? How much of a discount? Joe didn't know. He was more of a specialist in bedsheet hygiene. So he called the Sales Manager, who hauled over a batch of travel brochures, which he kept on his side of the table while he flipped through them at great speed, pausing occasionally to read parts of headlines to us as if they contained actual information.

The whole ordeal took over three hours, and it was not easy, but we got our merchandise: a calculator of the kind that you have eight or twelve dead ones at the bottom of your sock drawer at any given time because it's easier and cheaper to buy a new one than to try to put in new batteries, and an LCD watch that really does have five functions, if you count telling time as two functions (telling hours, and telling minutes).

I would say, even though the watch stopped working the next day, that it was a fun family outing, and I recommend that you try it, assuming you are fortunate enough to get through the strict screening procedure and receive an invitation. Those of you who are convicted felons might want to use your illegal handguns to bypass the Leisure Concept altogether and ask for the $1,000 cash up front.

I GOT TO THINKING ABOUT DIRTY WORDS THIS morning when I woke up and looked at the clock, realized I had once again overslept, and said a popular dirty word that begins with "S," which will hereinafter be referred to as "the S-word."

I say the S-word every morning when I look at the clock, because I'm always angry at the clock for continuing to run after I've turned off the alarm and gone back to sleep. What we need in this country, instead of Daylight Savings Time, which nobody really understands anyway, is a new concept called Weekday Morning Time, whereby at 7 A.M. every weekday we go into a space-launch-style "hold" for two or three hours, during which it just remains 7 A.M. This way we could all wake up via a civilized gradual process of stretching and belching and scratching, and it would still be only 7 A.M. when we were ready to actually emerge from bed.

But so far we are stuck with this system under which the clock keeps right on moving, which is what prompts me each morning to say the S-word. The reason I raise this subject is that this particular morning I inadvertently said it directly into the ear of my son, who is almost four and who sometimes creeps into our bedroom during the night because of nightmares, probably caused by the fact that he sleeps on *Return of the Jedi* sheets with illustrations of space creatures such as Jabba the Hut, who looks like a 6,000-pound intestinal parasite.

I felt pretty bad, saying the S-word right into my son's ear, but he was cool. "Daddy, you shouldn't say the S-word," he said. Only he didn't say "the S-word," you understand; he actually said the S-word. But he said it in a very mature way, indicating that he got no thrill from it, and that he was merely trying to correct my behavior.

I don't know where kids pick these things up.

Here's what strikes me as ironic: When I said the S-word this morning, I was in no way thinking of or trying to describe the substance that the S-word literally represents. No, I was merely trying to describe a feeling of great anguish and frustration, but I'd have felt like a fool, looking at the alarm clock and saying: "I feel great anguish and frustration this morning." So in the interest of saving time, I said the S-word instead, and I got a condescending lecture from a person who consistently puts his underpants on backwards.

The other irony is that for thousands of years, great writers such as William Shakespeare have used so-called dirty words to form literature. In *Romeo and Juliet,* for example, the following words appear in Act II, Scene VI, Row A, Seats 4 and 5:

> "O Romeo, Romeo;
> "Where the F-word art thou, Romeo?"

Today, of course, it is considered very poor taste to use the F-word except in major motion pictures. When we do use it, we are almost always expressing hostility toward somebody who has taken our parking space. This is also ironic, when you consider what act the F-word technically describes, and I imagine you psychiatrists out there could drone on for hours about the close relationship between sex and hostility, but frankly I think you psychiatrists are up to your necks in S-word.

What I think is that the F-word is basically just a convenient nasty-sounding word that we tend to use when we would really like to come up with a terrifically witty insult, the kind Winston Churchill always came up with when enormous women asked him stupid questions at parties. But most of us don't think of good insults until weeks later, in the shower, so in the heat of the moment many of us tend to go with the old reliable F-word.

I disapprove of the F-word, not because it's dirty, but because we use it as a substitute for thoughtful insults, and it frequently leads to violence. What we ought to do, when we anger each other, say, in traffic, is exchange phone numbers, so that later on, when we've had time to think of witty and learned insults or look them up in the library, we could call each other up:

YOU: Hello? Bob?

BOB: Yes?

YOU: This is Ed. Remember? The person whose parking space you took last Thursday? Outside of Sears?

BOB: Oh, yes! Sure! How are you, Ed?

YOU: Fine, thanks. Listen, Bob, the reason I'm calling is: "Madam, you may be drunk, but I am ugly, and . . ." No, wait. I mean: "You may be ugly, but I am Winston Churchill, and . . ." No, wait. (Sound of reference book thudding onto the floor.) S-word. Excuse me. Look, Bob, I'm going to have to get back to you.

BOB: Fine.

This would be much more educational than the F-word approach, plus it would eliminate a lot of unnecessary stabbings. On the other hand, to get back to my original point, we really ought to repeal any laws we have on the books against the S-word, which should henceforth be considered a perfectly acceptable and efficient way of expressing one's feelings toward alarm clocks and cars that break down in neighborhoods where a toxic-waste dump could be classified as urban renewal.

MOLECULAR HOMICIDE

WE HAVE THE FLU. I DON'T KNOW IF THIS PARTIC-
ular strain has an official name, but if it does, it must be
something like Martian Death Flu. You may have had it
yourself. The main symptom is that you wish you had another setting on your electric blanket, up past "HIGH," that
said: "ELECTROCUTION."

Another symptom is that you cease brushing your teeth
because (a) your teeth hurt and (b) you lack the strength.
Midway through the brushing process, you'd have to lie
down in front of the sink to rest for a couple of hours, and
rivulets of toothpaste foam would dribble sideways out of
your mouth, eventually hardening into crusty little toothpaste stalagmites what would bond your head permanently
to the bathroom floor, which is where the police would find
you.

You know the kind of flu I'm talking about.

I spend a lot of time lying very still and thinking flu-
related thoughts. One insight I have had is that all this time
scientists have been telling us the truth: Air really *is* made up
of tiny objects called "molecules." I know this because I can
feel them banging against my body. There are billions and
billions and billions of them, but if I concentrate, I can detect
each one individually, striking my body, especially my eyeballs, at speeds upwards of a hundred thousand miles per
hour. If I try to escape by pulling the blanket over my face,

they attack my hair, which has become almost as sensitive as my teeth.

There has been a mound of blankets on my wife's side of the bed for several days now, absolutely motionless except that it makes occasional efforts to spit into a tissue. I think it might be my wife, but the only way to tell for sure would be to prod it, which I wouldn't do even if I had the strength, because if it turned out that it was my wife, and she were alive, and I prodded her, it would kill her.

Me, I am leading a more active life-style. Three or four times a day, I attempt to crawl to the bathroom. Unfortunately this is a distance of nearly 15 feet, with a great many air molecules en route, so at about the halfway point I usually decide to stop and get myself into the fetal position and hope for nuclear war. Instead, I get Earnest. Earnest is our dog. She senses instantly that something is wrong, and guided by that timeless and unerring nurturing instinct that all female dogs have, she tries to lick my ears off.

For my son, Robert, this is proving to be the high point of his entire life to date. He has had his pajamas on for two, maybe three days now. He has a sense of joyful independence a five-year-old child gets when he suddenly realizes that he could be operating an acetylene torch in the coat closet and neither parent would have the strength to object. He has been foraging for his own food, which means his diet consists entirely of "food" substances that are advertised only on Saturday morning cartoon shows; substances that are the color of jukebox lights and that, for legal reasons, have their names spelled wrong, as in New Creemy Chock-'n'-Cheez Lumps o' Froot ("part of this complete breakfast").

Crawling around, my face inches from the carpet, I sometimes encounter traces of colorful wrappers that Robert has torn from these substances and dropped on the floor, where Earnest, always on patrol, has found them and chewed them into spit-covered wads. I am reassured by this. It means they are both eating.

38

The Martian Death Flu has not been an entirely bad thing. Since I cannot work, or move, or think, I have been able to spend more Quality Time with Robert, to come up with creative learning activities that we can enjoy and share together. Today, for example, I taught him, as my father had taught me, how to make an embarrassing noise with your hands. Then we shot rubber bands at the contestants on "Divorce Court." Then, just in case some parts of our brains were still alive, we watched professional bowling. Here's what televised professional bowling sounds like when you have the flu:

PLAY-BY-PLAY MAN: He left the 10-pin, Bob.

COLOR COMMENTATOR: Yes, Bill. He failed to knock it down.

PLAY-BY-PLAY MAN: It's still standing up.

COLOR COMMENTATOR: Yes. Now he must try to knock it down.

PLAY-BY-PLAY MAN: You mean the 10-pin, Bob?

The day just flew by. Soon it was 3:30 P.M., time to crawl back through the air molecules to the bedroom, check on my wife or whoever that is, and turn in for the night.

Earnest was waiting about halfway down the hall.

"Look at this," the police will say when they find me. "His ears are missing."

WAY TO GO!
ROSCOE!

WELL, IT LOOKS LIKE WE'VE FINALLY GOTTEN some tax reform. We've been trying to get tax reform for over 200 years, dating back to 17-something, when a small, brave band of patriots dressed up as Indians and threw tea into the Boston Harbor. Surprisingly, this failed to produce tax reform. So the brave patriots tried various other approaches, such as dressing up as tea and throwing Indians into the harbor, or dressing up as a harbor and throwing tea into Indians, but nothing worked.

And so, today, the tax system is a mess. To cite some of the more glaring problems:

• The big corporations pay nothing.
• The rich pay nothing.
• The poor pay nothing.
• I pay nothing.
• Nobody pays anything except you and a couple of people where you work.
• The commissioner of the Internal Revenue Service is named "Roscoe."

This unfair system has increasingly resulted in calls for reform. I personally called for reform nearly two years ago, when I proposed a simple and fair three-pronged tax system called the You Pay Only $8.95 Tax Plan, which worked as follows:

PRONG ONE: You would pay $8.95 in taxes.

PRONG TWO: Cheating would be permitted.

PRONG THREE: Anybody who parked his or her car diagonally across two parking spaces would be shot without trial. (This prong is not directly related to tax reform, but everybody I discussed it with feels it should be included anyway.)

The other major plan was proposed by President Reagan, who made tax reform the cornerstone of his second term, similar to the way he made tax reduction the cornerstone of his first term. Remember that? It was back when everybody was talking about "supply-side economics," which is the mysterious curve that became famous when an economist named Arthur Laffer drew it at a party, on a napkin belonging to U.S. Congressman Jack Kemp. I'm not making this up.

What the Laffer curve allegedly showed, when you held it in a certain light, was that if the government reduced everybody's taxes, it would make *more money*, and the federal budget deficit would go away. I admit that, looking back on it, this theory seems even stupider than throwing beverages into Boston Harbor, but, at the time, it had a very strong appeal. Congressman Kemp started showing his napkin around Washington and soon many people were excited about supply-side economics. It was similar to those stories you sometimes see in the newspaper about how some Third World village gets all riled up when a peasant woman discovers a yam shaped exactly like the Virgin Mary. President Reagan made tax reduction his first-term cornerstone, and Congress enacted it, and everybody waited for the budget deficit to go down, and it wasn't until recently that economists realized Kemp had been holding his napkin sideways.

So that was tax reduction. Now we're on tax *reform*, which as I said earlier is the president's second-term cornerstone. For a while, however, it appeared to be in big trouble

in Congress, because of the PACs. PACs are lobbying organizations with names like the American Nasal Inhaler Industry Committee for Better Government, which make large
contributions to your elected representatives so they can afford to make TV campaign commercials where they stand
around in shirt sleeves pretending that they actually care
about ordinary bozo citizens such as you.

The PACs did not care for the president's plan. They
were very concerned that the term "tax reform" might be
interpreted to mean "reforming the tax system in some way,"
which of course would destroy the economy as we now know
it. So they had all these amendments introduced, and, before
long, the president's tax-reform plan had been modified so
much that its only actual legal effect, had it been enacted,
would have been to declare July as Chalk Appreciation
Month. And so it looked as though the president might have
to come up with a new cornerstone for his second
term, something like: "Ronald Reagan: He never bombed
Canada." Or: "Ronald Reagan: Most of his polyps were
benign."

And then a wonderful thing happened. The Senate Finance Committee, a group of men who are not famous for
standing up to the special interests, a group of men who have
little slots in their front doors for the convenience of those
PACs wishing to make large contributions at night, suddenly
got their courage up. They took a hard look at themselves,
and they said: "Wait a minute. What are we? Are we a bunch
of prostitutes, taking large sums of money from the PACs
and giving them what they want? No! Let's take large sums
of their money and *not* give them what they want!" It was a
courageous step, a step that took the senators beyond pros-
titution, into the realm of fraud. All the editorial writers of
course hailed it as a Positive Step. And that is how we came
to have tax reform.

How will tax reform affect you? It will change your life
dramatically. Let's say you're a typical family of four with
both parents working and occasional car problems. Under

the new system, each year you'll get a bunch of unintelligible forms from the government, and you'll put off doing anything about them until mid-April, and you'll be confused by the directions, and you'll miss a lot of deductions, and you'll worry about being audited. Other than that things will remain pretty much the same. Roscoe will still be in charge.

NOTE: *This is my annual column on how to fill out our income-tax return. As you read it, please bear in mind that I am not a trained accountant. I am the Chief Justice of the United States Supreme Court. Nevertheless, if you have any questions whatsoever about the legality of a particular tax maneuver, you should call the special Toll-Free IRS Taxpayer Assistance Hotline Telephone Number in your area and listen to the busy signal until you feel you have a better understanding of the situation.*

There are a number (23,968,847) of significant differences between this year's tax form and last year's, but let's first look at the two things that have *not* changed:

1. The commissioner of Internal Revenue is *still* named "Roscoe," and

2. Roscoe is evidently still doing situps under parked cars, because he once again devotes the largest paragraph on page one to telling us taxpayers how we can send in "voluntary contributions to reduce the federal debt." As I interpret this statement, Roscoe, by using the word "voluntary," is saying that even though your government finds itself in serious financial trouble owing to the fact that every time an Acting Assistant Deputy Undersecretary of Something changes offices, he spends more on new drapes than your whole house is worth, the IRS does not *require* you to send in extra money, beyond what you actually owe. No sir. You also are allowed

to send in jewelry, stocks, canned goods, or clothing in good condition. Roscoe is a 42 regular.

Everything else about the tax form is different this year, but it shouldn't be too much trouble as long as you avoid Common Taxpayer Errors. "For example," reminds IRS Helpful Hint Division Chief Rexford Pooch, Jr., "taxpayers who make everything up should use numbers that sound sort of accurate, such as $3,847.62, rather than obvious fictions like $4,000. Also, we generally give much closer scrutiny to a return where the taxpayer gives a name such as Nick 'The Weasel' Testosterone."

With those tips in mind, let's look at some typical tax cases, and see how they would be handled under the new tax code.

TAX CASE ONE: Mrs. Jones, a 71-year-old widow living on social security with no other income, is sound asleep one night when she has an incredibly vivid dream in which her son dies in an automobile crash in California. Suddenly, she is awakened by the telephone; it is a member of the California Highway Patrol, calling to remind her that she does not have a son. Stunned, she suffers a fatal heart attack.

QUESTION: Does Mrs. Jones still have to file a tax return?

ANSWER: Yes. Don't be an idiot. She should use Form DPFS-65, "Dead Person Filing Singly," which she can obtain at any of the two nationwide IRS Taxpayer Assistance Centers during their normal working hour.

TAX CASE TWO: Mr. and Mrs. Smith, both 32, are a working couple with two dependent children and a combined gross net abstracted income of $27,000. During the first fiscal segment of the 1984 calendar year, they received IRS Form YAFN-12, notifying them that according to the federal computer, they owe $179 billion in taxes. They have a good laugh over this and show the notice to their friends, thinking that it is such an obvious mistake that the IRS will correct it right away and they might even get their names in the newspaper as the victims of a typical humorous government bone-head computer bungle.

QUESTION: Can the Smiths deduct the cost of the snake-related injuries they suffered when they were fleeing the federal dogs through the wilderness?

ANSWER: They may deduct 61 percent of the base presumptive adjusted mean allocated cost that is greater than, but not exceeding, $1,575, provided they kept accurate records showing they made a reasonable effort to save little Tina's ear. Except in states whose names consist of two words.

TAX CASE THREE: Mr. A. Pemberton Trammel Snipe-Treadwater IV has established a trust fund for his six children under which each of them, upon reaching the age of 21, will receive a subcontinent. One afternoon while preparing to lash a servant, Mr. Snipe-Treadwater has a vague recollection that in 1980—or perhaps it was in 1978, he is not sure—he might have paid some taxes.

QUESTION: What should Mr. Snipe-Treadwater do?

ANSWER: He should immediately summon his various senators and congressmen to soothe his brow with damp compresses until he can be named ambassador to France.

YUP THE ESTABLISHMENT

OBVIOUSLY, WE—AND WHEN I SAY "WE," I MEAN people who no longer laugh at the concept of hemorrhoids —need to come up with some kind of plan for dealing with the yuppies. In a moment I'll explain my personal proposal, which is that we draft them, but first let me give you some background.

If you've been reading the trend sections of your weekly newsmagazines, you know that "yuppies" are a new breed of serious, clean-cut, ambitious, career-oriented young person that probably resulted from all that atomic testing. They wear dark, natural-fiber, businesslike clothing even when no-body they know has died. In college, they major in Business Administration. If, to meet certain academic requirements, they have to take a liberal-arts course, they take Business Poetry.

In short, yuppies are running around behaving as if they were real grown-ups, and they are doing it at an age when persons of my generation were still playing Beatles records backwards and actively experimenting to determine what happens when you drink a whole bottle of cough syrup.

NOTE TO IMPRESSIONABLE YOUNG READERS: *Don't bother. All that happens is you feel like you could never, ever cough again, even if professional torturers armed with X-acto knives ordered you to, then you develop this intense, 10-to-12-hour interest in individual carpet*

47

fibers. So it's not worth it, plus I understand the manufacturers have done something wimpy to the formulas.

What bothers me about the yuppies is, they're destroying the normal social order, which is that people are supposed to start out as wild-eyed radicals, and then gradually, over time, develop gum disease and become conservatives.

This has always been the system. A good example is Franklin Roosevelt, who when he was alive was considered extremely liberal, but now is constantly being quoted by Ronald Reagan. Or take the Russian leaders. When they were young, they'd pull any kind of crazy stunt, kill the czar, anything, but now they mostly just lie around in state.

So I say the yuppies represent a threat to society as we know it, and I say we need to do something about them. One possibility would be to simply wait until they reproduce, on the theory that they'll give their children the finest clothing and toys and designer educations, and their children will of course grow up to absolutely loathe everything their parents stand for and thus become defiant, ill-dressed, unwashed, unkempt, violently antiestablishment drug addicts, and society will return to normal. The problem here is that yuppies have a very low birth rate, because apparently they have to go to Aspen to mate.

So we'll have to draft them. Not into the Armed Forces, of course; they'd all make colonel in about a week, plus they'd be useless in an actual war, whapping at the enemy with briefcases. Likewise we cannot put them in the Peace Corps, as they would cause no end of ill will abroad, crouching among the residents of some poverty-racked village in, say, Somalia, and attempting to demonstrate the water-powered Cuisinart.

No, what we need for the yuppies is a national Lighten Up Corps. First they'd go through basic training, where a harsh drill sergeant would force them to engage in pointless nonproductive activities, such as eating moon pies and watching "Days of Our Lives." Then they'd each have to

48

serve two years in a job that offered no opportunity whatsoever for career advancement, such as:

- bumper-car repairman;
- gum-wad remover;
- random street lunatic;
- bus-station urinal maintenance person;
- lieutenant governor;
- owner of a roadside attraction such as "World's Largest All-Snake Orchestra."

During their time of service in the Lighten Up Corps,
the yuppies would of course be required to wear neon-yellow
polyester jumpsuits with the name "Earl" embroidered over
the breast pocket.

PAIN & SUFFERING

AS AN AMERICAN, YOU ARE VERY FORTUNATE TO live in a country (America) where you have many legal rights. Bales of rights. And new ones are being discovered all the time, such as the right to make a right turn on a red light.

This doesn't mean you can do just *anything*. For example, you can't shout "FIRE!" in a crowded theater. Even if there *is* a fire, you can't shout it. A union worker has to shout it. But you can—I know this, because you always sit right behind me—clear your throat every 15 seconds all the way through an entire movie, and finally, at the exact moment of greatest on-screen drama, hawk up a gob the size of a golf ball. Nobody can stop you. It's your *right*.

The way you got all these rights is the Founding Fathers fought and died for them, then wrote them down on the Constitution, a very old piece of paper that looks like sick puppies have lived on it, which is stored in Washington, D.C., where you have the right to view it during normal viewing hours. The most important part of the Constitution, rightswise, appears in Article IX, Section II, Row 27, which states:

If any citizen of the United States shall ever at any time for any reason have any kind of bad thing happen to him or her, then this is probably the result of Negligence on the part of a large corporation with a lot of insurance. If you get our drift.

What the Constitution is trying to get across to you here is that the way you protect your rights, in America, is by suing the tar out of everybody. This is an especially good time to sue, because today's juries hand out giant cash awards as if they were complimentary breath mints.

So you definitely want to get in on this. Let's say your wedding ring falls into your toaster, and when you stick your hand in to retrieve it, you suffer Pain and Suffering as well as Mental Anguish. You would sue:

• The toaster manufacturer, for failure to include, in the instructions section that says you should never never never never *ever* stick your hand in the toaster, the statement: "Not even if your wedding ring falls in there."

• The store where you bought the toaster, for selling it to an obvious cretin like yourself.

• The Union Carbide Corporation, which is not directly responsible in this case, but which is feeling so guilty that it would probably send you a large cash settlement anyway.

Of course you need the help of a professional lawyer. Experts agree the best way to select a lawyer is to watch VHF television, where more and more of your top legal talents are advertising:

"Hi. I'm Preston A. Mantis, president of Consumers Retail Law Outlet. As you can see by my suit and the fact that I have all these books of equal height on the shelves behind me, I am a trained legal attorney. Do you have a car or a job? Do you ever walk around? If so, you probably have the makings of an excellent legal case. Although of course every case is different, I would definitely say that, based on my experience and training, there's no reason why you shouldn't come out of this thing with at least a cabin cruiser. Remember, at the Preston A. Mantis Consumers Retail Law Outlet, our motto is: "It is very difficult to disprove certain kinds of pain."

Another right you have, as an American, is the right to Speedy Justice. For an example of how Speedy Justice works, we turn now to an anecdote told to me by a friend who once worked as a clerk for a judge in a medium-sized city. My friend swears this is true. It happened to an elderly recent immigrant who was hauled before the judge one day. The thing to bear in mind is, this man was *not actually guilty of anything*. He had simply gotten lost and confused, and he spoke very little English, and he was wandering around, so the police had picked him up just so he'd have a warm place to sleep while they straightened everything out.

Unfortunately, this judge, who got his job less on the basis of being knowledgeable in matters of law than on the basis of attending the most picnics, somehow got the *wrong folder* in front of him, the folder of a person who had done something semiserious, so he gave the accused man a stern speech, then sentenced him to *six months in jail*. When this was explained to the man, he burst into tears. He was thinking, no doubt, that if he had only known they had such severe penalties for being elderly and lost in America, he would never have immigrated here in the first place.

Finally, about an hour later, the police figured out what happened, and after they stopped rolling around the floor and wetting their pants, they told the judge, and he sent them to fetch the prisoner back from jail. By now, of course, the prisoner had no *idea* what they're going to do to him. Shoot him, maybe. He was terrified. So put yourself in the judge's position. Here you have a *completely innocent* man in front of you, whom you have scared half to death and had carted off to jail because *you* made a stupid mistake. What is the only conceivable thing you can do? Apologize, right?

This just shows you have no legal training. What this judge did was give a speech. "*America*," it began. Just the one word, very dramatically spoken. My friend, who saw all this happen, still cannot recount this speech without falling most of the way out of his chair. The gist of it was that this is a Great Country, and since this was a First Offense, he, the judge, had had a Change of Heart, and had decided to give the accused a Second Chance.

Well. Once they explained *this* to the prisoner, that he

was not going to jail after all, that he was to be shown all this *mercy,* he burst into tears again, and rushed up and *tried to kiss the judge's hand.* Who could blame him? This was probably the greatest thing that had ever happened to him. What a *great* country! What *speedy* justice! I bet he still tells his grandchildren about it. I bet they tell him he should have sued.

THE DEADLY WIND

WHAT PROSPECTIVE BUYERS SAID, WHEN THEY looked at our house, was: "Huh! This is . . . *interesting*." They *always* said this. They never said: "What a nice house!" Or: "We'll take this house! Here's a suitcase filled with money!!" No, they said our house is *interesting*. What they meant was: "Who installed this paneling? Vandals?"

Sometimes, to cheer us up, they also said: "Well it certainly has a lot of possibilities!" Meaning: "These people have lived here for 10 years and *they never put up any curtains*."

We were trying to sell our house. We had elected to move voluntarily to Miami. We wanted our child to benefit from the experience of growing up in a community that is constantly being enriched by a diverse and ever-changing infusion of tropical diseases. Also they have roaches down there you could play polo with.

The first thing we did, when we decided to move, was we rented a dumpster and threw away the majority of our furniture. You think I am kidding, but this is only because you never saw our furniture. It was much too pathetic to give to The Poor. The Poor would have taken one look at it and returned, laughing, to their street grates.

What we did give to The Poor was all my college textbooks, which I had gone through, in college, using a yellow felt marker to highlight the good parts. You college graduates out there know what I'm talking about. You go back, years later, when college is just a vague semicomical memory, and read something you chose to highlight, and it's always a statement like: "Structuralized functionalism represents both a continuance of, and a departure from, functionalistic structuralism." And you realize that at one time you actually had *large sectors* of your brain devoted to this type of knowledge. Lord only knows what The Poor will use it for. Fuel, probably.

One book we did keep is called *Survive the Deadly Wind*. I don't know where we got it, but it's about hurricanes, and so we thought it might contain useful information about life in Miami. "Any large pieces of aluminum left in a yard are a definite hazard," it states. "Each piece has a potential for decapitation. Hurled on the tide of a 150-mile-an-hour wind, it can slice its way to, and through, bone." Ha ha! Our New Home!

After we threw away our furniture, we hired two men, both named Jonathan, to come over and fix our house up so prospective buyers wouldn't get to laughing so hard they'd fall down the basement stairs and file costly lawsuits. The two Jonathans were extremely competent, the kind of men who own winches and freely use words like "joist" and can build houses starting out with only raw trees. The first thing they did was rip out all the Homeowner Projects I had committed against our house back when I thought I had manual dexterity. They were trying to make the house look as nice as it did before I started improving it. This cost thousands of dollars.

I think there should be a federal law requiring people who publish do-it-yourself books to include a warning, similar to what the Surgeon General has on cigarette packs, right on the cover of the book, stating:

WARNING: ANY MONEY YOU SAVE BY DOING HOMEOWNER PROJ-ECTS YOURSELF WILL BE OFFSET BY THE COST OF HIRING COM-PETENT PROFESSIONALS TO COME AND REMOVE THEM SO YOU CAN SELL YOUR HOUSE, NOT TO MENTION THE EMOTIONAL TRAUMA ASSOCIATED WITH LISTENING TO THESE PROFESSION-

ALS, AS THEY RIP OUT LARGE CHUNKS OF A PROJECT, LAUGH, AND YELL REMARKS SUCH AS: "HEY! GET A LOAD OF THIS."

After the Jonathans took out all my projects, the house mostly consisted of holes, which they filled up with spackle. When prospective buyers asked: "What kind of construction is this house?" I answered: "Spackle."

The only real bright spot in the move was when I got even with the television set in our bedroom, which had been broken for years. My wife and I have had the same argument about it maybe 200 times, wherein I say we should throw it away, and she says we should get it repaired. My wife grew up in a very sheltered rural Ohio community and she still believes you can get things repaired.

Over the years, this television had come to believe that as long as my wife was around, it was safe, and it had grown very smug, which is why I wish you could have seen the look on its face when, with my wife weakened by the flu, I took it out and propped it up at the end of the dumpster, execution-style, and, as a small neighborhood crowd gathered, one of the Jonathans hurled a long, spear-like piece of Homeowner Project from 20 feet away right directly through the screen, into the very heart of its picture tube. It made a sound that I am sure our other appliances will not soon forget.

But the rest were mostly low points. I looked forward to the day when somebody bought our house, perhaps to use as a tourist attraction (SPACKLE KINGDOM, 5 MI.), and we could pack our remaining household possessions—a piano and 48,000 "He-Man" action figures—into cardboard boxes and move to Miami to begin our new life, soaking up the sun and watching the palm trees sway in the tropical breeze. At least until the aluminum sliced through them.

THE HOUSE OF THE SEVEN FIGURES

BEFORE MY WIFE, BETH, LEFT ON THE JET AIR-plane to buy us a new house, we sat down and figured out what our Price Range was. We used the standard formula where you take your income and divide it by three, which gives you the amount you would spend annually on housing if you bought a house that is much cheaper than the one you will actually end up buying.

With that figure in mind, Beth took off for our new home-to-be, South Florida, and my son and I, who had never been in charge of each other for this long before, embarked on the following rigorous nutritional program:

BREAKFAST: Frozen waffles heated up.

LUNCH: Hot dogs heated up.

DINNER: Choice of hot dogs or frozen waffles heated up.

Also in the refrigerator were many health-fanatic foods such as presliced carrot sticks placed there by Beth in hopes that we would eat something that did not have a label stating that it met the minimum federal standard for human armpit hair, but we rejected these because of the lengthy preparation time.

Some of you may be wondering why, considering that this is the most important financial transaction of our lives, I didn't go with Beth to buy the house. The answer is that I am a very dangerous person to have on your side in a sales situation. I develop great anxiety in the presence of salespeople, and the only way I can think of to make it go away is to buy whatever they're selling. This is not a major problem with, for example, pants, but it leads to trouble with cars and houses.

Here is how I bought our last car. I didn't dare go directly to the car dealership, so, for several consecutive days —this is the truth—I would park at a nearby Dairy Queen, buy a chocolate cone, then amble over to the car lot, disguised as a person just ambling around with a chocolate cone, and I would try to quickly read the sticker on the side of the car where they explain that the only part of the car included in the Base Sticker Price is the actual sticker itself, and you have to pay extra if you want, for example, transparent windows. After a few minutes, a salesman would spot me and come striding out, smiling like an entire Rotary Club, and I would adopt the expression of a person who had just remembered an important appointment and amble off at speeds approaching 40 miles per hour. What I'm saying is, I shopped for this car the way a squirrel hunts for acorns in a dog-infested neighborhood.

When I finally went in to buy the car, I was desperate to get it over with as quickly as possible. Here is how I negotiated:

SALESPERSON: (showing me a sheet of paper with figures on it): OK, Dave. Here's a ludicrously inflated opening price that only a person with Rice-A-Roni for brains would settle for.

ME: You got a deal.

I am worse with houses. The last time we were trying to buy a house, I made Beth crazy because I was willing to make a formal offer on whatever structure we were standing in at the time:

ME: This is perfect! Isn't this perfect?!

BETH: This is the real-estate office.

ME: Well, how much are they asking?

So this is why Beth went to Miami without me. Moments after she arrived, she ascertained that there were no houses there in our Price Range. Our Price Range turned out to be

58

what the average homeowner down there spends on roach control. (And we are not talking about *killing* the roaches. We are talking about sedating them enough so they let you into your house.)

Fortunately, Beth found out about a new financial concept they have in home-buying that is tailor-made for people like us, called Going Outside Your Price Range. This is where she started looking, and before long she had stumbled onto an even *newer* financial concept called Going Way Outside Your Price Range. This is where she eventually found a house, and I am very much looking forward to seeing it someday, assuming we get a mortgage.

They have developed a new wrinkle in mortgages since the last time we got one, back in the seventies. The way it worked then was, you borrowed money from the bank, and every month you paid back some money, and at the end of the year the bank sent you a computerized statement proving you still owed them all the money you borrowed in the first place. Well, they're still using that basic system, but now they also have this wrinkle called "points," which is a large quantity of money you give to the bank, right up front, for no apparent reason. It's as though the *bank* is the one trying to buy the house. You ask real-estate people to explain it, and they just say: "Oh yes, the points! Be sure to bring an enormous sum of money to the settlement for those!" And of course we will. We consumers will do almost anything to get our mortgages. Banks know this, so they keep inventing new charges to see how far they can go:

MORTGAGE OFFICER: OK, at your settlement you have to pay $400 for the preparation of the Certificate of Indemption.

CONSUMER: Yes, of course.

MORTGAGE OFFICER: And $430 for pastries.

But it will all be worth it, to get to our house. It sounds, from Beth's description, as though it has everything that I look for in a house: (1) a basketball hoop and (2) a fiberglass backboard. I understand it also has rooms.

CAN NEW YORK SAVE ITSELF?

AT THE *MIAMI HERALD* WE ORDINARILY DON'T provide extensive coverage of New York City unless a major news development occurs up there, such as Sean Penn coming out of a restaurant. But lately we have become very concerned about the "Big Apple," because of a story about Miami that ran a few weeks ago in the Sunday magazine of the *New York Times.* Maybe you remember this story: The cover featured an upbeat photograph of suspected Miami drug dealers being handcuffed face-down in the barren dirt next to a garbage-strewn sidewalk outside a squalid shack that probably contains roaches the size of Volvo sedans. The headline asked:

CAN MIAMI SAVE ITSELF?

For those readers too stupid to figure out the answer, there also was this helpful hint:

A City Beset by Drugs and Violence

The overall impression created by the cover was: *Sure Miami can save itself! And some day trained sheep will pilot the Concorde!*

The story itself was more balanced, discussing the pluses as well as the minuses of life in South Florida, as follows:

• *Minuses:* The area is rampant with violent crime and

poverty and political extremism and drugs and corruption and ethnic hatred.

• *Pluses:* Voodoo is legal.

I myself thought it was pretty fair. Our local civic leaders reacted to it with their usual level of cool maturity, similar to the way Moe reacts when he is poked in the eyeballs by Larry and Curly. Our leaders held emergency breakfasts and issued official statements pointing out that much of the information in the *New York Times* story was Ancient History dating all the way back to the early 1980s, and that we haven't had a riot for what, *months* now, and that the whole drugs-and-violence thing is overrated. Meanwhile, at newsstands all over South Florida, crowds of people were snapping up all available copies of the *New York Times*, frequently at gunpoint.

All of which got us, at the *Miami Herald*, to thinking. "Gosh," we thought. "Here the world-famous *New York Times*, with so many other things to worry about, has gone to all this trouble to try to find out whether Miami can save itself. Wouldn't they be thrilled if we did the same thing for them?" And so it was that we decided to send a crack investigative team consisting of me and Chuck, who is a trained photographer, up there for a couple of days to see what the situation was. We took along comfortable walking shoes and plenty of major credit cards, in case it turned out that we needed to rent a helicopter, which it turned out we did. Here is our report:

DAY ONE: We're riding in a cab from La Guardia Airport to our Manhattan hotel, and I want to interview the driver, because this is how we professional journalists take the Pulse of a City, only I can't, because he doesn't speak English. He is not allowed to, under the rules, which are posted right on the seat:

NEW YORK TAXI RULES
1. DRIVER SPEAKS NO ENGLISH.

61

2. DRIVER JUST GOT HERE TWO DAYS AGO FROM
   SOMEPLACE LIKE SENEGAL.
3. DRIVER HATES YOU.

Which is just as well, because if he talked to me, he might lose his concentration, which would be very bad because the taxi has some kind of problem with the steering, probably dead pedestrians lodged in the mechanism, the result being that there is a delay of 8 to 10 seconds between the time the driver turns the wheel and the time the taxi actually changes direction, a handicap that the driver is compensating for by going 175 miles per hour, at which velocity we are able to remain airborne almost to the far rim of some of the smaller potholes. These are of course maintained by the crack New York Department of Potholes (currently on strike), whose commissioner was recently indicted on corruption charges by the Federal Grand Jury to Indict Every Commissioner in New York. This will take some time, because New York has more commissioners than Des Moines, Iowa, has residents, including the Commissioner for Making Sure the Sidewalks Are Always Blocked by Steaming Fetid Mounds of Garbage the Size of Appalachian Foothills, and, of course, the Commissioner for Bicycle Messengers Bearing Down on You at Warp Speed with Mohawk Haircuts and Pupils Smaller Than Purely Theoretical Particles.

After several exhilarating minutes, we arrive in downtown Manhattan, where the driver slows to 125 miles so he can take better aim at wheelchair occupants. This gives us our first brief glimpse of the city we have come to investigate. It looks to us, whizzing past, as though it is beset by serious problems. We are reminded of the findings of the 40-member Mayor's Special Commission on the Future of the City of New York, which this past June, after nearly two years of intensive study of the economic, political, and social problems confronting the city, issued a 2,300-page report, which reached the disturbing conclusion that New York is "a nice place to visit" but the commission "wouldn't want to live there."

Of course they probably stayed at a nicer hotel than where we're staying. We're staying at a "medium-priced" hotel, meaning that the rooms are more than spacious enough for a family of four to stand up in if they are slightly built and hold their arms over their heads, yet the rate is just $135 per night, plus of course your state tax, your city tax, your occupancy tax, your head tax, your body tax, your soap tax, your ice bucket tax, your in-room dirty movies tax, and your piece of paper that says your toilet is sanitized for your protection tax, which bring the rate to $367.90 per night, or a flat $4,000 if you use the telephone. A bellperson carries my luggage—one small gym-style bag containing, primarily, a set of clean underwear—and I tip him $2, which he takes as if I am handing him a jar of warm sputum.

But never mind. We are not here to please the bellperson. We are here to see if New York can save itself. And so Chuck and I set off into the streets of Manhattan, where we immediately detect signs of a healthy economy in the form of people squatting on the sidewalk selling realistic jewelry. This is good, because a number of other businesses, such as Mobil Corp., have recently decided to pull their headquarters out of New York, much to the annoyance of Edward Koch, the feisty, cocky, outspoken, abrasive mayor who really gets on some people's nerves, yet at the same time strikes other people as a jerk. "Why would *anybody* want to move to some dirt-bag place like the Midwest?" Mayor Koch is always asking reporters. "What are they gonna do at *night*? Huh? *Milk the cows?* Are they gonna wear bib overalls and sit around *canning their preserves?* Huh? Are they gonna . . . Hey! Come back here!"

But why *are* the corporations leaving? To answer this question, a polling firm recently took a scientific telephone survey of the heads of New York's 200 largest corporations, and found that none of them were expected to arrive at work for at least two more hours because of massive transit delays caused by a wildcat strike of the 1,200-member Wildcat Strikers Guild. So you can see the corporations' point: It *is* an inconvenience, being located in a city where taxes are ludicrously high, where you pay twice your annual income to rent an apartment that could easily be carried on a commercial airline flight, where you spend two-thirds of your work day trying to get to and from work, but as Mayor Koch philosophically points out, "Are they gonna *slop the hogs?* Are they gonna. . . ."

Despite the corporate exodus, the New York economy continues to be robust, with the major industry being people from New Jersey paying $45 each to see *A Chorus Line*. Employment remains high, with most of the new jobs opening up in the fast-growing fields of:

• Person asking everybody for "spare" change.
• Person shrieking at taxis.
• Person holding animated sidewalk conversation with beings from another dimension.
• Person handing out little slips of paper entitling the bearer to one free drink at sophisticated nightclubs with names like The Bazoom Room.

As Chuck and I walk along 42nd Street, we see a person wearing an enormous frankfurter costume, handing out coupons good for discounts at Nathan's Famous hot dog stands. His name is Victor Leise, age 19, of Queens, and he has held the position of giant frankfurter for four months. He says he didn't have any connections or anything; he just put in an application and, boom, the job was his. Sheer luck. He says it's OK work, although people call him "Frank" and sometimes sneak up and whack him on the back. Also there is not a lot of room for advancement. They have no hamburger costume.

"Can New York save itself?" I ask him.

"If there are more cops on the street, there could be a possibility," he says, through his breathing hole.

Right down the street is the world-famous Times Square. Although this area is best known as the site where many thousands of people gather each New Year's Eve for a joyous and festive night of public urination, it also serves as an important cultural center where patrons may view films such as *Sex Aliens, Wet Adulteress,* and, of course, *Sperm Busters* in comfortable refrigerated theaters where everybody sits about 15 feet apart. This is also an excellent place to shop for your leisure product needs, including The Bionic Woman ("An amazingly lifelike companion") and a vast selection of latex objects, some the size of military pontoons. The local residents are very friendly, often coming right up and offering to engage in acts of leisure with you. Reluctantly, however, Chuck and I decided to tear ourselves away, for we have much more to see, plus we do not wish to spend the rest of our lives soaking in vats of penicillin.

As we leave the area, I stop briefly inside an Off-Track Betting parlor on Seventh Avenue to see if I can obtain the Pulse of the City by eavesdropping on native New Yorkers in casual conversation. Off-Track Betting parlors are the kinds of places where you never see signs that say, "Thank You for Not Smoking." The best you could hope for is, "Thank You for Not Spitting Pieces of Your Cigar on My Neck." By listening carefully and remaining unobtrusive, I am able to overhear the following conversation:

FIRST OFF-TRACK BETTOR: I like this (*very bad word*) horse here.

SECOND OFF-TRACK BETTOR: That (*extremely bad word*) couldn't (*bad word*) out his own (*comical new bad word*).

FIRST OFF-TRACK BETTOR: (*bad word*).

Listening to these two men share their innermost feelings, I sense concern, yes, but also an undercurrent of hope, hope for a Brighter Tomorrow, if only the people of this great city can learn to work together, to look upon each other with respect and even, yes, love. Or at least stop shoving one another in front of moving subway trains. This happens a fair amount in New York, so Chuck and I are extremely alert as we descend into the complex of subway tunnels under Times Square, climate-controlled year-round at a comfortable 172 degrees Fahrenheit.

Although it was constructed in 1536, the New York subway system boasts an annual maintenance budget of nearly $8, currently stolen, and it does a remarkable job of getting New Yorkers from point A to an indeterminate location somewhere in the tunnel leading to point B. It's also very easy for the "out-of-towner" to use, thanks to the logical, easy-to-understand system of naming trains after famous letters and numbers. For directions, all you have to do is peer up through the steaming gloom at the informative signs, which look like this:

A 5 N 7 8 C 6 AA MID-DOWNTOWN 7⅜

EXPRESS LOCAL ONLY LL 67 ♦

DDD 4♠ 1K ☆ AAAA 9 ONLY

EXCEPT CERTAIN DAYS BB ®® 3

MIDWAY THROUGH TOWN 1 7 D

WALK REAL FAST AAAAAAAAA 56

LOCALIZED EXPRESS-6

"YY" ♣ 1,539

AAAAAAAAAAAAAAAAAAA

If for some reason you are unsure where to go, all you have to do is stand there looking lost, and within seconds a helpful New Yorker will approach to see if you have any "spare" change.

Within less than an hour, Chuck and I easily located what could well be the correct platform, where we pass the time by perspiring freely until the train storms in, colorfully decorated, as is the tradition in New York, with the spray-painted initials of all the people it has run over. All aboard!

Here is the correct procedure for getting on a New York subway train at rush hour:

1. As the train stops, you must join the other people on the platform in pushing forward and forming the densest possible knot in front of each door. You want your knot to be so dense that, if the train were filled with water instead of people, not a single drop would escape.

2. The instant the doors open, you want to push forward as hard as possible, in an effort to get onto the train *without letting anybody get off.* This is *very important.* If anybody does get off, it is legal to tackle him and drag him back on. I once watched three German tourists—this is a true anecdote —attempt to get off the northbound No. 5 Lexington Avenue IRT train at Grand Central Station during rush hour. "Getting off please!" they said, politely, from somewhere inside a car containing approximately the population of Brazil, as if they expected people to actually *let them through.* Instead of course, the incoming passengers propelled the Germans, like gnats in a hurricane, *away* from the door, deeper and deeper into the crowd, which quickly compressed them into dense little wads of Teutonic tissue. I never did see where they actually got off. Probably they stumbled to daylight somewhere in the South Bronx, where they were sold for parts.

Actually, there is reason to believe the subways are safer now. After years of being fearful and intimidated, many New Yorkers cheered in 1985 when Bernhard Goetz, in a highly controversial incident that touched off an emotion-charged nationwide debate, shot and killed the New York subway commissioner. This resulted in extensive legal proceedings, culminating recently when, after a dramatic and highly publicized trial, a jury voted not only to acquit Goetz, but also to dig up the commissioner and shoot him again.

Chuck and I emerge from the subway in Lower Manhattan. This area has been hard hit by the massive wave of immigration that has threatened to rend the very fabric of society, as the city struggles desperately to cope with the social upheaval caused by the huge and unprecedented influx of a group that has, for better or for worse, permanently altered the nature of New York: young urban professionals. They began arriving by the thousands in the 1970s, packed two and sometimes three per BMW sedan, severely straining the city's already-overcrowded gourmet-ice cream facilities. Soon they were taking over entire neighborhoods, where longtime residents watched in despair as useful businesses such as bars were replaced by precious little restaurants with names like The Whittling Fig.

And still the urban professionals continue to come, drawn by a dream, a dream that is best expressed by the words of the song "New York, New York," which goes:

> *Dum dum da de dum*
> *Dum dum da de dum*
> *Dum dum da de dum*
> *Dum dum da de dum dum.*

It is a powerfully seductive message, especially if you hear it at a wedding reception held in a Scranton, Pennsylvania, Moose Lodge facility and you have been drinking. And so you come to the Big Apple, and you take a peon-level position in some huge impersonal corporation, an incredibly awful, hateful job, and you spend $1,250 a month to rent an apartment so tiny that you have to shower in the kitchen, and the only furniture you have room for—not that you can afford furniture anyway—is your collection of back issues of *Metropolitan Home* magazine, but you stick it out, because this is the Big Leagues (*If I can make it there, I'll make it anywhere*), and you know that if you show them what you can do, if you really *go for it*, then, by gosh, one day you're gonna wake up, in The City That Never Sleeps, to find that the corporation has moved its headquarters to Plano, Texas.

Now Chuck and I are in Chinatown. We pass an outdoor market where there is an attractive display consisting of a tub containing I would estimate 275,000 dead baby eels. One of the great things about New York is that, if you ever need dead baby eels, you can get them. Also there is opera here. But tonight I think I'll just try to get some sleep.

At 3:14 A.M. I am awakened by a loud crashing sound, caused by workers from the city's crack Department of Making Loud Crashing Sounds during the Night, who are just outside my window, breaking in a new taxicab by dropping it repeatedly from a 75-foot crane. Lying in bed listening to them, I can hardly wait for . . .

DAY TWO: Chuck and I decide that since we pretty much covered the economic, social, political, historical and cultural aspects of New York on Day One, we'll devote Day Two to sightseeing. We decide to start with the best-known sight of all, the one that, more than any other, exemplifies what the Big Apple is all about: the Islip Garbage Barge. This is a barge of world-renowned garbage that originated on Long Island, a place where many New Yorkers go to sleep on those occasions when the Long Island Railroad is operating.

The Islip Garbage Barge is very famous. Nobody really remembers *why* it's famous; it just *is*, like Dick Cavett. It has traveled to South America. It has been on many television shows, including—I am not making this up—"Donahue." When we were in New York, the barge—I am still not making this up—was on trial. It has since been convicted and sentenced to be burned. But I am not worried. It will get out on appeal. It is the Claus von Bülow of garbage barges.

Chuck and I find out from the Director of Public Affairs at the New York Department of Sanitation, who is named Vito, that the barge is anchored off the coast of Brooklyn, so we grab a cab, which is driven by a man who of course speaks very little English and, as far as we can tell, has never heard of Brooklyn. By means of hand signals we direct him to a place near where the barge is anchored. It is some kind of garbage-collection point.

There are mounds of garbage everywhere, and if you really concentrate, you can actually see them giving off smell rays, such as you see in comic strips. Clearly no taxi has ever been here before, and none will ever come again, so we ask the driver to wait. "YOU WAIT HERE," I say, speaking in capital letters so he will understand me. He looks at me suspiciously. "WE JUST WANT TO SEE A GARBAGE BARGE," I explain.

We can see the barge way out on the water, but Chuck decides that, to get a good picture of it, we need a boat. A sanitation engineer tells us we might be able to rent one in a place called Sheepshead Bay, so we direct the driver there ("WE NEED TO RENT A BOAT"), but when we get there we realize it's too far away, so we naturally decide to rent a helicoper, which we find out is available only in New Jersey. ("NOW WE NEED TO GO TO NEW JERSEY. TO RENT A HELICOPTER.") Thus we end up at the airport in Linden, New Jersey, where we leave the taxi driver with enough fare money to retire for life, if he ever finds his way home.

Chuck puts the helicoper on his American Express card. Our pilot, Norman Knodt, assures me that nothing bad has ever happened to him in a helicopter excepting getting it shot up nine times, but that was in Vietnam, and he foresees no problems with the garbage-barge mission. Soon we are over the harbor, circling the barge, which turns out to be, like so many celebrities when you see them up close, not as tall as you expected. As I gaze down at it, with the soaring spires of downtown Manhattan in the background gleaming in the brilliant sky, a thought crosses my mind: I had better write at *least* 10 inches about this, to justify our expense reports.

Later that day, I stop outside Grand Central Station, where a woman is sitting in a chair on the sidewalk next to a sign that says:

TAROT CARDS

PALM READINGS

I ask her how much it costs for a Tarot card reading, and she says $10, which I give her. She has me select nine cards, which she arranges in a circle. "Now ask me a question," she says.

"Can New York save itself?" I ask.

She looks at me.

"That's your question?" she asks.

"Yes," I say.

"OK," she says. She looks at the cards. "Yes, New York can save itself for the future."

She looks at me. I don't say anything. She looks back at the cards.

"New York is the Big Apple," she announces. "It is big and exciting, with very many things to see and do."

After the reading I stop at a newsstand and pick up a copy of *Manhattan Living* magazine, featuring a guide to condominiums. I note that there are a number of one-bedrooms priced as low as $250,000.

Manhattan Living also has articles. "It is only recently," one begins, "that the word 'fashionable' has been used in conjunction with the bathroom."

DAY THREE: Just to be on the safe side, Chuck and I decide to devote Day Three to getting back to the airport. Because of a slip-up at the Department of Taxi Licensing, our driver speaks a fair amount of English. And it's a darned good thing he does, because he is kind enough to share his philosophy of life with us, in between shouting helpful instructions to other drivers. It is a philosophy of optimism and hope, not just for himself, but also for New York City, and for the world:

"The thing is, you got to look on the lighter side, because HEY WHAT THE HELL IS HE DOING! WHAT THE HELL ARE YOU DOING YOU (*very bad word*)! Because for me, the thing is, respect. If a person shows me respect, then HAH! YOU WANT TO SQUEEZE IN FRONT NOW?? YOU S.O.B.!! I SQUEEZE YOU LIKE A LEMON!! So I am happy here, but you Americans, you know, you are very, you know WHERE IS HE GOING??

You have to look behind the scenery. This damn CIA, something sticky is going on WHERE THE HELL IS THIS STUPID S.O.B. THINK HE IS GOING??? behind the scenery there, you don't think this guy what his name, Casey, you don't LOOK AT THIS S.O.B. you don't wonder why he *really* die? You got to look behind the scenery. I don't trust *nobody*. I don't trust my own *self*. WILL YOU LOOK AT . . .

By the time we reach La Guardia, Chuck and I have a much deeper understanding of life in general, and it is with a sense of real gratitude that we leap out of the cab and cling to the pavement. Soon we are winging our way southward, watching the Manhattan skyline disappear, reflecting upon our many experiences and pondering the question that brought us here:

Can New York save itself? Can this ultrametropolis—crude yet sophisticated, overburdened yet wealthy, loud yet obnoxious—can this city face up to the multitude of problems besetting it and, drawing upon its vast reserves of spunk and spirit, as it has done so many times before, emerge triumphant?

And, who cares?

A BOY AND HIS DIPLODOCUS

WE HAVE BEEN DEEPLY INTO DINOSAURS FOR some time now. We have a great many plastic dinosaurs around the house. Sometimes I think we have more plastic dinosaurs than plastic robots, if you can imagine.

This is my son's doing, of course. Robert got into dinosaurs when he was about three, as many children do. It's a power thing: Children like the idea of creatures that were much, much bigger and stronger than mommies and daddies are. If a little boy is doing something bad, such as deliberately pouring his apple juice onto the television remote-control device, a mommy or daddy can simply snatch the littly boy up and carry him, helpless, to his room. But they would not dare try this with Tyrannosaurus Rex. No sir. Tyrannosaurus Rex would glance down at Mommy or Daddy from a height of 40 feet and casually flick his tail sideways, and Mommy or Daddy would sail directly through the wall, leaving comical cartoon-style Mommy-or-Daddy–shaped holes and Tyrannosaurus Rex would calmly go back to pouring his apple juice onto the remote-control device.

So Robert spends a lot of time being a dinosaur. I recall the time we were at the beach and he was being a Gorgosaurus, which, like Tyrannosaurus Rex, is a major dinosaur, a big meat-eater (Robert is almost always carnivorous). He was stomping around in the sand and along came an elderly tourist couple, talking in German. They sat down near us. Robert watched them.

"Tell them I'm a Gorgosaurus," he said.

"*You* tell them," I said.

"Gorgosauruses can't talk," Robert pointed out, rolling his eyes. Sometimes he can't believe what an idiot his father is.

Anybody who has ever had a small child knows what happened next. What happened was Robert, using the powerful whining ability that Mother Nature gives to young children to compensate for the fact that they have no other useful skills, got me to go over to this elderly foreign couple I had never seen before, point to my son, who was looking as awesome and terrifying as a three-year-old can look lumbering around in a bathing suit with a little red anchor sewn on the crotch, and say: "He's a Gorgosaurus."

The Germans looked at me the way you would look at a person you saw walking through a shopping mall with a vacant stare and a chain saw. They said nothing.

"Ha ha!" I added, so they would see I was in fact very normal.

They continued to say nothing. You could tell this had never happened to them over in Germany. You could just tell that in Germany, they have a strict policy whereby people who claim their sons are dinosaurs on public beaches are quickly sedated by the authorities. You could also tell that this couple agreed with that policy.

"Tell them I'm a meat-eater," the Gorgosaurus whispered.

"He's a meat-eater," I told the couple. God only knows why.

They got up and started to fold their towels.

"Tell them I can eat more in ONE BITE than a mommy and a daddy and a little boy could eat in TWO WHOLE MONTHS," urged the Gorgosaurus, this being one of the many dinosaur facts he got from the books we read to him at bedtime. But by then the Germans were already striding off, glancing back at me and talking quietly to each other about which way they would run if I came after them.

"Ha ha!" I called after them, reassuringly.

Gorgosaurus continued to stomp around, knocking over whole cities. I had a hell of a time getting him to take a nap that day.

Sometimes when he's tired and wants to be cuddled, Robert is a gentle plant-eating dinosaur. I'll come into the living room, and there will be this lump on my wife's lap, whimpering, with Robert's blanket over it.

"What's that?" I ask my wife.

"A baby Diplodocus," she answers. (Diplodocus looked sort of like Brontosaurus, only sleeker and cuter.) "It lost its mommy and daddy."

"No!" I say.

"So it's going to live with us forever and ever," she says.

"Great!" I say.

The blanket wriggles with joy.

Lately, at our house we have become interested in what finally happened to the dinosaurs. According to our bedtime books, all the dinosaurs died quite suddenly about 60 million years ago, and nobody knows why. Some scientists—this is the truth, it was in *Time* magazine—think the cause was a Death Comet that visits the earth from time to time. Robert thinks this is great. A Death Comet! That is *serious* power. A Death Comet would *never* have to brush its teeth. A Death Comet could have pizza *whenever it wanted.*

Me, I get uneasy, reading about the Death Comet. I don't like to think about the dinosaurs disappearing. Yet another reminder that nothing lasts forever. Even a baby Diplodocus has to grow up sometime.

YOUNG FRANKINCENSE

MY MOST VIVID CHILDHOOD MEMORY OF CHRIST-mas that does not involve opening presents, putting batteries in presents, playing with presents, and destroying presents before sundown, is the annual Nativity Pageant at St. Stephen's Episcopal Church in Armonk, New York. This was a major tradition at St. Stephen's, which had quite a few of them. For example, at Easter, we had the Hoisting of the Potted Hyacinths. Each person in the congregation was issued a potted hyacinth, and we'd sing a song that had a lot of "alleluias" in it, and every time we'd get to one, we'd all hoist our pots over our heads. This is the truth. Remember it next time somebody tells you Episcopalians never really get loose.

But the big event was the Nativity Pageant, which almost all the Sunday School kids were drafted to perform in. Mrs. Elson, who had experience in the Legitimate Theater, was the director, and she would tell you what role you would play, based on your artistic abilities. Like, if your artistic abilities were that you were short, you would get a role as an angel, which involved being part of the Heavenly Host and gazing with adoration upon the Christ Child and trying not to scratch yourself. The Christ Child was played by one of those dolls that close their eyes when you lay them down because they have weights in their heads. I know this because Neil Thompson and I once conducted a research experiment

wherein we scientifically opened a doll's head up with a hammer. (This was not the doll that played the Christ Child, of
course. We used a doll that belonged to Neil's sister, Penny,
who once tied her dog to the bumper of my mother's car
roughly five minutes before my mother drove the car to
White Plains. But that is another story.)

Above your angels, you had your three shepherds.
Shepherd was my favorite role, because you got to carry a
stick, plus you spent most of the pageant waiting back in the
closet with a rope that led up to the church bell and about
750,000 bats. Many were the happy rehearsal hours we shepherds spent back there, in the dark, whacking each other
with sticks and climbing up the ladder so as to cause bat
emission products to rain down upon us. ("And lo, when the
shepherds did looketh towards the heavens, they did see,
raining down upon them, a multitude of guano. . . .")

When it was our turn to go out and perform, we shepherds would emerge from the closet, walk up the aisle, and
hold a conference to determine whether or not we should go
to Bethlehem. One year when I was a shepherd, the role of
First Shepherd was played by Mike Craig, who always, at
every rehearsal, would whisper: "Let's ditch this joint." Of
course this does not strike *you* as particularly funny, but believe me, if you were a 10-year-old who had spent the past
hour in a bat-infested closet, it would strike you as amusing
in the extreme, and it got funnier every time, so that when
Mike said it on Christmas Eve *during the actual pageant,* it was
an awesome thing, the hydrogen bomb of jokes, causing the
shepherds to almost pee their garments as they staggered
off, snorting, toward Bethlehem.

After a couple of years as shepherd, you usually did a
stint as a Three King. This was not nearly as good a role,
because (a) you didn't get to wait in the closet, and (b) you
had to lug around the gold, the frankincense, and of course
the myrrh, which God forbid you should drop because they
were played by valuable antique containers belonging to Mrs.
Elson. Nevertheless, being a Three King was better than

being Joseph, because Joseph had to hang around with Mary, who was played by (YECCCCCHHHHHHH) a girl. You had to wait backstage with this girl, and walk in with this girl, and needless to say you felt like a total wonk, which was not helped by the fact that the shepherds and the Three Kings were constantly suggesting that you *liked* this girl. So during the pageant Joseph tended to maintain the maximum allowable distance from Mary, as though she were carrying some kind of fatal bacteria.

On Christmas Eve we were all pretty nervous, but thanks to all the rehearsals, the pageant generally went off with only 60 or 70 hitches. Like, for example, one year Ernie Dobbs, a Three King, dropped the frankincense only moments before showtime, and he had to go on carrying, as I recall, a Rolodex. Also there was the famous incident where the shepherds could not get out of the bat closet for the longest while, and thus lost their opportunity for that moment of dramatic tension where they confer and the audience is on the edge of its pews, wondering what they'll decide. When they finally emerged, all they had time to do was lunge directly for Bethlehem.

But we always got through the pageant, somehow, and Mrs. Elson always told us what a great job we had done, except for the year Ernie broke the frankincense. Afterwards, whoever had played Joseph would try to capture and destroy the rest of the male cast. Then we would go home to bed, with visions of Mattel-brand toys requiring six "D" cell batteries (not included) dancing in our heads. Call me sentimental, but I miss those days.

PEACE ON EARTH, BUT NO PARKING

ONCE AGAIN WE FIND OURSELVES ENMESHED IN the Holiday Season, that very special time of year when we join with our loved ones in sharing centuries-old traditions such as trying to find a parking space at the mall. We traditionally do this in my family by driving around the parking lot until we see a shopper emerge from the mall, then we follow her, in very much the same spirit as the Three Wise Men, who 2,000 years ago followed a star, week after week, until it led them to a parking space.

We try to keep our bumper about four inches from the shopper's calves, to let the other circling cars know that she belongs to us. Sometimes two cars will get into a fight over whom the shopper belongs to, similar to the way great white sharks will fight over who gets to eat a snorkeler. So we follow our shoppers closely, hunched over the steering wheel, whistling "It's Beginning to Look a Lot Like Christmas" through our teeth, until we arrive at her car, which is usually parked several time zones away from the mall. Sometimes our shopper tries to indicate that she was merely planning to drop off some packages and go back to shopping, but when she hears our engine rev in a festive fashion and sees the holiday gleam in our eyes, she realizes she would never make it.

And so we park and clamber joyously out of our car through the windows, which is necessary because the crack

Mall Parking Space Size Reduction Team has been at work again. They get out there almost every night and redo the entire parking lot, each time making the spaces smaller, until finally, they are using, say, a Jell-O box to mark the width between lines. "Let's see them fit in there," they say, laughing, because they know we will try. They know that if necessary, we will pull into the parking space balanced on two left-side wheels, like professional stunt drivers, because we are holiday shoppers.

I do not mean to suggest that the true meaning of the holiday season is finding a parking space. No, the true meaning of the holiday season is finding a sales clerk. The way to do this is, look around the store for one of those unmarked doors, then burst through it without warning. There you will find dozens of clerks sitting on the floor, rocking back and forth and whimpering from weeks of exposure to the holiday environment. Of course as soon as they see you, a shopper, they will bolt for the window. This is why you must carry a tape recorder.

"Hold it!" you shout, freezing them in their tracks. "I have a tape recorder here, and unless somebody lets me make my holiday purchases, I'm going to play 'Frosty the Snowman.'"

Cruel? Inhuman? Perhaps. But you have no choice. Because this is the holiday season, and you have to buy thoughtful gifts for all of your Loved Ones, or they will hate you. Here are some helpful suggestions:

GIFTS FOR CHILDREN: To find out what children want this year, I naturally called up the headquarters of the Toys Backward 'R' Us Corporation, which as you parents know is now larger than the Soviet Union. I talked with a spokesperson who told me that last year the corporation's net sales were $2.4 billion (I assume she meant in my immediate neighborhood).

The spokesperson told me that one of the hot toys for boys this year, once again, is the G.I. Joe action figure and "accessories," which is the toy-industry code word for "guns," as in: "Don't nobody move! I got an accessory!" The little boy on your list can have hours of carefree childhood fun with this G.I. Joe set, engaging in realistic armed-forces adventures such as having G.I. Joe explain to little balding congressional committee figures how come he had to use his optional Action Shredder accessory.

Another hot item is Captain Power and the Soldiers of the Future, a toy system that—here is a concidence for you —is featured on a Saturday-morning TV show. The heart of this system is an electronic accessory that the child shoots at the TV screen to actually kill members of the Bio Dread Empire. The spokesperson did not say whether it also would work on Geraldo Rivera.

For little girls, the toy industry is once again going way out on a limb and offering a vast simpering array of dolls. The big news this year, however, is that many of these dolls have computer chips inside them, so they can do the same things that a real baby would do if it had a computer chip inside it. Some dolls even respond according to the time of day. In the morning, they say: "I'm hungry!" In the evening, they say: "I'm sleepy!" And late at night, when the house is dark and quiet, they whisper into the child's ear: "I think I hear Mr. Eyeball Plucker in the closet again!"

GIFTS FOR GROWN-UPS: I don't want to get too corny here, but I think the nicest gift you can give a grown-up, especially one you really care about, is not something you buy in a store. In fact, it costs nothing, yet it is a very precious gift, and one that only you can give. I'm talking about your parking space.

HEY BABE HUM BABE HUM BABE HEY...

THE CRACK OF THE BAT...THE ROAR OF THE crowd . . . the sight of slug-shaped, saliva-drenched gobs of tobacco seeping into the turf and causing mutations among soil-based life forms. . . .

Baseball. For me, it's as much a part of summer as sitting bolt upright in bed at 3:30 A.M. and trying to remember if I filed for an extension on my tax return. And the memories baseball season brings back! Ebbetts Field, for example. That's all I remember: Ebbetts Field. What the hell does it mean? Is it anything important? Maybe one of you readers can help.

Why does baseball hold such great appeal for Americans? A big factor, of course, is that the Russians can't play it. Try as they might, they can't seem to master infield chatter, which is what the members of the infield constantly yell at the pitcher. A typical segment of infield chatter would be:

Hey babe hum babe hum babe hey no batter hey fire that ball hum that pellet whip that hose baby sling that sphere c'mon heave that horsehide right in there c'mon dammit we're bored we're really bored bored bored bored out here hunched over in these cretin pants c'mon let's fling that orb let's unload that globe you sum-bitch let's THROW that ball please for God's sake let's . . .

The infield's purpose in chattering at the pitcher like this is to get him so irritated that he deliberately throws the ball at the batter's face, which minimizes the danger that the batter will swing and thus put the infield in the position of having to stand in the path of a potentially lethal batted ball. American boys learn infield chatter as very young children, but the Russians have tremendous trouble with it. The best they've been able to do so far is "Holy mackerel, you are putting forth some likely shots now, ho ho!" which is pretty good for only five years' effort, but hardly the level of chatter they'll need in international competition.

Another reason why Americans are Number One in baseball is the phrases yelled by fans to encourage the players. American fans generally use the three basic phrases:

- Boo.
- You stink.
- You really stink, you stupid jerk.

These phrases of encouragement have dominated baseball since the 1920s, when the great George Herman Ruth made baseball history at Yankee Stadium by pointing his bat at the stands and correctly identifying them in only four attempts. But in recent years, a large cold-air mass of change has begun to form in the North, where fans of the Montreal Expos, who all know how to speak French because there's nothing else to do in Canada after 4 P.M., have developed some new and very competitive phrases, such as:

- Vous bumme, il y a un poisson dans votre bibliotheque. (You bum, there is a fish in your library.)
- Boux. (Boo.)

Thus encouraged, the Expos have become a baseball powerhouse. They probably would have won the World Series by now except that the players refuse to return from spring training until Labor Day.

So the United States is still the best, and you can bet the mortgage that the World Series, which is open to any city in the world that has a major-league franchise, will this year be won once again by a team consisting of U.S. citizens plus maybe two dozen guys named Julio from friendly spider-infested nations to the south. In fact, the only real problem facing major-league baseball at the moment is that everybody associated with it in any way is a drug addict. This is beginning to affect the quality of the game:

ANNOUNCER: For those viewers who are just joining us, the game has been delayed slightly because the umpires really wanted some nachos, and also the Yankees keep turning into giant birds. I can't remember seeing that happen before in a regular season game, can you, Bob?

COLOR COMMENTATOR *(shrieking)*: THESE aren't my crayons!

So baseball has problems. So who doesn't? It's still a very national pastime, and I for one always feel a stirring of tremendous excitement as we approach the All-Star Game. I'm assuming here that we haven't already passed the All-Star Game.

What I like about the All-Star Game is that the teams aren't picked by a bunch of experts who use computers and care only about cold statistics—what a player's batting average is, how well he throws, whether he's still alive, etc. No, the All-Star teams are chosen by the fans, the everyday folks who sit out in the hot sun hour after hour, cursing and swilling beer that tastes like it has been used to launder jockstraps. The fans don't care about statistics: They vote from the heart, which is why last year's starting American League lineup included Lou Gehrig, O.J. Simpson, and Phil Donahue.

And what lies ahead, after the All-Star break? I look for several very tight pennant races, with many games ending in scores of 4–2, 5–1, and in certain instances 2–0. In the National League, I think we'll see a sharp late-season increase in the number of commercials wherein players employ inappropriate baseball imagery, such as, "Hit a home run against nasal discharge." And in the American League, I look for Dave Winfield to be attacked by seagulls. As always, pitching will be the key.

RED, WHITE, AND BEER

LATELY I'VE BEEN FEELING VERY PATRIOTIC, ES-
pecially during commercials. Like, when I see those strongly
pro-American Chrysler commercials, the ones where the
winner of the Bruce Springsteen Sound-Alike Contest sings
about how The Pride Is Back, the ones where Lee Iacocca
himself comes striding out and practically challenges the
president of Toyota to a knife fight, I get this warm, proud
feeling inside, the same kind of feeling I get whenever we
hold routine naval maneuvers off the coast of Libya.

But if you want to talk about *real* patriotism, of course,
you have to talk about beer commercials. I would have to say
that Miller is the most patriotic brand of beer. I grant you it
tastes like rat saliva, but we are not talking about taste here.
What we are talking about, according to the commercials, is
that Miller is by God an *American* beer, "born and brewed in
the U.S.A.," and the men who drink it are American men,
the kind of men who aren't afraid to perspire freely and
shake a man's hand. That's mainly what happens in Miller
commercials: Burly American men go around, drenched in
perspiration, shaking each other's hands in a violent and
patriotic fashion.

You never find out exactly why these men spend so
much time shaking hands. Maybe shaking hands is just their
simple straightforward burly masculine American patriotic
way of saying to each other: "Floyd, I am truly sorry I drank

all that Miller beer last night and went to the bathroom in your glove compartment." Another possible explanation is that, since there are never any women in the part of America where beer commercials are made, the burly men have become lonesome and desperate for any form of physical contact. I have noticed that sometimes, in addition to shaking hands, they hug each other. Maybe very late at night, after the David Letterman show, there are Miller commercials in which the burly men engage in slow dancing. I don't know.

I do know that in one beer commercial, I think this is for Miller—although it could be for Budweiser, which is also a very patriotic beer—the burly men build a house. You see them all getting together and pushing up a brand-new wall. Me, I worry some about a house built by men drinking beer. In my experience, you run into trouble when you ask a group of beer-drinking men to perform any task more complex than remembering not to light the filter ends of cigarettes.

For example, in my younger days, whenever anybody in my circle of friends wanted to move, he'd get the rest of us to help, and, as an inducement, he'd buy a couple of cases of beer. This almost always produced unfortunate results, such as the time we were trying to move Dick "The Wretch" Curry from a horrible fourth-floor walk-up apartment in Manhattan's Lower East Side to another horrible fourth-floor walk-up apartment in Manhattan's Lower East Side, and we hit upon the labor-saving concept of, instead of carrying The Wretch's possessions manually down the stairs, simply dropping them out the window, down onto the street, where The Wretch was racing around, gathering up the broken pieces of his life and shrieking at us to stop helping him move, his emotions reaching a fever pitch when his bed, which had been swinging wildly from a rope, entered the apartment two floors below his through what had until seconds earlier been a window.

This is the kind of thinking you get, with beer. So I figure what happens, in the beer commercial where the burly men are building the house, is they push the wall up so it's vertical, and then, after the camera stops filming them, they just keep pushing, and the wall crashes down on the other side, possibly onto somebody's pickup truck. And then they all shake hands.

But other than that, I'm in favor of the upsurge in retail patriotism, which is lucky for me because the airwaves are saturated with pro-American commercials. Especialy popular are commercials in which the newly restored Statue of Liberty—and by the way, I say Lee Iacocca should get some kind of medal for that, or at least be elected president— appears to be endorsing various products, as if she were Mary Lou Retton or somebody. I saw one commercial strongly suggesting that the Statue of Liberty uses Sure brand underarm deodorant.

I have yet to see a patriotic laxative commercial, but I imagine it's only a matter of time. They'll show some actors dressed up as hardworking country folk, maybe at a church picnic, smiling at each other and eating pieces of pie. At least one of them will be a black person. The Statue of Liberty will appear in the background. Then you'll hear a country-style singer singing:

> *"Folks 'round here they love this land;*
> *They stand by their beliefs;*
> *An' when they git themselves stopped up;*
> *They want some quick relief."*

Well, what do you think? Pretty good commercial concept, huh?

Nah, you're right. They'd never try to pull something like that. They'd put the statue in the *foreground.*

WHY NOT THE BEST?

EXCELLENCE IS *THE* TREND OF THE EIGHTIES. Walk into any shopping-mall bookstore, go to the rack where they keep the bestsellers such as *Garfield Gets Spayed*, and you'll see a half-dozen books telling you how to be excellent: *In Search of Excellence, Finding Excellence, Grasping Hold of Excellence, Where to Hide Your Excellence at Night So the Cleaning Personnel Don't Steal It*, etc.

The message of these books is that, here in the eighties, "good" is no longer good enough. In today's business environment, "good" is a word we use to describe an employee whom we are about to transfer to a urinal-storage facility in the Aleutian Islands. What we want, in our eighties business executive, is somebody who demands the best in *everything;* someone who is *never satisfied;* somebody who, if he had been in charge of decorating the Sistine Chapel, would have said: "That is a good fresco, Michelangelo, but I want a *better* fresco, and I want it by tomorrow morning."

This is the kind of thinking that now propels your top corporations. Take the folks at Coca-Cola. For many years, they were content to sit back and make the same old carbonated beverage. It was a *good* beverage, no question about it; generations of people had grown up drinking it and doing the experiment in sixth grade where you put a nail into a glass of Coke and after a couple of days the nail dissolves and the teacher says: "Imagine what it does to your *teeth!*" So Coca-Cola was solidly entrenched in the market, and the management saw no need to improve.

But then along came Pepsi, with the bold new marketing concept of saying that its carbonated beverage was *better,* a claim that Pepsi backed up by paying $19 trillion to Michael Jackson, the most excellent musical genius of all time according to the cover story in *Newsweek* magazine. And so the folks at Coca-Cola suddenly woke up and realized that, hey, these are the *eighties,* and they got off their butts and *improved* Coke by letting it sit out in vats in the hot sun and adding six or eight thousand tons of sugar, the exact amount being a trade secret.

Unfortunately, the general public, having failed to read the market surveys proving that the new Coke was better, refused to drink it, but that is not the point. The point is, the Coke executives decided to *strive for excellence,* and the result is that the American consumer is now benefiting from the most vicious carbonated-beverage marketing war in history. It wouldn't surprise me if, very soon, one side or the other offered to pay $29 trillion to Bruce Springsteen, who according to a *Newsweek* magazine cover story is currently the most excellent musical genius of all time, preceded briefly by Prince.

This striving for excellence extends into people's personal lives as well. When eighties people buy something, they buy the best one, as determined by (1) price and (2) lack of availability. Eighties people buy imported dental floss. They buy gourmet baking soda. If an eighties couple goes to a restaurant where they have made a reservation three weeks in advance, and they are informed that their table is available, they stalk out immediately, because they know it is not an excellent restaurant. If it were, it would have an enormous crowd of excellence-oriented people like themselves, waiting, their beepers going off like crickets in the night. An excellent restaurant wouldn't have a table ready immediately for anybody below the rank of Liza Minnelli.

An excellence-oriented eighties male does not wear a regular watch. He wears a Rolex, because it weighs nearly six pounds and is advertised only in excellence-oriented publications such as *Fortune* and *Rich Protestant Golfer Magazine*. The advertisements are written in incomplete sentences, which is how advertising copywriters denote excellence:

"The Rolex Hyperion. An elegant new standard in quality excellence and discriminating handcraftsmanship. For the individual who is truly able to discriminate with regard to excellent quality standards of crafting things by hand. Fabricated of 100 percent 24-karat gold. No watch parts or anything. Just a great big chunk of gold on your wrist. Truly a timeless statement. For the individual who is very secure. Who doesn't need to be reminded all the time that he is very successful. Much more successful than the people who laughed at him in high school. Because of his acne. People who are probably nowhere near as successful as he is now. Maybe he'll go to his twentieth reunion, and they'll see his Rolex Hyperion. Hahaha-hyahahahahaha."

Nobody is excused from the excellence trend. *Babies* are not excused. Starting right after they get out of the womb, modern babies are exposed to instructional flashcards designed to make them the best babies they can possibly be, so they can get into today's competitive preschools. Your eighties baby sees so many flashcards that he never gets an unobstructed view of his parents' faces. As an adult, he'll carry around a little wallet card that says "7 x 9 = 63," because it will remind him of mother.

I recently saw a videotape of people who were teaching their babies while they (the babies) were *still in the womb*. I swear I am not making this up. A group of pregnant couples sat in a circle, and, under the direction of an Expert in These Matters, they crooned instructional songs in the direction of the women's stomachs. Mark my words: We will reach the point, in our lifetimes, where babies emerge from their mothers fully prepared to assume entry-level management positions. I'm sure I'm not the only person who has noticed, just wandering around the shopping mall, that more and more babies, the really brand-new modern ones, tend to resemble Lee Iacocca.

MAKING THE WORLD SAFE FOR SALAD

I'VE BEEN THINKING ABOUT TECHNOLOGY OF late, because, as you are no doubt aware (like fudge, you are), we recently celebrated the 25th anniversary of the Etch-a-Sketch. I think we can all agree that, except for long-lasting nasal spray, this is the greatest technological achievement of all time. Think, for a moment, of the countless happy childhood hours you spent with this amazing device: Drawing perfect horizontals; drawing perfect verticals; drawing really spastic diagonals; trying to scrape away the silver powder from the window so you could look inside and try to figure out how it works (Mystery Rays from space, is what scientists now believe); and just generally enjoying the sheer childhood pleasure of snatching it away from your sister and shaking it upside down after she had spent 40 minutes making an elaborate picture of a bird.

Think how much better off the world would be if everybody—young and old, black and white, American and Russian, *Time* and *Newsweek*—spent part of each day playing with an Etch-a-Sketch. Think how great it would be if they had public Etch-a-Sketches for you to use while you were waiting in line at the Department of Motor Vehicles. And imagine what would happen if, instead of guns, our young soldiers carried Etch-a-Sketches into battle! They would be cut down like field mice under a rotary mower! So we can't carry this idea too far.

So anyway, as I said, this got me to thinking about technology in general. Too often—three or four times a week, according to some figures—we take technology for granted. When we drop our money into a vending machine at our place of employment and press the button for a tasty snack selection of crackers smeared with "cheez," a nondairy petroleum subproduct approved for use on humans, we are blithely confident that the machine will automatically, much of the time, hurl our desired selection down into the pickup bin, using a computerized electronic snack-ejection device that gives our snack a bin impact velocity of nearly 70 miles an hour, which is what is required to reduce our crackers to a fine, dayglow-orange grit. We rarely stop to consider that without this device, the only way the vending-machine manufacturers would be able to achieve this kind of impact velocity would be to use gravity, which means the machines would have to be 40 feet tall!

Of course, not all technology is good. Some is exactly the opposite (bad). The two obvious examples of this are the hydrogen bomb and those plastic "sneeze shields" they put over restaurant salad bars for your alleged hygiene protection. I have said this before, but it needs to be said again: *Sneeze shields actually spread disease,* because they make it hard for a squat or short-armed person to reach back to the chick peas and simulated bacon, and some of these people inevitably are going to become frustrated and spit in the House Dressing (a creamy Italian).

But this does not mean we should be against technology in general. Specifically, we should not be so hostile toward telephone-answering machines. I say this because I own one, and I am absolutely sick unto death of hearing people say— they *all* say this; it must be Item One on the curriculum in Trend College—"I just *hate* to talk to a *machine!*" They say this as though it is a major philosophical position, as opposed to a description of a minor neurosis. My feeling is, if you have a problem like this, you shouldn't go around *trumpeting* it; you should stay home and practice talking to a machine you can feel comfortable with, such as your Water Pik, until you are ready to assume your place in modern society, OK?

Meanwhile, technology marches on, thanks to new inventions conceived of by brilliant innovative creative geniuses such as a friend of mine named Clint Collins. Although he is really a writer, Clint has developed an amazingly simple yet effective labor-saving device for people who own wall-to-wall carpeting but don't want to vacuum it. Clint's concept is, you cut a piece of two-by-four so it's as long as your vacuum cleaner is wide, and just before company comes, you drag it across your carpet, so it leaves parallel marks similar to the ones caused by a vacuum. Isn't that great? The only improvement I can think of would be if they wove those lines into the carpet right at the factory, so you wouldn't even need a two-by-four.

Another recent advantage in technology comes from Joseph DiGiacinto, my lawyer, who has developed a way to fasten chopsticks together with a rubber band and a little wadded-up piece of paper in such a way that you can actually pick up food with them one-handed. You don't have to ask your waiter for a fork, which makes you look like you just tromped in from Des Moines and never even heard of sweet and sour pork. If you'd like to get in on this high-tech culinary advance, send an envelope with your address and a stamp on it to: Chopstick Concept, c/o Joseph DiGiacinto, Legal Attorney at Law, 235 Main Street, White Plains, NY 10601, and he'll send you , free, a Chopstick Conversion Kit —including a diagram, a rubber band, and instructions that can be wadded up for use as your paper wad—just as soon as I let him know that he has made this generous offer. He also does wills.

And what other advances does the future hold, technol-

ogywise? Even as you read these words, white-coated labo-
ratory geeks are working on a revolutionary new camera that
not only will focus automatically, set the exposure automatically, flash automatically, and advance the film automatically,
but will also automatically refuse to take stupid pictures, such
as of the wing out the airplane window.

TROUBLE ON THE LINE

I WANT THEM TO STOP EXPLAINING MY LONG-DIS-
tance options to me. I don't want to *know* my long-distance
options. The more I know about my long-distance options,
the more I feel like a fool.

They did this to us once before, with our financial options. This was back in the seventies. Remember? Up until
then, if you had any excess money, you put it in a passbook
savings account paying 5¼ percent interest, and your only
financial options were, did you want the toaster or the electric blanket. For a really slick high-finance maneuver, you
could join the Christmas Club, where you gave the bank
some money each week, and, at the end of the year, the bank
gave you your money *back*. These were simple, peaceful
times, except for the occasional Asian land war.

And then, without warning, they made it legal for consumers to engage in complex monetary acts, many of them
involving "liquidity." Today, there are a whole range of pro-
grams in which all that happens is people call up to ask what
they should do with their money:

"Hi, Steve? My wife and I listen to you all the time, and
we just love your show. Now here is the problem: We're 27
years old, no kids, and we have a combined income of
$93,000, and $675,000 in denatured optional treasury instruments of accrual, which will become extremely mature
next week."

Now to me, those people do not have a problem. To me, what these people need in the way of financial advice is: "Lighten up! Buy yourself a big boat and have parties where people put on funny hats and push the piano into the harbor!" But Mr. Consumer Radio Money Advisor, he tells them complex ways to get even *more* money and orders them to tune in next week. These shows make me feel tremendously guilty, as a consumer, because I still keep my money in accounts that actually get smaller, and sometimes disappear, like weekend guests in an old murder mystery, because the bank is always taking out a "service charge," as if the tellers have to take my money for walks or something.

So I feel like a real consumer fool about my money, and now I have to feel like a fool about my phone, too. I liked it better back when we all had to belong to the same Telephone Company, and phones were *phones*—black, heavy objects that were routinely used in the movies, as murder weapons (try *that* with today's phones!). Also, they were permanently attached to your house, and only highly trained Telephone Company personnel could "install" them. This involved attaching four wires, but the Telephone Company always made it sound like brain surgery. It was part of the mystique. When you called for your installation appointment, the Telephone Company would say: "We will have an installer in your area between the hours of 9 A.M. October 3 and the following spring. Will someone be at home?" And you would say yes, if you wanted a phone. You would stay at home, the anxious hours ticking by, and you would wait for your Phone Man. It was as close as most people came to experiencing what heroin addicts go through, the difference being that heroin addicts have the option of going to another supplier. Phone customers didn't. They feared the power of the Telephone Company.

I remember when I was in college, and my roommate Rob somehow obtained a phone. It was a Hot Phone. Rob hooked it up to our legal, wall-mounted phone with a long wire, which gave us the capability of calling the pizza-delivery man without getting up off the floor. This capability was essential, many nights. But we lived in fear. Because we knew we were breaking the rule—not a local, state, or federal rule, but a *Telephone Company* rule—and that any moment, agents of the Telephone Company, accompanied by heavy black dogs, might burst through the door and seize the Hot Phone and write our names down and *we would never be allowed to have phone service again*. And the dogs would seize our pizza.

So the old Telephone Company could be tough, but at least you knew where you stood. You never had to think about your consumer long-distance options. Whereas today you cannot turn on the television without seeing Cliff Robertson, standing in some pathetic rural community with a name like Eye Socket, Montana, telling you that if you don't go with his phone company, you won't be able to call people in rural areas like this, in case you ever had a reason to, such as you suddenly needed information about heifers. Which sounds reasonable, but then Burt Lancaster tells you what a jerk you are if you go with Cliff because it costs more. But that's exactly what Joan Rivers says about Burt! And what about Liz? Surely Liz has a phone company!

So it is very confusing, and yet you are expected to somehow make the right consumer choice. They want you to fill out a *ballot*. And if you don't fill it out, they're going to *assign you a random telephone company*. God knows what you could wind up with. You could wind up with the Soviet Union Telephone Company. You could wind up with one of those phone companies where you have to crank the phone, like on "Lassie," and the operator is always listening in, including when you call the doctor regarding intimate hemorrhoidal matters.

So you better fill out your ballot. I recommend that you go with Jim & Ed's Telephone Company & Radiator Repair. I say this because Jim and Ed feature a service contract whereby you pay a flat $15 a month, and if you have a problem, Jim or Ed will come out to your house (Jim is preferable, because after 10 A.M. Ed likes to drink Night Train wine and shoot at religious lawn statuary) and have some coffee with you and tell you that he's darned if *he* can locate the problem, but if he had to take a stab, he'd guess it was probably somewhere in the wires.

READ THIS FIRST

CONGRATULATIONS! YOU HAVE PURCHASED AN extremely fine device that would give you thousands of years of trouble-free service, except that you undoubtedly will destroy it via some typical bonehead consumer maneuver. Which is why we ask you to PLEASE FOR GOD'S SAKE READ THIS OWNER'S MANUAL CAREFULLY BEFORE YOU UNPACK THE DEVICE. YOU ALREADY UNPACKED IT, DIDN'T YOU? YOU UNPACKED IT AND PLUGGED IT IN AND TURNED IT ON AND FIDDLED WITH THE KNOBS, AND NOW YOUR CHILD, THE SAME CHILD WHO ONCE SHOVED A POLISH SAUSAGE INTO YOUR VIDEOCASSETTE RECORDER AND SET IT ON "FAST FORWARD," THIS CHILD ALSO IS FIDDLING WITH THE KNOBS, RIGHT? AND YOU'RE JUST STARTING TO READ THE INSTRUCTIONS, RIGHT??? WE MIGHT AS WELL JUST BREAK ALL THESE DEVICES RIGHT AT THE FACTORY BEFORE WE SHIP THEM OUT, YOU KNOW THAT?

We're sorry. We just get a little crazy sometimes, because we're always getting back "defective" merchandise where it turns out that the consumer inadvertently bathed the device in acid for six days. So, in writing these instructions, we naturally tend to assume that your skull is filled with dead insects, but we mean nothing by it. OK? Now let's talk about:

1. UNPACKING THE DEVICE: The device is encased in foam to protect it from the Shipping People, who like nothing more than to jab spears into the outgoing boxes. PLEASE

INSPECT THE CONTENTS CAREFULLY FOR GASHES OR IDA MAE BARKER'S ENGAGEMENT RING WHICH SHE LOST LAST WEEK, AND SHE THINKS MAYBE IT WAS WHILE SHE WAS PACKING DEVICES. Ida Mae really wants that ring back, because it is her only proof of engagement, and her fiancé, Stuart, is now seriously considering backing out on the whole thing inasmuch as he had consumed most of a bottle of Jim Beam in Quality Control when he decided to pop the question. It is not without irony that Ida Mae's last name is "Barker," if you get our drift.

WARNING: DO NOT EVER AS LONG AS YOU LIVE THROW AWAY THE BOX OR ANY OF THE PIECES OF STYROFOAM, EVEN THE LITTLE ONES SHAPED LIKE PEANUTS.

If you attempt to return the device to the store, and you are missing one single peanut, the store personnel will laugh in the chilling manner exhibited by Joseph Stalin just after he enslaved Eastern Europe.

Besides the device, the box should contain:

• Eight little rectangular snippets of paper that say: "WARNING"

• A plastic packet containing four 5/17″ pilfer grommets and two chub-ended 6/93″ boxcar prawns.

YOU WILL NEED TO SUPPLY: a matrix wrench and 60,000 feet of tram cable.

IF ANYTHING IS DAMAGED OR MISSING: You *immediately* should turn to your spouse and say: "Margaret, you know why this country can't make a car that can get all the way through the drive-thru at Burger King without a major transmission overhaul? Because nobody cares, that's why." (Warning: This Is Assuming Your Spouse's Name Is Margaret.)

2. PLUGGING IN THE DEVICE: The plug on this device represents the latest thinking of the electrical industry's Plug Mutation Group, which, in the continuing effort to prevent consumers from causing hazardous electrical current to flow through their appliances, developed the Three-Pronged

Plug, then the Plug Where One Prong Is Bigger Than the Other. Your device is equipped with the revolutionary new Plug Whose Prongs Consist of Six Small Religious Figurines Made of Chocolate. DO NOT TRY TO PLUG IT IN! Lay it gently on the floor near an outlet, but out of direct sunlight, and clean it weekly with a damp handkerchief.

WARNING: WHEN YOU ARE LAYING THE PLUG ON THE FLOOR, DO NOT HOLD A SHARP OBJECT IN YOUR OTHER HAND AND TRIP OVER THE CORD AND POKE YOUR EYE OUT, AS THIS COULD VOID YOUR WARRANTY.

3. OPERATION OF THE DEVICE:

WARNING: WE MANUFACTURE ONLY THE ATTRACTIVE DESIGNER CASE. THE ACTUAL WORKING CENTRAL PARTS. OF THE DEVICE ARE MANUFACTURED IN JAPAN. THE INSTRUCTIONS WERE TRANS- LATED BY MRS. SHIRLEY PELTWATER OF ACCOUNTS RECEIVABLE, WHO HAS NEVER ACTUALLY BEEN TO JAPAN BUT DOES HAVE MOST OF *SHOGUN* ON TAPE.

INSTRUCTIONS: For results that can be the finest, it is our advising that: Never to hold these buttons two times!! Except the battery. Next, taking the (something) earth section may cause a large occurrence! However. If this is not a trouble, such rotation is a very maintenance action, as a kindly (something) viewpoint from Drawing B.

4. WARRANTY: Be it hereby known that this device, together with but not excluding all those certain parts thereunto, shall be warrantied against all defects, failures, and malfunctions as shall occur between now and Thursday afternoon at shortly before 2, during which time the Manufacturer will, at no charge to the Owner, send the device to our Service People, who will emerge from their caves and engage in rituals designed to cleanse it of evil spirits. This warranty does not cover the attractive designer case.

WARNING: IT MAY BE A VIOLATION OF SOME LAW THAT MRS. SHIRLEY PELTWATER HAS *SHOGUN* ON TAPE.

THE URBAN PROFESSIONALS

I'M GOING TO START A ROCK 'N' ROLL BAND. NOT a *good* band, where you have to be in tune and wear makeup. This will be a band consisting of people who are Approaching Middle Age, by which I mean they know the words to "Wooly Bully." This will be the kind of band whose members often miss practice for periodontal reasons and are always yelling at their kids for leaving Popsicles on the amplifiers. We will be called the "Urban Professionals." I will be lead guitar.

I miss being in a band. The last band I was in, the "Phlegmtones," dissolved a couple of years ago, and even that was not truly a formal band in the sense of having instruments or playing them or anything. What it was, basically, was my friend Randall and myself drinking beer and trying to remember the words to "Runaround Sue," by Dion and the Belmonts.

Before that, the last major band I was in was in college, in the sixties. It was called the "Federal Duck," which we thought was an extremely hip name. We were definitely 10 pounds of hipness in a 5-pound bag. We had the first strobe light of any band in our market area. We were also into The Blues, which was a very hip thing to be into, back in the sixties. We were always singing songs about how our woman she done lef' us and we was gon' jump into de ribba an' drown. This was pretty funny, because we were extremely

103

white suburban-style college students whose only actual insight into the blues came from experiences such as getting a C in Poli Sci.

In terms of musical competence, if I had to pick one word to describe us, that word would be "loud." We played with the subtlety of aboveground nuclear testing. But we made up for this by being cheap. We were so cheap that organizations were always hiring us sight unseen, which resulted a number of times in our being hired by actual grown-ups whose idea of a good party band was elderly men in stained tuxedos playing songs from *My Fair Lady* on accordions at about the volume of a drinking fountain.

When we would come in and set up, with our mandatory long hair and our strobe light and our 60,000 pounds of amplifiers, these people would watch us in wary silence. But once we started to play, once the sound of our pulsating beat filled the air, something almost magical would happen: They would move farther away. They'd form hostile little clots against the far wall. Every now and then they'd send over an emissary, who would risk lifelong hearing damage to cross the dance floor and ask us if we knew any nice old traditional slow-dance fox-trot-type songs such as "Smoke Gets In Your Eyes," which of course we didn't, because it has more than four chords. So we'd say: "No, we don't know that one, but we do know another one you might like." Then we'd play "Land of 1,000 Dances," a very big hit by Cannibal and the Headhunters on Rampart Records. This is a song with only one chord (E). Almost all of the lyrics consist of the statement, *I said a na,* as follows:

> *I said a na*
> *Na na na na*
> *Na na na na, na na na, na na na;*
> *Na na na na.*

Our best jobs were at fraternity parties. The only real problem we'd run into there was that every now and then they'd set fire to our equipment. Other than that, fraternity brothers made for a very easygoing audience. Whatever song they requested, we'd play "Land of 1,000 Dances," and they'd be happy. They were too busy throwing up on their dates to notice. They are running the nation today.

Me, I am leading a quiet life. Too quiet. This is why I'm going to form the Urban Professionals. Right now I am actively recruiting members. So far I've recruited one, an editor named Tom whose musical qualifications are that he is 32 years old. He's going to play some instrument of the type you got handed in rhythm band in elementary school, such as the tambourine. Just judging from my circle of friends, I think The Urban Professionals are going to have a large tambourine section.

Once we start to catch on, we'll make a record. It will be called: "A Moderate Amount of Soul." After it comes out, we'll go on a concert tour. We'll stay in Holiday Inns, and sometimes we'll "trash" our rooms by refusing to fill out the Guest Questionnaire. Because that's the kind of rebels the Urban Professionals will be. But our fans will still love us. When we finish our act, they'll be overcome by emotion. They'll all rise spontaneously to their feet, and they'll try, as a gesture of appreciation, to hold lighted matches over their heads. Then they'll all realize they quit smoking, so they'll spontaneously sit back down.

THE PLASTIC, FANTASTIC COVER

I HAVE JUST ABOUT GIVEN UP ON THE TUPPER-
ware people. I've been trying to get them interested in a song
I wrote, called "The Tupperware Song," which I am sure
would be a large hit. I called them about it two or three times
a week for several weeks.

"You wrote a song?" they would say.

"Yes," I would say.

"About Tupperware?" they would say.

"Yes," I would say. "It's kind of a blues song."

"We'll have somebody get back to you," they would say.

For quite a while there I thought I was getting the runaround, until finally a nice Tupperware executive named
Dick called me up. He was very honest with me. "There's a
fairly limited market for songs about Tupperware," he said.

"Dick," I said. "This is a killer song." Which was true. It
gets a very positive reaction whenever I perform it. Of
course, I perform it only in those social settings where people
have loosened up to the point where they would react posi-
tively if you set their clothing on fire, but I still think this
song would have widespread appeal.

I wrote it a while back, when friends of mine named Art
and Dave had a big Tupperware party in their apartment. It
was the social event of the month. Something like 50 people
showed up. When the Tupperware Lady walked in, you
could tell right away from her facial expression that this was

not the kind of Tupperware crowd she was used to. She was used to a subdued all-female crowd, whereas this was a large coeducational crowd with some crowd members already dancing on the refrigerator. The Tupperware Lady kept saying things like: "Are you sure this is supposed to be a Tupperware party?" And: "This doesn't look like a Tupperware party." She wanted to go home.

But we talked her into staying, although she never really accepted the fact that Art and Dave were her Tupperware hostesses. She wanted to deal with a woman. All of her communications with Art and Dave had to go through a woman interpreter:

TUPPERWARE LADY (*speaking to a woman*): Where do you want me to set up?

WOMAN (*speaking to Art, who is standing right there*): Art, where do you want her to set up?

ART: How about right over here on the coffee table?

WOMAN (*to the Tupperware Lady*): Art says how about right over here on the coffee table.

TUPPERWARE LADY: Fine.

Once we got everybody settled down, sort of, the Tupperware Lady wanted us to engage in various fun Tupperware party activities such as "brain teasers" wherein if we could name all the bodily parts that had three letters, we would win a free grapefruit holder or something. We did this for a while, but it was slowing things down, so we told the Tupperware Lady we had this song we wanted to perform.

The band consisted of me and four other highly trained journalists. You know what "The Tupperware Song" sounds like if you ever heard the song "*I'm a Man*" by Muddy Waters, where he sings about the general theme that he is a man, and in between each line the band goes Da-DA-da-da-DUM, so you get an effect like this:

MUDDY WATERS: *I'm a man.*
BAND: Da-DA-da-da-DUM

MUDDY WATERS: *A natural man.*
BAND: Da-DA-da-da-DUM
MUDDY WATERS: *A full-grown man.*

And so on. This is the general approach taken in *The Tupperware Song,* except it is about Tupperware. It starts out this way:

Some folks use waxed paper
Some folks use the Reynolds Wrap
Some folks use the Plastic Baggie
To try to cover up the gap
You can use most anything
To keep your goodies from the air
But nothing works as well
As that good old Tupperware

(CHORUS)

'Cause it's here
Whooaaa
Take a look at what we got
If you don't try some and buy some
Don't blame me when your turnips rot.

It has two more verses covering other important Tupperware themes. Verse Two stresses the importance of "burping" the air out of your container to make sure your lid seals securely, and Verse Three points out that you can make money by holding a Tupperware party in your home.

As you might imagine, the crowd was completely blown away by this song. The Tupperware Lady herself was near tears. But the important thing was, people bought a *lot* of Tupperware that night. People bought Tupperware they would never in a million years need. Single men who lived in apartments and never cooked anything, ever, that could not be heated in a toaster, were ordering Tupperware cake transporters. It was obvious to me right then and there that "The Tupperware Song" was a powerful marketing tool.

I explained all this to Dick, of the Tupperware company, and he said I could send him a cassette tape of the song. Which I did, but I haven't heard a thing. Not that I'm worried. I'm sure there are plenty of other large wealthy corporations out there that would be interested in a blues song about Tupperware. In fact, I'm getting offers in the mail almost every day. Most of them are for supplementary hospitalization insurance, but that's obviously just a negotiating ploy.

BANG THE TUPPERWARE SLOWLY

WHEN I DIE, I WANT MY OBITUARY TO READ AS follows:

"Dave Barry is dead. Mr. Barry and his band, the Urban Professionals, once performed 'The Tupperware Song' before 1,000 Tupperware distributors."

This is the truth. We really did perform before 1,000 Tupperware distributors, and they gave us a standing ovation, although in the interest of accuracy, I should tell you that just before we performed, they also gave a standing ovation to a set of ovenware. But I don't care. This was without question the highlight of my entire life.

The way it came about was, the Tupperware people finally saw the musical light and decided to invite me to perform my original composition, "The Tupperware Song," before a large sales conference at Tupperware headquarters, located in Orlando, Florida, right next to Gatorland, an attraction where (this is true) alligators jump into the air and eat dead chickens hung from wires. Naturally I accepted the invitation. A break like this comes along once in your career.

I formed a new band, the Urban Professionals, especially for this performance. I chose the members very carefully, based on their ability to correctly answer the following question: "Do you want to go to Orlando at your own expense and perform before Tupperware distributors?" (The correct answer was: "Yes.") Using this strict screening procedure, I obtained three band members, all trained members of the *Miami Herald* staff. I'm the lead guitar player and singer and also (I'm not bragging here; these are simply facts) the only person in the band who knows when the song has started or ended. The other members of the band just sort of stand around looking nervous until I've been going for a while, and then, after it penetrates their primitive musical consciousnesses that the song has begun, they become startled and lurch into action. Likewise it takes them up to 30 seconds to come to a complete stop after the song is technically over.

The only other normal instrument in the band is a harmonica, played by Gene. Gene has been attempting to play the harmonica for a number of years, and has developed a repertoire of several songs, all of which sound exactly like "Oh, Susannah!" "Here's another one!" he'll say, and then he plays "Oh, Susannah!" He plays it very rapidly, totally without pauses, as if he's anxious to get back to journalism, so if you tried to sing along, you'd have to go: "Icomefromalabamawithmybanjoonmyknee," etc., and pretty soon you'd run out of oxygen and keel over onto your face, which Gene wouldn't notice because he'd be too busy trying to finish the song on schedule.

The other two instruments in the band are actually Tupperware products, played rhythmically by Tom and Lou, who also dance. How good are they? Let me put it this way: If you can watch them perform and not wet your pants then you are legally blind. For one thing, they are both afflicted with severe rhythm impairment, the worst cases I have ever seen, worse even than Republican convention delegates. You ask Lou and Tom to clap along to a song and not only will they never once hit the beat, but they will also never, no matter how eternally long the song goes on, both clap at the same time. On top of which you have the fact that they do not have your classic dancer's build, especially Lou, who is, and I say this with all due respect, the same overall shape as a Krispy Kreme jelly doughnut.

111

When we got to the Tupperware convention center we became a tad nervous, because (a) it turns out that Tupperware is a large business venture that many people take very seriously and (b) we had never even practiced as a total band. The bulk of our musical preparation to that point had consisted of deciding that our band outfits should include sunglasses.

Fortunately, the Tupperware distributors turned out to be extremely peppy people, prone to applauding wildly at the slightest provocation. They especially loved Lou and Tom lunging around waving their Tupperware products in what they presumably thought was unison, looking like the Temptations might look if they were suddenly struck onstage with severe disorders of the central nervous system.

After we got off the stage, Lou announced that it was the most exciting thing he had ever done. Gene kept saying: "A professional musician. I'm a *professional musician.*" A Tupperware person came up and asked if we'd be willing to perform again, and of course we said yes, although I am becoming concerned. Tom has announced, several times, that he thinks next time the dancers should get a singing part. I can see already that unless we hold our egos in check, keeping this thing in perspective, we could start having the kind of internal conflicts that broke up the Beatles, another very good band.

BITE THE WAX TADPOLE!

NOW WE'RE GOING TO LOOK AT SOME IMPORTANT new developments in the U.S. advertising industry, which continues to be a hotbed of innovation as well as a source of pride to all Americans regardless of intelligence. This country may no longer be capable of manufacturing anything more technologically sophisticated than breakfast cereal, but by God when it comes to advertising, we are still—and I mean this sincerely—Number One.

Our first bit of advertising news will come as a happy surprise to those of you who lie awake nights asking yourselves: "Whatever happened to Mikey, the lovable chubby-cheeked child who hated everything until he tasted Life brand breakfast cereal in the heartwarming television commercial that we all saw 63,000 times back in the seventies?"

The good news is: Mikey is coming back, as part of a major advertising campaign! The Quaker Oats Co. sent me *two* large press kits on this, both quoting a Quaker Oats executive as saying: "We've received thousands of letters over the years asking what's become of him. . . . We thought it would be fun to satisfy America's curiosity by conducting a nationwide search to reveal his present-day identity."

Ha ha! Fun is hardly the word! I don't know about you, but I'm going to be waiting on tenterhooks until the big moment comes when the Quaker Oats Co., in a national press conference, finally reveals what "tenterhooks" are. No, seriously, they're going to reveal who Mikey is, so that the thousands of people who wrote to them about this important matter can go back to learning how to eat with real utensils.

Speaking of adorable and talented young actors whose moving commercial performances have tugged at the heart-strings of our minds, I wonder whatever happened to that little boy who used to do the Oscar Mayer commercials. Remember? The one who claimed his baloney had a first name, and it was O-S-C-A-R? I wonder if that child didn't run into problems later in life. ("OK, pal. You and Oscar there are under arrest.").

Another commercial personality I was wondering about is the man who used to promote Ti-D-bol brand automatic commode freshener by rowing his boat around inside the tank of a giant toilet. I mean, it must have been difficult for him, going back to normal life after having reached a show business pinnacle like that. So I called the Knomark company, which makes Ti-D-bol, and I found out an amazing fact: The role of the original Ti-D-bol man was played by none other than "Miami Vice" 's Don Johnson! Isn't that an incredible celebrity gossip tidbit? I hope to see it reprinted in leading supermarket tabloids everywhere, although in the interest of fairness and objectivity I should point out that I just now made it up.

The actual truth, according to Bill Salmon, Knomark's marketing director, is that there were a number of Ti-D-bol men. "The Ti-D-bol man," he said, "was anybody who put on the blazer and the white hat and got in the boat." The current Ti-D-bol man, he said, is a cartoon character who remains on dry land. "Right now he is not in a toilet tank in a rowboat, but that does not mean we would not use the Ti-D-bol man in the tank again at a future time," Salmon stressed.

By the way, I was disappointed to learn from Salmon that the rowboat commercials were done with trick photography, meaning there never was a 50-foot-high toilet. I think they should build one, as a promotional concept. Wouldn't that be great? They could split the cost with the Jolly Green Jolly Green Giant. I bet he sure could use it. I bet he's making a mess out of his valley. Ho ho ho!

I found our next news item in the *Weekly World News*, a leading supermarket tabloid, and it is just so wonderful that I will reprint it verbatim:

"The Coca-Cola Company has changed the name of its soft drink in China after discovering the words mean 'bite the wax tadpole' in Chinese."

I called Coca-Cola, and a woman named Darlene confirmed this item. She also said the company decided to go with a different name over in China, which I think is crazy. "Bite the Wax Tadpole" is the best name I ever heard for a soft drink. Think of the commercials:

(The scene opens up with a boy in a Little League uniform, looking very sad. His father walks up.)

FATHER: What's the matter, Son?

SON: *(bursting into tears):* Oh Dad, I struck out and lost the big game. *(Sobs.)*

FATHER *(putting his arm around the boy's shoulders):* Hey! Forget it! Let's have a nice cold can of Bite the Wax Tadpole!

SON: And then I murdered a policeman.

THE RULES

RECENTLY I READ THIS NEWS ITEM STATING that the U.S. Senate Finance Committee had printed up 4,500 copies of a 452-page document with every single word crossed out. The Senate Finance Committee did this on purpose. It wasn't the kind of situation where they got the document back from the printer and said: "Hey! Every single word in this document is crossed out! We're going to fire the zitbrain responsible for this!" No. A 452-page document with all the words crossed out was exactly what the Senate Finance Committee wanted.

This news item intrigued me. I said to myself: There has to be a logical explanation for this. So I called Washington, D.C., and over the course of an afternoon I spoke to, I don't know, maybe 15 or 20 people, and sure enough it turned out there was an extremely logical explanation: The Senate Finance Committee was following the Rules. As well it should. You have to have rules. This is true in government just as much as in sports. Think what professional baseball would be like if the pitcher could just throw the ball right at the batter whenever he felt like it, or the batter could turn around after a called third strike and try to whomp a major cavity in the umpire's skull. It would be great. I'd buy season tickets. But you can't have that kind of behavior in your government.

This is why, back when we bombed Libya, the Reagan

administration made such a large point of the fact that we were *not* trying to kill Moammar Khadafy. I think most of us average citizens had assumed, since the administration had been going around announcing that it had absolute proof that Khadafy was an international baby-murdering scumball, that the whole *point* of the raid was to kill him, and although we didn't want to see innocent persons hurt, we certainly wouldn't have minded if say a half dozen fatal bombs had detonated inside Moammar's personal tent.

So I, for one, was quite surprised when right after the raid, President Reagan himself said, and this is a direct quote: "We weren't out to kill anybody." My immediate reaction, when I read this statement, was to assume that this was another of those unfortunate instances where the president's advisers, caught up in the excitement of planning a major military operation, had forgotten to advise the president about it. But then other top administration officials started saying the same thing, that we weren't trying to kill anybody, and specifically we *weren't trying to kill Khadafy*. You following this? We announced we have proof the guy is a murderer; we announce that we are by God going to Do Something about It; we have large military airplanes fly over there and drop bombs all over his immediate vicinity; but *we weren't trying to kill him*. You want to know why? I'll tell you why: The Rules.

That's right. It turns out that we have this law, signed in 1976 by Gerald Ford, who coincidentally also pardoned Richard M. Nixon, under which it is illegal for our government to assassinate foreign leaders. So we can't just hire a couple of experienced persons named Vito for 100 grand to sneak over there one night in dark clothing and fill up Moammar's various breathing apertures with plumber's putty. No, that would be breaking a Rule. So what we do is spend several hundred million dollars to crank up the entire Sixth Fleet and have planes fly over from as far away as England, not to mention that we lose a couple of airmen, to achieve the purpose of *not* killing Moammar Khadafy. We did kill various other random Libyans, but that is OK, under the Rules. Gerald Ford signed nothing to protect them.

OK? Everybody understand the point here? The point is: You have to follow the Rules. Without Rules, you would have *anarchy*.

And that is exactly why the Senate Finance Committee had to print up 4,500 copies of a 452-page document with every single word crossed out. What this document was, originally, was the tax-reform bill passed by the House of Representatives. It seemed the Senate Finance Committee didn't like it, so they wrote a whole new bill, with all different words. Their new bill is 1,489 pages long. Also they wrote another 1,124 pages to explain how it works. (Sounds like our new reformed tax system is going to be mighty simple, all right! I can't wait!)

OK. So the Finance Committee had 2,613 pages worth of tax reform to print up, but that was not all. They also printed the entire House bill, the one they rejected, with all the words crossed out to show where they disagreed with it. According to the 15 or 20 people I talked to on the phone, the committee had to do this. I asked them if maybe it wouldn't have been more economical, and just as informative, if the Finance Committee had stuck a note on the front of their bill saying something like: "We thought the whole House Bill was pig doots and we chucked it," but the 15 or 20 people assured me that, no, this was not possible, under the Rules. I was skeptical at first, but I heard this same explanation over and over, all afternoon, from people who all sounded like very bright college graduates, so that by the end of the day I was beginning to think that, yes, of course, it made perfect sense to print 4,500 copies of a document with every word crossed out. I felt like a fool for even bothering to think about it.

By the way: This document is for sale. This is the truth. You can actually buy a document that your government has used your tax money to print up with all the words crossed out. It's called HR 3838 As Reported in the Senate, Part I.

The Government Printing Office is selling it for—I swear—
$17. So far they have sold *1,800 copies.* And I *don't even want
to know* who is buying them. I am sure that whoever they are,
they're going to claim *every single cent they spent on these docu-
ments as a tax deduction.* But I don't *care.* I'm *through* asking
questions.

I also don't want to know how much we spend each year
for the upkeep on Richard M. Nixon.

THE $8.95 TAX PLAN

I'D LIKE TO TAKE JUST A MOMENT HERE TO DIS-cuss my tax plan, which I call the You Pay Only $8.95 Tax Plan, because the way this particular plan works, you would pay only $8.95 in taxes. There would be no deductions, but you would still be permitted to cheat.

I imagine many of you have questions about the details of this plan, so I'll try to answer them here in the informative question-and-answer format:

Q. How much money will your tax plan raise?

A. To answer your question, I punched some figures into my personal home computer, using the following "Basic" computer language program:

ME: HOW MUCH WOULD WE RAISE IF EVERY-BODY PAID $8.95 IN TAXES? ROUGHLY.

COMPUTER: SYNTAX ERROR.

ME: NO, A SYNTAX ERROR WOULD BE "ME HIT COMPUTER IN SCREEN WITH BIG ROCK."

COMPUTER: ROUGHLY $2 BILLION.

ME: THANK YOU.

Q. But the federal government wishes to spend $830 billion this year. Where will the other $828 billion come from?

A. It would come from people who elect to purchase the new American Express Platinum Card, which costs $250, making it even more prestigious than the Gold Card, which

120

is of course much more prestigious than the Green Card, which is advertised to lowlife scum like yourself on television. According to the American Express brochure, the new Platinum Card is "beyond the aspirations and reach of all but a few of our Cardmembers," and "sets its possessor on a new plateau of recognition." Under my plan, people who buy the Platinum Card would be taxed $500 million each, and if they complained the slightest little bit they would be thrown into federal prisons so lonely that inmates pay spiders for sex.

Q. What about nuns?

A. Nuns would be taxed at a reduced rate of $5.95, because they do so little damage to our nation's crumbling infrastructure. For example, you have probably noticed that they drive really slow. This makes quite a difference, as the following statistical analysis shows:

ME: WHAT PERCENTAGE OF THE DAMAGE TO THE INTERSTATE HIGHWAY SYSTEM IS CAUSED BY NUNS?

COMPUTER: WHAT?

ME: PERHAPS THIS HOT SOLDERING IRON WILL REFRESH YOUR MEMORY.

COMPUTER: A VERY SMALL PERCENTAGE.

Q. What about Mark Goodson and Bill Todman?

A. Who?

Q. The highly successful game-show producers. How would they be affected by your new tax plan?

A. They would have their bowels ripped out by wolves.

Q. Good. In the cartoon series "Tom and Jerry," which one is Tom?

A. Well, I say it's the cat. My four-year-old son says it's the mouse, but he also says dinosaurs could talk.

COMPUTER: IT'S DEFINITELY THE CAT, AS IN "TOM CAT."

A. Yes, that's what I say, but my son claims he knows of mice named Tom.

COMPUTER: HA HA! WHAT A CRETIN.

121

Q. What are the steps involved in getting this tax plan passed by Congress?

A. Well, first it has to be formally introduced as a bill on "Meet the Press"; then various congressional committees and subcommittees have to go to Aruba with their spouses for several weeks to see if there are any similar tax plans operating in the Caribbean; then interested groups such as the American Eggplant Council have to modify it so that members of the eggplant industry are exempt from paying any taxes ever and get flown free wherever they want on Air Force jets; then Senator Jesse Helms has to attach an amendment making it legal, during the months of May and June, to shoot homosexuals for sport, except of course for homosexual tobacco farmers; then the bill has to be signed by President Reagan; then the Supreme Court has to check it to make sure he didn't forget and sign "Best Wishes, Ron" again.

Q. Dave, the You Pay Only $8.95 Tax Plan makes a lot of sense to me. How can I let my Congressperson know how I feel on this issue?

A. The easiest way is to simply steal into his bedroom in the dead of night and stand over his sleeping form until he senses your presence and wakes up, then express your views clearly.

Q. Fine.

A. Be sure to use sweeping arm gestures.

MUTANT FLEAS TERRORIZE MIDWEST

I WAS GOING TO WRITE ABOUT HOW THE PRESI-
dent's revolutionary new tax plan will affect you, but it occurred to me that I really don't care how the president's
revolutionary new tax plan will affect you. So instead I'm
going to write about the giant vampire fleas that are on this
pet-killing rampage in the Midwest.

You probably read about these fleas recently in the *Sun*,
a weekly supermarket newspaper with a circulation of 18
trillion. According to the *Sun* article, what happened was that
the American farmer, all the while we were feeling sorry for
him, was deluging the soil with herbicides, despite the known
scientific fact that chemicals cause insects to mutate and become enormous, as has been documented in countless Japanese movies. So the result is that the Midwest is now infested
with giant mutant fleas that, according to the *Sun*, "are themselves as large as the small dogs they kill, draining them dry
of life fluids in as little as two minutes." The *Sun* even printed
an actual artist's depiction of a dog being attacked by a flea
the size of Sylvester Stallone.

Of course you don't believe a word of it. You think publications like the *Sun* make everything up. I used to think
that, too, before I checked into a story the *Sun* published a
few months ago headlined "GIANT FLYING CAT TERRI-
FIES STATES." Remember? The article that featured the
actual artist's depiction of an enormous cat? Flying? With

123

wings? Well, I did some checking, and you will be interested to learn that every single word in the headline is true except for "GIANT," "FLYING," "TERRIFIES," AND "STATES." It turns out that some people in Harrington, Delaware, have indeed seen a largish cat. The local editor says he thinks it's an escaped exotic pet, because it has a collar and has been declawed. He said it does not have any actual wings per se, but it jumps pretty well, especially considering that, to judge from its tracks, it has only three legs. They think it eats birds.

But the point is that the central thrust of the *Sun* headline ("CAT") was right on target, which gives us every reason to accept the giant-mutant-flea article at face value. Nevertheless, I thought I should check it out, so I called the Midwest, which is in Iowa, and talked with Donald Lewis, extension entomologist for Iowa State University. He said: "I haven't heard anything even remotely similar to that. We do have periodic flea outbreaks, but each flea is still small." Naturally, this made me suspicious, so I called Lysle Waters of the University of Iowa, who said: "I haven't heard anything about that. And I definitely would have heard about giant fleas."

And that was all the proof I needed. Because when two men from separate universities that are miles apart and have completely different nicknames ("Cyclones" vs. "Hawkeyes") used *almost exactly the same words*—"I haven't heard anything"—to deny having heard anything, then you don't have to be a seasoned journalist such as myself to know they are covering up a giant mutant flea rampage. My guess is they don't want to scare off the seven or eight tourists who flock to the Midwest each summer looking for directions.

How serious is this problem? To help answer that question, the *Sun* has published a direct quotation from a "Cornbelt sheriff" who, as you can well imagine, asked not to be identified. He states that these giant fleas "are almost impossible to catch" because "they can jump 50 times their own height without warning."

The Cornbelt sheriff does not specify *why* he would wish

to catch the giant mutant flea or what kind of warning he feels the flea should give. ("Stand back! I am about to jump 50 times my own height!") But he does point out that once the fleas have eaten all the smaller animals in the Midwest, they "will have to go somewhere else to eat the larger livestock, chicken ranches, city streets, and homes."

"Little children will be completely at their mercy," he notes.

I have mixed feelings about all this. On the one hand, I have never liked small dogs. There are these two in particular that live near me, both about the size of the wads of cotton they put in aspirin bottles to keep you from getting at the aspirin. They're always yapping at me when I go by, and quite frankly the only thing I would enjoy more than watching them have all their life fluids sucked out by a giant mutant flea would be watching this happen in slow motion. But I draw the line at larger livestock, chicken ranches, and most little children.

Step One, of course, is to send Vice President Bush out there to the Midwest to frown at the affected area from a federal helicopter. Step Two is to develop a plan. I think we should try an approach that has been used on other insect pests in the past, namely: You get a hold of a whole bunch of the males, sterilize them, and drop them from airplanes onto the affected area, where they mate with the females, who don't get pregnant, and there you are.

Of course, we have to solve some technical problems first. We need to figure out a way to sterilize giant mutant fleas. My guess is this job will call for highly paid personnel with soothing voices and tremendous manual dexterity. Also, we will need some kind of special parachute system, because otherwise we're going to have giant, federally neutered fleas crashing through the roofs of cornbelt dwellings, thus further depressing the American farmer. Of course, all of this will cost money, which fortunately is the very thing the government will continue to relieve you of in large amounts under the president's revolutionary new tax plan.

BOOKED TO DEATH

I'M ON A BOOK TOUR. I'M GOING ON RADIO AND TV shows, being a Guest, selling a book. I've been on this tour two, maybe three weeks now. Maybe 10 weeks. Hard to tell. Been in a lot of time zones. Been on a lot of planes. Had a lot of complimentary honey-roasted peanuts whapped onto my tray table by hostile flight attendants. "Would you care for some peanuts, sir?" WHAP. Like that. The flight attendants hate us passengers, because we're surly to them because our flight is delayed. Our flight is always delayed. The Russians will never be able to get their missiles through the dense protective layer of delayed flights circling over the United States in complex, puke-inducing holding patterns.

Our flight is also always very crowded. This is because air fares are now assigned by a machine called the Random Air Fare Generator, which is programmed to ensure that on any given flight (1) no two people will pay the same fare, and (2) everybody else will pay less than you. People are flying across the country for less than you paid for your six-week-old corn muffin at the airport snack bar. Anybody can afford to fly these days. You see Frequent Flyers with bare feet and live carry-on chickens.

And so the planes are crowded and noisy and late, and everybody hates everybody. If armed terrorists had tried to hijack any of the flights I've been on lately, we passengers would have swiftly beaten them to death with those hard rolls you get with your in-flight meal. Funny, isn't it? The airlines go to all that trouble to keep you from taking a gun on board, then they just hand you a dinner roll you could kill a musk ox with.

Me, I eat the roll. Got to eat. Got to keep my strength up, on the book tour, so I can be perky when I get interviewed by the cheerful talk-show host. You want to sound as perky and enthusiastic as possible, on a book tour, so your listening audience won't suspect that you really, deep down inside, don't want to talk about your book ever ever ever again. You have come to hate your book. Back at the beginning, you kind of liked it, but now you think of it as a large repulsive insect that cheerful hosts keep hauling out and sticking in your face and asking you to pet.

But you do it, because the alternative is gainful employment. You put on your perky face, and you chat with the host about why you wrote the book. Why you wrote it, of course, is money. I'm very up front about this. "Buy my book," I always advise the listening audience. "Or just send me some money in a box."

I've had some fun times, on my various book tours. The most fun was when I was promoting a book about do-it-yourself home repair. This book was, of course, totally worthless, not a single fact in it, but I ended up on a whole bunch of radio shows where the hosts, who had not had time to look at the book personally, thought I had written a *real* book about home repair. So the interviews went like this:

HOST: Dave, what's the best place to add insulation?
ME: Bob, I recommend the driveway.
HOST: Ha ha! Seriously, Dave.
ME: I am serious, Bob.
HOST: My guest has been Dave Barry.

I have also been on some very interesting TV shows. I was on a show in Cleveland where the other guests were a sex therapist and a Swedish gynecologist, who were supposed to have a sensitive discussion about the Male Perspective on sexuality with an all-male audience that had been bused in especially for the show. It turned out, however, that there was also beer on the bus, so the Male Perspective on sexuality consisted almost entirely of hooting and snickering. Somebody would ask the sex-therapist where the "G-spot" was, and she'd start to answer, and somebody in the back would yell: "It's in Germany!" Then there would be a violent eruption of hoots and snickers and we'd break for a commercial.

Recently, in Boston, I was on a show where the other two guests were—this is true—a police officer who explained how to avoid getting your purse snatched, and a woman named "Chesty Morgan" who once served in the Israeli army and currently dances topless and has the largest natural bosom in the world. She said she wears a size double-P bra. She has it made specially in Waco, Texas. She has a very interesting and tragic life story, and I wouldn't be surprised if, in the near future, she comes out with a book.

HOT BOOKS AND HOT COALS

TIME NOW FOR THE ANNUAL LITERARY SURVEY
and firewalking report:

First, I am pleased to report that millions of units of new literature will soon be arriving at bookstores near you. I know this because I recently went to San Francisco to attend the American Booksellers Association's annual convention, at which all the big publishing companies reveal their fall literary lines. And on hand were a number of top authors such as Mister T, who was there to stress to the young people of America that they should read a lot of books or he will break all the bones in their faces; and Mary Lou Retton, who discussed a new book she has written about (get ready!) physical fitness. This is certainly a topic we need a *lot* more books on, because at present we have only enough fitness books to cover the Midwest to a depth of 60,000 feet.

Some other exciting book concepts you can look forward to seeing this fall include:

• A great many books telling you how to become so extremely successful in business, so totally *excellent*, that one day, during a budget meeting, you just *vanish* in a blinding flash of total managerial perfection, and the next thing you know you are on a distant misty mountain top wearing a white robe and talking about motivation with Lee Iacocca;

• Biographies of two of the three Stooges;

• A book called *How to Find a Husband in 30 Days* (Get

Ready . . . Get Set . . . Get Married!), which is a terrific literary concept, the only problem being that it is written by the same person who wrote the best-selling *Thin Thighs in 30 Days,* which also seemed like a terrific concept except that it did not work, in the sense that if you glance around with your eyes angled slightly downward you will note that the general population continues to have thighs the size of research submarines.

And here is a major piece of literary excitement for you; Parker Brothers has unveiled a new group of cute licensed characters for children. This is the one thing we need even *more* than we need another fitness book. These licensed characters are called "The Hugga Bunch," and I am pleased to report that they are just about the most lovable little wads of cuteness to mince down the pike since Rainbow Brite. You parents of preschool children are definitely going to hear a *lot* of high-pitched whining about these exciting characters.

Which brings us to the firewalking portion of our report. One of the authors at the convention was a person named Tolly Burkan, who is one of the top, if not *the* top firewalker in the United States. For the benefit of those of you who do not watch "Donahue," I should explain that firewalking is a very important new emerging growth trend where people walk on hot coals in bare feet. You will never in a million jillion years guess what state this concept has gained great popularity in: California(!). Out in California, you can pay people money, and they let you walk on their hot coals.

Besides doing firewalking seminars, Tolly Burkan has produced various cassette tapes and books, including his hardcover book *Dying to Live,* in which he explains how he used to be really messed up and try to kill himself all the time, but now he is all straightened out and goes around encouraging people to walk barefoot on hot coals. Also he supervises fasting. According to a brochure I got at his firewalking demonstration, you pay him $35 a day, in return for which you get not to eat under his personal supervision. Also for $500 he will whack you in both kneecaps with a ballpeen hammer.

Ha ha! Just kidding! I think!

The firewalking demonstration took place at a parking lot near the convention hall, and there were maybe a hundred of us on hand to watch. Tolly, who had a wireless microphone and who has that extremely mellow California-spiritual-leader style of speech similar to what you would get if you gave Mister Rogers a horse tranquilizer, explained the basic theory of firewalking, which as I understand it is that if you really believe you can do something, then by golly you can just *do* it, even if it seems impossible. I happen to agree with this theory. I think it explains, for example, how large heavy commercial airplanes get off the ground despite the fact that they are clearly too heavy to fly, especially when their beverage carts are fully loaded.

So anyway, at the firewalking demonstration, Tolly raked out a six-foot-long bed of very hot coals from a bed of cedar and oak logs (he has also walked on mesquite) and taught the onlookers a little chant they were supposed to chant when the walkers walked across the coals. This being San Francisco, they chanted it. In New York, they would have stolen his wireless microphone. Then Tolly brought on some of his veteran walkers, who each took a couple of quick steps across the coals the way you would step if you were walking on some very hot coals. Then Tolly walked on the coals a couple of times for a newspaper photographer, including once when he pretended that while he was walking he was reading his book, which by the way is for sale.

These people actually do walk across hot coals. It is quite impressive. To find something comparable in my experience I have to go back to when I was eight years old, and Charles Ringwald ate a worm, only he did it without any assistance in the form of chanting. So if you're looking for a way to find total happiness in your life, I urge you to walk on hot coals as soon as possible, provided of course that you have taken a seminar run by a responsible professional.

Also, Charles Ringwald, if you're out there, please get in touch with me as soon as possible, because I have a terrific idea for a book.

THE HAIR APPARENT

I HAVE A LETTER HERE FROM MRS. BELLE EHR-lich, of San Jose, California, who feels I should get a new hairdo. To quote her directly: "I enjoy reading most of your columns . . . but your hairdo in your photo sure looks DATED and NOT at all flattering or becoming, to say the least. If you are still sporting that awful hairdo, I suggest you go to a good hair stylist to give you a new and better hairdo. I hope you don't mind my criticism, it's nothing personal— just a suggestion."

Mind? Ha ha! MIND? Of course not, Mrs. Belle Ehrlich of San Jose! As a journalist who seeks to inform his readers about topics of vital concern to the nation and the world, I *welcome* insulting remarks about my hair!

OK, perhaps I am a bit sensitive about my hair. I have been sensitive about my hair since second grade, when the Kissing Girls first swung into action. You probably had Kissing Girls at your elementary school too: they roamed the playground, chasing after selected boys and trying to kiss them. We boys carried on as though we would have preferred to undergo the Red-Ants-Eat-Your-Eyelids-Off Torture than get kissed, but of course we wanted desperately to be selected. And I almost never was. The boys who were selected had wavy hair. Wavy hair was big back then, and I did not have it. I had straight hair, and it did not help that my father cut it.

You should know that my father was a fine, decent, and sensitive man, but unfortunately he had no more fashion awareness than a baked potato. His idea of really el snazzo dressing was to wear a suit jacket and suit pants that both originated as part of the same suit. He would have worn the same tie to work for 42 consecutive years if my mother had let him. So, the way he would cut my hair is, he'd put me on a stool, and he'd start cutting hair off one side of my head with the electric clippers, then he'd walk around me and attempt, relying on memory, to make the other side of my head look similar. Which, of course, he could never quite do, so he would head back around to take a stab at Side One again, and he'd keep this up for some time, and all I can say is, thank heavens they had a little plastic guard on the electric clippers so that you couldn't make the hair any shorter than a quarter-inch, because otherwise my father, with the best of intentions, trying to even me up, would have started shaving off slices of actual tissue until eventually I would have been able to turn my head sideways and stick it through a mail slot. As it was, in photographs taken back then, I look like an extremely young Marine, or some kind of radiation victim.

It also did not help that in third grade I became the first kid in the class to get glasses, and we are talking serious 1950s horn rims of the style that when you put them on a third-grade child, especially one with a comical haircut, you get a Mister Peepers effect such that everybody assumes the child must be a Goody-Two-Shoes Teacher's Pet science-oriented little dweeb. And it also did not help that I was a late developer, pubertywise. I was *ready* for puberty. All of us boys were. We wanted to catch up to the girls, who about two years earlier had very suddenly, in fact I think it was all on the same day, shown up at school a foot taller than us and with bosoms and God knows what else. So I was definitely looking forward to puberty as the Dawn of a New Era in the looks department, and you can just imagine how *betrayed* I felt when it started happening to the other boys, even boys whom I had considered my friends, well before it happened to me. They got ahead of me then, and sometimes I think I never really caught up. I am 38 years old now, and I have yet to develop hair on my arms. Isn't that supposed to happen, in puberty? I see men much younger than myself, with hairy arms, and I think: Does this mean I'm not done with puberty *yet*?

I realize I sound insecure here, but if you really wanted to see insecure, you should have seen me in eighth grade. I was a mess. That was why I developed a sense of humor. I needed something to do at parties. The other boys, the boys who had wavy hair and reasonable hormone-activity levels, would be necking with girls, and I would be over by the record player, a short radiation victim in horn-rimmed spectacles, playing 45s and making jokes to entertain the 10-year-old brother of whoever was holding the party. Now that I'm grown up, I keep reading magazine articles about these surveys where they ask you women what you really want most in a man, and you always say: A Sense of Humor. And I think to myself: Right. Sure. Great. *Now* you want a sense of humor. But back in the eighth grade, back when it really mattered, what you wanted was puberty.

And I am not even going to mention here that for several years my hands were covered with warts.

So anyway, Mrs. Belle Ehrlich of San Jose, what I'm trying to say here is: Thanks, thanks a million for taking the time to drop me a note informing me that my hair looks awful. Because now I'm grown up (except in terms of arm hair) and have contact lenses, and I have finally come to think of myself as very nearly average in appearance, I can handle this kind of helpful criticism, and I will definitely see if I can't find a good hair stylist. This is assuming that I ever leave my bedroom again.

THE TURNING POINT, IN TERMS OF MY GIVING IN
to the concept of being a Television Personality, was when I
let them put the styling mousse on my hair. Hair has always
been my dividing line between television personalities and us
newspaper guys. We newspaper guys generally have hair
that looks like we trim it by burning the ends with Bic light-
ers. We like to stand around and snicker at the TV guys,
whose hair all goes in the same direction and looks as though
it's full-bodied and soft, but which in fact has been per-
meated with hardened petrochemical substances to the point
where it could deflect small-caliber bullets. We newspaper
guys think these substances have actually penetrated the
skulls and attacked the brain cells of the TV guys, which we
believe explains why their concept of a really major journal-
istic achievement is to interview Mr. T.

So I need to explain how I became a Television Personality. A while back, a public-television station asked me to be
the host of a new TV series they want to start for parents of
young children, and I said, sure, what the heck. I remember
saying, "Sounds like fun." And thus I became a talent. That's
what TV people call you if you go in front of the camera: a
"talent." They call you that right to your face. Only after a
while you realize they don't mean that you have any actual
talent. In fact, it's sort of an insult. In the TV business, "talent" means "not the camera, lighting, or sound people, all of

whom will do exactly what they're supposed to do every single time, but the bonehead with the pancake makeup who will make us all stay in the studio for two extra hours because he cannot remember that he is supposed to say 'See you next *time*' instead of 'See you next *week*.' " It reminds me of the way people in the computer industry use the word "user," which to them means "idiot."

When you are a TV talent, you are meat. People are always straightening your collar, smearing things on your face, and talking about you in the third person, saying things like: "What if we had him sitting down?" and "Can we make his face look less round?" and "Can we do anything about his nose?" This is how my hair came to contain several vats of styling mousse, which is this gunk that looks like shaving cream and which you can just tell was invented by a French hair professional whom, if you met him, you would want to punch directly in the mouth. The TV people felt it made me look older. I felt it made me look like a water bed salesman, but hey, I'm just a talent.

Still, I thought I'd be all right, once we got into the studio. What I pictured was, I would saunter in front of the camera, and say something like, "Hi! Welcome to our show! Here's an expert psychological authority to tell you what it means when your child puts the cat in the Cuisinart! And sets it on 'mince'!" Then I would just sit back and listen to the expert, nodding my head and frowning with concern from time to time. And every now and then I might say something spontaneous and riotously funny.

As it turns out, *nothing* happens spontaneously in a television studio. Before anything can happen, they have to spend several hours shining extremely bright lights on it from different angles, then they have to stand around frowning at it, then they have to smear it and dust it with various substances to get it to stop the glare from those bright lights that they are shining on it, and then they have to decide that it has to be moved to a completely different place so they can start all over.

Once they get all set up, once they're satisfied that the lights are as bright and as hot as they can possibly get them, it's time for the talent to come in and make a fool out of itself. On a typical day, I would have to do something like walk up to a table, lean on it casually, say some witty remarks to one camera, turn to the right and say some more witty remarks to another camera, and walk off. This sounds very easy, right? Well, here's what would happen. I would do my little performance, and there would be a lengthy pause while the director and the producer and the executive producer and all the assistant producers back in the control room discussed, out of my hearing, what I had done wrong.

Now I can take criticism. I'm a writer and my editor is always very direct with me. "Dave, this column bites the big one," is the kind of thing he'll say by way of criticism. And I can handle it. But in the TV world, they never talk to you like that. They talk to you as though you're a small child, and they're not sure whether you're just emotionally unbalanced or actually retarded. They take tremendous pains not to hurt your feelings. First of all, they *always* tell you it was great.

"That was great, Dave. We're going to try it again, with just a little more energy, OK? Also, when you walk in, try not to shuffle your feet, OK? Also, When you turn right, dip your eyes a bit, then come up to the next camera, because otherwise it looks odd, OK? Also, don't bob your head so much, OK? And try not to smack your lips, OK? Also, remember you're supposed to say next *time*, not next *week*, OK? So just try to be natural, and have some fun with it, OK? I think we're almost there."

So I had to do everything a great many times, and of course all my jokes, which I thought were absolute killers when I wrote them in the privacy of my home, soon seemed, in this studio where I was telling them over and over to camera persons who hadn't even laughed the first time, remarkably stupid, or even the opposite of jokes, antihumor, somber remarks that you might make to somebody who had just lost his whole family in a boat explosion. But I kept at it, and finally after God knows how many attempts, would come the voice from the control room: "That was perfect, Dave. Let's try it again with a little more energy. Also you forgot to say your name."

THE EMBARRASSING TRUTH

HAVE YOU EVER REALLY EMBARRASSED YOUR-self? Don't answer that, stupid. It's a rhetorical question. Of course you've embarrassed yourself. Everybody has. I bet the pope has. If you were to say to the pope: "Your Holy Wor-shipfulness, I bet you've pulled some blockheaded boners in your day, huh?" he'd smile that warm, knowing, fatherly smile he has, and then he'd wave. He can't hear a word you're saying, up on that balcony.

But my point is that if you've ever done anything humil-iating, you've probably noticed that *your brain never lets you forget it.* This is the same brain that never remembers things you *should* remember. If you were bleeding to death and the emergency-room doctor asked you what blood type you were, you'd say: "I think it's B. Or maybe C. I'm pretty sure it's a letter." But if your doctor asked you to describe the skirt you were wearing when you were do-ing the Mashed Potatoes in the ninth-grade dance com-petition in front of 350 people, and your underwear, which had holes in it, fell to your ankles, you'd say, with-out hesitating for a millisecond, "It was gray felt with a pink flocked poodle."

Your brain cherishes embarrassing memories. It likes to take them out and fondle them. This probably explains a lot of unexplained suicides. A successful man with a nice family and a good career will be out on his patio, cooking hamburgers, seemingly without a care in the world, when his brain, rummaging through its humiliating-incident collection, selects an old favorite, which it replays for a zillionth time, and the man is suddenly so overcome by feelings of shame that he stabs himself in the skull with his barbecue fork. At the funeral, people say how shocking it was, a seemingly happy and well-adjusted person choosing to end it all. They assume he must have had a terrible dark secret involving drugs or organized crime or dressing members of the conch family in flimsy undergarments. Little do they know he was thinking about the time in Social Studies class in 1963 when he discovered a hard-to-reach pimple roughly halfway down his back, and he got to working on it, subtly at first, but with gradually increasing intensity, eventually losing track of where he was, until suddenly he realized the room had become silent, and he looked up, with his arm stuck halfway down the back of his shirt, and he saw that *everybody in the class, including the teacher, was watching what he was doing,* and he knew they'd give him a cruel nickname that would stick like epoxy cement for the rest of his life, such as when he went to his 45th reunion, even if he had been appointed Chief Justice of the U.S. Supreme Court, the instant his classmates saw him, they'd shriek: "Hey look! It's ZIT!"

Everybody has incidents like this. My mother is always reliving the time she lost her car in a shopping-center parking lot, and she was wandering around with several large shopping bags and two small children, looking helpless, and after a while other shoppers took pity on her and offered to help. "It's a black Chevrolet," she told them, over and over. And they searched and searched and searched for it. They were extremely nice. They all agreed that it can be darned easy to lose your car in these big parking lots. They had been there for an hour, some of them, searching for this black Chevrolet, and it was getting dark, when my mother remembered that several days earlier we had bought a new car. "I'm sorry!" she told the people, smiling brightly so they would see what a humorous situation this was. "It's *not* a black Chevrolet! It's a yellow Ford!" She kept on smiling as they edged away, keeping their eyes on her.

My own personal brain is forever dredging up the time in 11th grade when I took a girl, a very attractive girl on whom I had a life-threatening crush, to a dance. I was standing in the gym next to her, holding her hand, thinking what a sharp couple we made—Steve Suave and His Gorgeous Date—when one of my friends sidled up to me and observed that, over on the other side, my date was using her spare hand to hold hands with another guy. This was of course a much better-looking guy. This was Paul Newman, only taller.

Several of my friends gathered to watch. I thought: What am I supposed to do here? Hit the guy? That would have been asking for a lifetime of dental problems. He was a varsity football player; I was on the Dance Committee. I also had to rule out hitting my date. The ideal move would have been to spontaneously burst into flames and die. I have read that this sometimes happens to people. But you never get a break like that when you need it.

Finally I turned to my date, dropped her hand, looked her square in the eye, and said: "Um." Just like that: "Um." My brain absolutely loves to remember this. "Way to go, Dave!" it shrieks to me, when I'm stopped at red lights, 23½ years later. Talk about eloquent! My brain can't get over what a jerk I was. It's always coming up with much better ideas for things I could have said. I should start writing them down, in case we ever develop time travel. I'd go back to the gym with a whole Rolodex file filled with remarks, and I'd read them to my date over the course of a couple of hours. Wouldn't *she* feel awful! Ha ha!

It just occurred to me that she may be out there right now, in our reading audience, in which case I wish to state for the record that I am leading an absolutely wonderful life, and I have been on the Johnny Carson show, and I hope things are equally fine with you.

Twice. I was on Carson twice.

A MILLION WORDS

IT WAS TIME TO GO HAVE MY LAST WORDS WITH my father. He was dying, in the bedroom he built. He built our whole house, even dug the foundation himself, with a diaper tied around his head to keep the sweat out of his eyes. He was always working on the house, more than 35 years, and he never did finish it. He was first to admit that he really didn't know how to build a house.

When I went in to see him, he was lying in the bedroom, listening to the "People's Court." I remember when he always would be on those Sunday-morning television talk shows, back in the fifties and sixties. Dr. Barry, they called him. He was a Presbyterian minister, and he worked in inner-city New York. They were always asking him to be on those shows to talk about Harlem and the South Bronx, because back then he was the only white man they could find who seemed to know anything about it. I remember when he was the Quotation of the Day in the *New York Times*. The Rev. Dr. David W. Barry.

His friends called him Dave. "Is Dave there?" they'd ask, when they called to talk about their husbands or wives or sons or daughters who were acting crazy or drinking too much or running away. Or had died. "Dave," they'd ask, "what can I do?" They never thought to call anybody but him. He'd sit there and listen, for hours, sometimes. He was always smoking.

The doctor told us he was dying, but we knew anyway. Almost all he said anymore was thank you, when somebody brought him shaved ice, which was mainly what he wanted, at the end. He had stopped putting his dentures in. He had stopped wearing his glasses. I remember when he yanked his glasses off and jumped in the Heyman's pool to save me.

So I go in for my last words, because I have to go back home, and my mother and I agree I probably won't see him again. I sit next to him on the bed, hoping he can't see that I'm crying. "I love you, Dad," I say. He says: "I love you, too. I'd like some oatmeal."

So I go back out to the living room, where my mother and my wife and my son are sitting on the sofa, in a line, wating for the outcome and I say, "He wants some oatmeal." I am laughing and crying about this. My mother thinks maybe I should go back in and try to have a more meaningful last talk, but I don't.

Driving home, I'm glad I didn't. I think: He and I have been talking ever since I learned how. A million words. All of them final, now. I don't need to make him give me any more, like souvenirs. I think: Let me not define his death on my terms. Let him have his oatmeal. I can hardly see the road.

SUBHUMANIZE YOUR LIVING ROOM

TODAY WE'RE GOING TO TALK ABOUT REDECOR-
ating your home. My guess is you're unhappy with your current decor, especially if you have small children around, the
result being that all of your furniture and carpeting, no matter what the original color scheme, is now the color of mixed-
fruit juice.

Fortunately for you, home decor is an area I happen to
know a great deal about, as I have done my own decorating,
without professional assistance, ever since my college days,
when I shared a dormitory suite with several other design-
conscious young men. Our watchword, decorwise, was "func-
tionality." For the floor covering in our bedrooms, we chose
the comfortable, carefree casualness of unlaundered jockey
shorts. By the end of a semester, there would be six, maybe
seven hundred pairs of shorts per bedroom, forming a pulsating, bed-high mound.

For our living-room-wall treatment we opted for a
very basic, very practical, and very functional decorating
concept called "old college dormitory paint, the color of
the substance you might expect to see oozing from an
improperly treated wound." We highlighted this with an
interesting textural effect that you can obtain by having
a Halloween party and throwing wads of orange and black
crepe paper soaked in beer up against the wall and then
leaving it there for a couple of months to harden and

trying to scrape it off with the edge of an economics text-book.

But our *pièce de résistance* (French, meaning "piece of resistance") was our living-room furniture, which was a two-piece grouping consisting of:

- An orange emergency light that flashed when you plugged it in.
- A "Two-Man Submarine," which we purchased for only $9.95 via an advertisement in a Spider-Man comic book. It was made of sturdy cardboard and measured five feet long when fully assembled. It was not only very attractive but also quite functional inasmuch as you could sit inside it and pretend you were actually deep beneath the ocean surface, driving a real submarine made of sturdy cardboard.

As you might imagine, the overall effect created by these design elements was quite impressive, especially when we had dates and we really spruced up the place. We'd stack the deceased pizza boxes in the corner, and we'd create a romantic atmosphere by spraying a couple of cans of Right-Guard brand deodorant on the jockey-short mounds, and believe me it was a real treat to see the look on the face of a date as she entered our suite for the first time and, seeing the striking visual effect created by the orange emergency light flashing on the "Two-Man Submarine," she realized what a suave kind of college man she was having a date with.

But enough about my qualifications. Let's talk about your own home. Clearly you need new furniture. To select exactly what you want, you need to have some Creative Decorating Ideas, which you get by purchasing about $65 worth of glossy magazines with names like *Unaffordable Home Design*. Inside these magazines will be exquisite color photographs of the most wondrously perfect, profoundly clean rooms anybody has ever seen, rooms where even the air molecules are arranged in attractive patterns. How, you ask yourself, can rooms look like this? Where are the hand smudges? Where is the dark spot on the carpet where the dog threw up the unidentified reptile? And how come there are *never any people* in these photographs?

The answer is: *These rooms are only four inches high.* The magazines have them built by skilled craftsmen solely for the purpose of making your home look, by comparison, like a Roach Motel. In fact, occasionally a magazine will slip up, and you'll see through the window of what is allegedly a rich person's living room, what appears to be a 675-pound thumb.

OK! Now that you have your Creative Decorating Ideas, you get a sheet of graph paper, and you make an elaborate scale drawing of your existing floor plan, showing exactly to the inch where you would put all your nice new furniture, if you were a major cocaine dealer and could afford nice new furniture. Unfortunately the furniture you can afford comes from places with names like Big Stu's World of Taste and is made of compressed bran flakes. So, frankly, if I were you, I'd spread my glossy interior-design magazines around so they covered as much of my current decor as possible.

THE LURE OF THE WILD

THE FIRST TIME I TAUGHT MY SON, ROBERT, HOW to fish was when he was two. I did it the old-fashioned way: I took him to the K-Mart with Uncle Joe, our old friend and lawyer, to pick out a Complete Fishing Outfit for $12.97. Then we went to a pond, where Robert sat in the weeds and put pond muck in his hair while Uncle Joe and I tried to bait the hook with a living breathing thinking feeling caring earthworm. This is a very difficult thing emotionally, and not just for the earthworm. It would be different if worms gave you some reason to feel hostile toward them, such as they had little faces that looked like Geraldo Rivera. That would be no problem, "Let's go bait some worms purely for amusement," you would frequently hear me call out.

But the way worms are now, they make it very hard, writhing around and conveying, by means of body language and worm guts squirting out, the concept of "Please please oh PLEASE Mr. Human Being don't stick this hook into me." For my money, worms are far better at this kind of nonverbal communication than those people called "mimes," who paint their faces all white and repeatedly attempt to entertain you at street festivals, although to be absolutely certain, we would have to run an experiment wherein we baited a hook with a live mime. (All those in favor of doing this, raise your hands. I thought so!)

148

I think it would be more humane if we just forgot about bait altogether and shot the fish directly with guns, the way we do with rabbits and deer. I saw Roy Scheider take this approach to angling in the movie *Jaws I,* and he got himself a real prize trophy shark using a rifle for a weapon and Richard Dreyfuss for bait. Unfortunately, this turned out to be a violation of our outmoded game laws, so Roy had to *throw the shark back,* which turned out to be highly fatal to several dozen teen-agers and a helicopter in *Jaws II.* This is a totally unnecessary outrage, if you ask me, especially when you consider that it is *not* illegal to catch deer with rod and reel in most states. *(Editor's Note: He's raving. Pay no attention.)*

Nevertheless, Robert and Uncle Joe and I did manage to land a fish, the kind veteran anglers call a "bluegill." It was three to four ounces of well-contained fury, and it fought like a frozen bagel. Many times at airport newsstands I have examined sportsperson-oriented magazines with names like *Tackle 'n' Bait,* and I have noted that the covers often feature pictures of bold sportspersons struggling to land extremely muscular, violent-looking fish the size of guest bathrooms, whose expressions say: "Yes, you had better kill me, Mr. Sportsperson, because otherwise I will evolve legs and lungs and talons and fangs and come to your suburban home and wreck your riding mower and *have my way with your women hahahahahaha.*"

But the fish we caught was a cute fish, a fish that would star in a Walt Disney animated cartoon featured called *Billy Bluegill Learns the True Meaning of Christmas.* Robert looked at it, then he looked at Uncle Joe and me with a look of great upsettedness in his two-year-old eyes and we realized, being responsible grown-ups, that it was time to lie.

"The fish doesn't feel it!" we announced brightly, almost in unison. "You see this sharp barbed metal hook going right through his lip?! It doesn't hurt a bit! Ha ha!!" Meanwhile Billy the Bluegill was of course edging out the worm for the Academy Award for Best Performance by a Cold-Blooded Animal Gasping and Writhing Around to Indicate Extreme

Pain. And so Uncle Joe, being an attorney, got Billy off the hook (get it?) and we put him (Billy) back into the pond.

After that Robert and I didn't go fishing for several years, until last Christmas, when we went up to New York and Uncle Phil—who is not our attorney but Robert affectionately calls him "uncle" anyway because he is my brother —bought Robert *another fishing rod,* meaning I had to teach him *again.* Fortunately, there were no worms available, as they had all formed up into characteristic V-shaped patterns and attempted to migrate South, getting as far as the toll booths on the New Jersey Turnpike.

So Robert and I used "lures," which are these comical devices that veteran anglers instinctively buy from catalogs. You would think that, to be effective, lures would have to look like creatures that a fish might actually eat, but, in fact, they look like what you would expect to see crawling around on the Planet Zork during periods of intense radioactivity. For example, many lures have propellers, which you rarely see in the Animal Kingdom. In my opinion, the way lures actually work is that the fish see one go by, and they get to laughing so hard and thrashing around that occasionally one of them snags itself on the hook. Back in the Prepuberty Era I used to spend hundreds of hours lure-fishing with my friend Tom Parker and his faithful dog Rip, and the only distinct memory I have of us catching anything besides giant submerged logs was the time Tom was using a lure called a Lazy Ike and it was attacked with stunning ferocity by his faithful dog Rip, resulting in a very depressing situation, veterinarianwise.

So, fortunately Robert and I didn't catch anything the second time I taught him to fish, and I think he's now old enough to remember it clearly and thus never ask me to teach him again. That's the good news. The bad news is, I am sure that one of these days he's going to want to have a "catch."

EARNING A COLLIE DEGREE

WE HAVE A NEW DOG, WHICH MEANS WE'RE GOING through this phase where we spend a lot of time crouching and stroking and going "Yessss! That's a GOOD girl!" and otherwise practically awarding a Nobel Prize to her for achievements such as not pooping on the rug.

Her name is Earnest, which I realize is not a traditional girl's name, but it describes her very well. Most dogs are earnest, which is why most people like them. You can say any fool thing to a dog, and the dog will give you this look that says, "My God, you're RIGHT! I NEVER would have thought of that!" So we come to think of dogs as being understanding and loving and compassionate, and after a while we hardly even notice that they spend the bulk of their free time circling around with other dogs to see which one can sniff the other the most times in the crotch.

We are not sure yet whether Earnest has a working brain. You can't tell, early on, with dogs. When we got our previous dog, Shawna, we thought she was smart as a whip, because she was a purebred German shepherd who had this extremely *alert* look. At first we took this to mean that she was absorbing every tiny detail of her environment with her keen senses and analyzing it with computerlike speed, but it turned out to be her way of expressing the concept: "What?"

Shawna would be sitting in our yard, looking very sharp, and a squirrel would scurry *right* past her, a squirrel whose

151

presence was instantly detected by normal, neighborhood dogs hundreds of yards away, causing them to bark rigorously, and also by us humans, causing us to yell helpfully: "Look! Shawna! A *squirrel!!*" And after a few seconds of delay, during which her nervous system would send the message via parcel post from her ears to her brain that something was going on, Shawna would turn in the exact opposite direction from whichever way the squirrel was, adopt a pose of great canine readiness, and go: "What?"

The only dog I ever met that was dumber than Shawna belongs to my editor. This dog, a collie named Augie, also *looks* smart, if you grew up watching "Lassie." Lassie looked brilliant, in part because the farm family she lived with was made up of idiots. Remember? One of them was always getting pinned under the tractor, and Lassie was always rushing back to the farmhouse to alert the other ones. She'd whimper and tug at their sleeves, and they'd always waste precious minutes saying things: "Do you think something's *wrong?* Do you think she wants us to *follow* her? What *is* it, girl?" as if this had never happened before, instead of every week. What with all the time these people spent pinned under the tractor, I don't see how they managed to grow any crops whatsoever. They probably got by on federal crop supports, which Lassie filed the applications for.

So anyway I thought Augie, being a collie, would have at least some intelligence, despite the fact that when my editor and I would walk into his house, Augie would not notice us, sometimes for upwards of a half hour. When she finally did notice us, talking and drinking beer, she would bark as though the Manson gang had just burst in, so my editor would have to go over and sort of say, "Look! It's me! The person you have lived with for 10 years!" This would cause Augie's lone functioning brain cell to gradually quiet down and go back to sleep.

But I still thought she was roughly on par with Shawna, IQ-wise, until the night—you may remember the night; it was the longest one we ever had—that I slept on my editor's couch in his living room, which is also where Augie sleeps. Only she doesn't sleep. What she does is, first, she lies down. Then she scratches herself. Then she engages in loud personal hygiene. Then she thinks, "Maybe I can go out!" and she walks across the floor, which is made of a special kind of very hard wood so that when a dog walks on it, it goes TICK TICK TICK TICK at exactly the volume you would use to get maximum benefit from the Chinese Ticking Torture. When Augie gets to the front door, which is of course closed —it is always closed at night; even the domestic insects have learned this by now—she bumps into it with her head. Then she backs up and bumps into it with her head a couple more times, in case there has been some mistake. Then she senses, somehow, that there is a person sleeping on the couch, and she has the most innovative idea she has ever thought of, which is: "Maybe *he* will let me out!" So she walks over to me and noses me in the face, using the same nose she uses for hygiene, and I say, "Dammit, Augie! Go to sleep!" So she lies down for *one minute,* which is how long it takes for her brain cell to forget everything that has ever happened to her since she was born. And then she starts again: SCRATCH SCRATCH SCRATCH SLURP SLURP SLURP (think) TICK TICK TICK TICK BUMP (think) BUMP (think) BUMP (think) TICK TICK TICK NOSE "DAMMIT, AUGIE! GO TO SLEEP!" TICK TICK TICK TICK (pause) SCRATCH . . .

I don't know yet about Earnest. One day soon I will give her the dog intelligence test, where you show her the ball, then you put the ball under a blanket, and then you see if she can find the ball. Shawna never could find the ball. I doubt Augie could find the blanket. I'm hoping Earnest does better, but I'm not counting my chickens. I am also not looking forward to receiving a lot of violent letters from you dog lovers out there, the ones with the "I (heart) my (breed of dog)" bumper stickers, asking how dare I say dogs are stupid when your dog can add, subtract, land the space shuttle, etc.

So please note, dog lovers: I never said *your* dog is stupid. I said *my* dog might be stupid. I know for a fact that she can't be *too* intelligent, because here I've written a fairly insulting column about her species, and despite the fact that she's lying right at my feet, it hasn't occurred to her to pull the plug on my word proces

SOME THOUGHTS ON THE TOILET

BOTH OF OUR HOUSEHOLD TOILETS BROKE RE-cently, on the same day. They work together, toilets. You know those strange sounds your plumbing makes at night? The ones that worry you much more than, for example, the threat of nuclear war? Those are your toilets, talking to each other. They communicate via plumbing sounds, similar to whales. "It's New Year's Eve," they'll say. "We break tonight."

I happen to know a great deal about toilets, although that was not the original plan. The original plan was for me to become profoundly wealthy by investing in real estate. I had read a book about it, which made the whole process sound as easy as getting insurance offers from Ed McMahon by mail. The trick, according to this book, was that when you purchase your real estate, you *never used your own money*. You used *other people's* money. The way the book described it, you strode into the bank, and you said: "Hi! I'd like to become filthy rich via real estate, but I don't wish to use my own money!" And the bank would say: "Well then! Here! Take some of ours!!"

So I got some partners who also had a sincere interest in becoming rich, and we hatched a plan wherein we would, using other people's money, buy a couple of small apartment buildings, after which we would sit around drinking gin and tonic and amassing great wealth due to Depreciation and Leverage, two characters who appeared often in the real-

155

estate book, performing amazing financial feats. They reminded me of Batman and Robin.

So my partners and I went around presenting our proposal to various bankers, and they thought it was the greatest thing they had every heard. They would set up extra chairs and invite all their banker friends over, and they'd make us go through our proposal again and again, and when we'd get to the part about not using any of our own money, they'd fall over backwards and hurl their loan application forms into the air and laugh until there was spittle all over their vests. They had evidently not read the book.

So eventually we worked out a compromise arrangement whereby my partners and I would each provide our life's savings, and the bank would provide a Closing Ceremony, which is when you go into a little room with unfamiliar lawyers and you sign every piece of paper they have managed to acquire in their lives, including book reports. This is how we came to acquire, as an investment, eight toilets. The Head Toilet, of course, immediately fired off an urgent message to the others. "We have been purchased," the message said, "by people who have read *a real estate investment book.*" As you can imagine, the sound of hysterical gurgling went on well into the night.

I became intimately familiar with every single one of these investment toilets. See, my partners all had useful skills, such as carpentry, whereas my only area of proven competence was listening to the radio, so we agreed that I would learn how to be the plumber. Gradually, I learned that there are two major toilet facts:

TOILET FACT NUMBER ONE: The only way to prevent a toilet part from leaking is to tighten it until it breaks.

TOILET FACT NUMBER TWO: Circling the Earth, at this very moment, is an alien spacecraft that is sending down powerful radio beams that affect the brains of tenants in such a way that they *must put inappropriate objects in the toilet.* They cannot help themselves. "Find an inappropriate object!" the beam commands them. "Put it in the toilet RIGHT

NOW!" You landlords out there, you know I'm telling the truth, right? And the tenants, they don't even remember what they have done. "How in the world did THAT get in there?" they say, when you show them, for example, a harmonica. "Ha ha!" they add. "Ha ha," you agree, all the while calculating the various angles and forces involved in killing them with your wrench.

Because of these two facts, I soon got to know all eight toilets personally, as individuals. I would call them by name. "So, Bob," I would say. "Leaking again, eh? How would you like to be *replaced*, Bob? How would you like to be taken outside and have your smooth white porcelain body *smashed repeatedly with a hammer?* Because there are plenty more toilets, down at the Home Center, who would *love* to have your job." But Bob would just chuckle, knowing that even if I could somehow manage to install an entire new toilet, it would quickly become part of the cadre.

This went on for several years, during which I amassed the world's largest privately held collection of broken toilet parts, but not, surprisingly enough, great wealth, so finally I ceased playing an active role in the investment property. But I have used the knowledge I acquired, in my home. When our toilets break, I call the plumber, and I am able to describe the problem in technical plumbing terms. "It's our toilets," I say. "They are broken." And he comes out and fixes them, and I don't care how much he charges. "That will be $68,000," he could tell me, and I would come up with it, somehow, because anything is better than having to deal with the toilets directly. Particularly the one in the hall bathroom. Norman.

THE ELEMENTS OF ELEGANCE

TODAY WE'RE GOING TO TALK ABOUT HOW YOU can hold an elegant dinner party in your home. Well, not really *your* home, of course. You'll need a much more elegant home, one where there is fine nonvelveteen art on the walls and a harp in the corner of the living room and some effort has been made over the years to clean behind the toilets.

You'll also need elegant guests, by which I mean not your friends. You want to invite socially prominent people, which means people who do not object to being called Thad and Bootsie right to their faces and who are directly affected by oil-company mergers. The best way to lure such people to your dinner party is to tell them it has something to do with disease. Socially prominent people are very fond of disease, because it gives them a chance to have these really elaborate charity functions, and the newspaper headlines say "EVENING IN PARIS BALL RAISES MONEY TO FIGHT GOUT" instead of "RICH PEOPLE AMUSE THEMSELVES."

Now let's plan your menu. The most elegant and sophisticated dishes are those that involve greasy little unsanitary birds with no meat and about 60 billion bones, such as grouse. If your local supermarket doesn't carry grouse, your best bet is to go into the woods and tramp around the underbrush until you hear something rustling, then cut loose with

30-second bursts from an automatic weapon until all rustling ceases. Then you merely squat down and scoop up anything that looks like a grouse or some other protein-based life form. It would also be a good idea to take along a pig, which will automatically without any prior training root around for truffles, a kind of delicacy that is very popular among pigs and French people. When you see the pig chewing something, fire a few warning shots over its head and collect whatever it spits out in a Mason jar.

To prepare your grouse, remove the feathers or fur, open up the bodies, remove the organs and parasites and mulch them in the blender until they turn to pâté. Now place the grouse corpses on a stout pan and insert them into a heated oven, dousing them from time to time with A-1 sauce.

When your guests arrive, your first responsibility is to make them feel at ease. I strongly suggest you get a copy of the *Complete Book of Games and Stunts* published in MCLVI by Bonanza Books and authored by Darwin A. Hindman, Ph.D., professor of physical education at the University of Missouri, available at garage sales everywhere. I especially recommend the "Funnel Trick" described in Chapter Four ("Snares"), wherein you tell the victim that the object is to place a penny on his forehead and tilt his head forward so the penny drops into a funnel stuck into his pants. However —get this—while he's got his head tilted back, you pour a pitcher of water into the funnel and get his pants soaking wet! Be sure to follow this with a lighthearted remark ("You look like a cretin, Thad!") and offer everybody a swig from the liqueur bottle.

Once your guests are loosened up, have them sit around the dinner table, and start by serving them each a small wad of truffles with a side wad of pâté. Then bring on the grouse, after whanging each corpse briskly against the kitchen table so as to knock off the char. As your guests enjoy their meal, show great facial interest in whatever conversational topics they choose ("Grouse don't have any teeth, do they?" "These aren't truffles! These are cigarette filters drenched in pig saliva!") Dessert should be something that has been set on fire.

After dinner, the men will gather around the radial-arm saw for cigars and brandy while the women head for the bathroom en masse to make pasta or whatever it is they do in there. Then you should herd everybody back into the living room for a cultural activity, such as humming and paging through one of those enormous $26.95 coffee-table books with names like *The Tractors of Spain* that people give you for Christmas when they get desperate.

Your guests will signal when they're ready to leave by darting out of the room the instant you turn your back; be sure to intercept them at the door to say goodbye and obtain written statements to the effect that they had a wonderful time and will invite you over on a specific date. You really shouldn't have to do this, but unfortunately many people today have forgotten even the basics of etiquette.

RESTROOMS AND OTHER RESORTS

WHAT WE HAD IN MIND WAS A FUN AND SPONTA-neous getaway weekend in Key West with our son, Robert, our friends Gene and Arlene, and their two children, Molly and Danny. So we tossed several thousand child-related objects into our two cars and off we went in a little spontaneous convoy, and, after a couple of hours, we stopped at a nice restaurant for lunch, Except, of course, the children didn't want to eat lunch. Children never want to eat in restaurants. What they want to do is to play under the table until the entrées arrive, then go to the bathroom.

And so we grown-ups sat there, trying to be relaxed, while our table, possessed from below by unseen forces, shrieked and vibrated like the furniture in the little girl's bedroom in *The Exorcist.* In accordance with federal restaurant regulations, the people seated around us had no children of any kind whatsoever, probably never had, probably were there to discuss important corporate mergers, and so occasionally we'd dart our heads under the table and hiss "STOP THAT!" like some deranged type of duck. We kept this up until the entrées arrived, and it was time to accompany the children to the restroom.

The men's room was very small and had not been cleaned since the Westward Expansion. Robert, seeing this, immediately announced that he had to do Number Two, and of course he insisted that I stand right outside the stall. I

161

hate this situation, because when strangers come in to pee, there I am, apparently just hanging around for fun in this tiny repulsive bathroom. So to indicate that I'm actually there on official business, guarding a stall, I feel obligated to keep a conversation going with Robert, but the only topic I can ever think of to talk about, under the circumstance, is how the old Number Two is coming along. You'd feel like a fool in that situation, talking about, say, Iran. So I say: "How're you doing in there, Robert?" in a ludicrously interested voice. And Robert says: "You just ASKED me that!" which is true. And I say "Ha ha!" to reassure the peeing stranger that I am merely engaging in parenthood and there is no cause for alarm.

And so, finally, we all got out of the restrooms, and we parents grabbed quick violent bites from our nice cold entrées in between checking young Danny's head for signs of breakage after he walked into adjacent tables. Eventually, the waitress took the children's plates, untouched, back to the kitchen to be frozen and reused hundreds of times as entrees for other children. Many modern efficient restaurants are now making their children's entrées entirely out of plastic.

Eventually, we got ourselves back on the road, which was the signal for the children to announce that they were hungry, and, of course, they ate potato chips all the rest of the way to Key West. Once at the hotel we were totally unpacked in a matter of hours, and we decided to go to a restaurant, thus proving that long car trips do indeed damage your brain. We found a charming Italian place with fairly clean restrooms and a lovely illuminated fountain with a dangerous electrical cord to attract the children, especially young Danny, who is only two, but has already figured out hundreds of ways to kill himself.

At the sight of the entrées arriving, the children of course fled like startled deer, so we had one of those restaurant meals where you are constantly whirling your head around as you eat, trying to locate the children, with the ever-present danger that you'll get your timing off and stab yourself in the side of the head with your fork. And then it was time to go back to the hotel for an intimate evening of sitting on the floor drinking beer and watching the older children bounce on the bed and eat potato chips while young Danny located bureaus to bang his head into.

For breakfast we found a charming buffet-style restaurant with medium restrooms and a cigarette machine that three small children, if they worked together, could pull over onto their heads.

After breakfast, we went back to our hotel so the children could get something to eat, and then we decided that the women would go shopping and the men, being Caring and Sharing eighties-style males, would take the children. Gene and I thought it would be fun to go to the beach, so off we went, unfortunately forgetting to take any of the items usually associated with the beach, such as toys, suntan lotion, rafts, or bathing suits. We did, however, remember to bring the children. Call it instinct.

Of course, as soon as we got to the beach, little Molly announced that she had to go to the bathroom, and so I watched Danny and Robert fill their shorts with beach muck while Gene and Molly hiked off in search of a restroom, which they eventually found a half-mile away. It took them a long time to get back, because Molly refuses to go into the men's room and Gene can't go into the women's room, so he had to hang around right outside like a sex offender while Molly went in alone, only she came back five minutes later and reported that she couldn't find the toilets. You wonder how we got this far as a species.

Finally, they got back, and we decided we'd better head back to the hotel, because one of the many things we had forgotten was young Danny's diaper bag, and he was wearing his Big Boy underpants, making him, in Gene's words, a "time bomb."

That night, spontaneously, we hired a babysitter.

REVENGE OF THE PORK PERSON

OK, LADIES, I WANT YOU ALL TO LINE UP ACCORD-
ing to height and prepare to receive your fashion orders for
the fall season. You ladies want to be up-to-date, right? You
don't want to show up at work dressed in some dowdy old
thing from last year, looking like Beaver Cleaver's mother,
do you? Of course not! You want to look the very best you
possibly can, given your various physical deformities.

Ha ha! I'm just teasing you ladies, because I know how
sensitive you tend to be about the way you look. I have never
met a woman, no matter how attractive, who wasn't convinced, deep down inside, that she was a real woofer. Men
tend to be just the opposite. A man can have a belly you
could house commercial aircraft in and a grand total of eight
greasy strands of hair, which he grows real long and combs
across the top of his head so that he looks, when viewed from
above, like an egg in the grasp of a giant spider, plus this
man can have B.O. to the point where he interferes with
radio transmissions, and he will still be convinced that, in
terms of attractiveness, he is borderline Don Johnson.

But not women. Women who look perfectly fine to other
people are always seeing horrific physical flaws in themselves.
I have this friend, Janice, who looks very nice and is a highly
competent professional with a good job and a fine family, yet
every now and then she will get very depressed, and do you
want to know why? Because she thinks she has *puffy ankles*.

This worries her much more than, for example, the arms race. Her image of herself is that when she walks down the street, people whisper: "There she goes! The woman with the *puffy ankles!*"

Likewise my wife, who it goes without saying has a great figure and excellent legs, is convinced, and nothing will change her mind, that she has inadequate calves. This has resulted in a situation where—I can produce documentation to prove this—the number of lifetime fitness-club memberships she has purchased *actually exceeds the total number of her legs.*

What women think they should look like, of course, is the models in fashion advertisements. This is pretty comical, because when we talk about fashion models, we are talking about mutated women, the results of cruel genetic experiments performed by fashion designers so lacking in any sense of human decency that they think nothing of putting their initials on your eyeglass lenses. These experiments have resulted in a breed of fashion models who are 8 and sometimes 10 feet tall, yet who weigh no more than an abridged dictionary due to the fact that they have virtually none of the bodily features we normally associate with females such as hips and (let's come right out and say it) bosoms. The leading cause of death among fashion models is falling through street grates. If a normal human woman puts on clothing designed for these unfortunate people, she is quite naturally going to look like Revenge of the Pork Person.

This was particularly true last year, when the Fashion Concept that we here in the fashion industry decided to thrust upon you ladies was the Big Shoulder Look. Remember that? What fun! I cannot tell you how many hours of enjoyment we got from watching you trying to have serious business careers while looking like Green Bay Packers in drag. At one point, we considered having you wear actual helmets, but we couldn't figure out how to fit all our initials on them.

But that was last year. This year we, of course, have an

entirely new concept. We have been working on it for just months and months now, and we are extremely proud of it, because it is so highly innovative. Are you ready? Here it is:

Gray.

Everybody got that? Better write it down! If we find any ladies out on the street without their gray on, we are going to be *very upset*. Also we are asking you to purchase certain mandatory accessories in the form of several thousand dollars worth of handbags, shoes, belts, and watch straps made from dead crocodiles. NO, YOU MAY *NOT* ASK WHY! JUST *DO* IT!

Sorry for that emotional outburst, ladies. It's just that we work so hard to come up with these concepts, and it really frosts our shorts when we find ourselves being questioned by some bimbo *consumer,* pardon our French.

Looking ahead to the future, we see some very exciting developments looming on the fashion horizon for you ladies. Here, for example, is a real quotation from a recent issue of *Vogue* magazine, which uses capital letters for important fashion bulletins:

"THE LOOK OF THE MODERN WOMAN? IN MODERNIST ANDRÉE PUTMAN'S EYES, SHE'S STRONG-SHOULDERED, HIGH-BREASTED, ALMOST AMAZONIAN AND COMES WITH BUILT-IN HIGH HEELS. AT LEAST, THAT'S THE LOOK OF THE NEW PUTMAN-DESIGNED MANNEQUINS MAKING THEIR FIRST PUBLIC APPEARANCE NOW AT BARNEY'S NEW YORK. COME FALL, THE CREATURES WILL PROLIFERATE TO OTHER STORES, OTHER CITIES."

Isn't this *exciting,* ladies? There could come a time, perhaps in your very lifetimes, when we are no longer designing clothes even for mutated fashion models, but for mannequins based on *entirely new concepts of what the female body really should look like,* from deep thinkers such as Andrée Putman. You could see the day when you can't even buy shoes without getting large heel implants! Let's all toss our hats into the air with joy! Our hats, by the way, should be gray porkpies.

SLOPE FLAKE

AS THOSE OF YOU WHO OWN DIGITAL WATCHES are already aware, the winter months are approaching, which means now is the time to start planning that ski vacation.

I understand that some of you may be reluctant to plan ski vacations because you've seen the snippet of film at the beginning of "Wide World of Sports" wherein the Agony of Defeat is depicted by an unfortunate person who loses control of himself going off the end of a ski-jump launcher and various organs come flying out of his body. If you're concerned that something like this could happen to you, here's a statistic from the National Ski Resort Association that should be very reassuring: the so-called castorbean tick, which sucks blood from sheep, will respond to a temperature change of as little as 0.5 degrees centigrade! Wait a minute, there seems to be a mistake here: that reassuring statistic actually comes from the *Encyclopedia Britannica.* Perhaps someone in our reading audience can come up with something more closely related to skiing safety.

Meanwhile, the rest of you should decide what kind of skiing you want to engage in. One option is cross-country skiing, which has become very popular in recent years because it is highly "aerobic," a term health experts use to describe how dull an activity is. What you do is find a patch of country and slog across on skis for no apparent reason in a manner very much reminiscent of a herd of cattle, except of course that cattle have the excuse that if they stop, armed men will ride up and kick them with pointed boots. A more fun option is downhill skiing, which is when a machine takes you up a hill and you have to get down.

Whatever kind of skiing you decide to do, your next important task—in fact, your most important task—is to make sure you have proper ski equipment. When your great grandfather was a boy, of course, he'd simply take two barrel staves and tie them to his feet. This could well be an indication that there is some kind of congenital mental illness in your family, and I urge you to look into it immediately.

Next you'll want to select a ski resort. The important thing here is to decide whether or not you are rich. If you are, you'll want to ski at an exclusive resort, the kind your congressperson goes to, where you have to examine your pillow before you go to bed at night lest you wind up with a complimentary miniature Swiss chocolate lodged in your ear. But even if you belong to the middle or lower class, there are plenty of newer resorts with names like "Large Rugged Wolf Mountain Ski Resort and Driving Range" that entrepreneurs have constructed in places such as South Carolina by piling industrial sludge on top of discarded appliances.

Just before you leave home, you should call the resort and ask for a frank and honest appraisal of the slope conditions, because it would make little sense to go and spend money if the resort operator did not frankly and honestly feel it would be worth your while. Most resorts use the Standardized Ski Resort Four-Stage Slope Condition Description System:

"REALLY INCREDIBLY SUPERB": This means the entire slope is encased in a frozen substance of some kind.

"REALLY SUPERB": This means there are large patches of bare industrial sludge, but persons with good motor skills can still slide all the way to the bottom.

"SUPERB": This means persons wishing to get to the bottom will have to remove their skis at several points and clamber over rusted dishwashers with sharp exposed edges.

"EXCELLENT": This means it is July.

OK! You've reached the resort, and now it's finally time to "hit the slopes." Not so fast! First attach skis of approximately equal length to each of your feet, discarding any leftovers, and check the bindings to make sure they release automatically just before your ankles break. Now grasp your poles and try to stand up. We'll wait right here.

(Three-hour pause.)

Ha ha! It's not as easy as it looks, is it? I mean, here are all these people around you, and *they* can do it, and their *kids* can do it, really *little* kids, *babies* practically, skiing past you without a care in the world, and there you are, thrashing around on your back in the snow right smack in front of the ski lodge, making an even bigger fool of yourself than Richard Nixon did the time he resigned and made that speech about his mother! Ha ha! Years from now you'll look back on this and laugh, but for now you can lash out with your poles and try to inflict puncture wounds on the other skiers' legs.

Now that you're comfortable with the equipment, summon several burly ski patrol persons and have them carry you over to the chairlift. While you're riding up to the summit, you'll have an opportunity to admire the spectacular sweeping panoramic view of the little tiny wire that you and the chairs and the other skiers are all hanging from. It looks far too frail to hold all that weight, doesn't it? But you can rest assured that it was designed and build on the basis of countless careful measurements and calculations done by scientists and engineers who are not currently up there hanging from the wire with you.

SHARK TREATMENT

I HAVE COME UP WITH A SURE-FIRE CONCEPT FOR a hit television show, which would be called "A Live Celebrity Gets Eaten by a Shark." To help you understand why I think this show would be a success, let me give you a little background.

The human race has been fascinated by sharks for as long as I can remember. Just like the bluebird feeding its young, or the spider struggling to weave its perfect web, or the buttercup blooming in spring, the shark reveals to us yet another of the infinite and wonderful facets of nature, namely the facet that can bite your head off. This causes us humans to feel a certain degree of awe.

I know what I'm talking about here, because I once had —this is the truth—an encounter with a shark. It was in 1973, in the Bahamas, where I was sailing with a group of friends. One day, we were anchored near a little island that had a vast shallow sandy-bottomed lagoon next to it, maybe a foot deep, and a friend of mine named Richard and I were wading around in there, and lo and behold we saw this shark. It was a small shark, less than two feet long. The only conceivable way it could have been a threat to a human being would be if it somehow got hold of, and learned to use, a gun.

So Richard and I decided to try to catch it. With a great deal of strategy and effort and shouting, we managed to maneuver the shark, over the course of about a half-hour, to a sort of corner of the lagoon, so that it had no way to escape other than to flop up onto the land and evolve. Richard and I were inching toward it, sort of crouched over, when all of a sudden it turned around and—I can still remember the sensation I felt at that moment, primarily in the armpit area —*headed right straight toward us.*

Many people would have panicked at this point. But Richard and I were not "many people." We were experienced waders, and we kept our heads. We did exactly what the textbook says you should do when you're unarmed and a shark that is nearly two feet long turns on you in water up to your lower calves: We sprinted I would say 600 yards in the opposite direction, using a sprinting style such that the bottoms of our feet never once went below the surface of the water. We ran all the way to the far shore, and if we had been in a Warner Brothers cartoon you would have seen these two mounds of sand racing across the island until they bonked into trees and coconuts fell onto their heads.

So I know the fascination of the shark, and thus I have been particularly interested in all these shark documentaries on television. You've probably noticed them. Any given night, you tune into a channel at random and odds are you'll see divers hurling themselves into shark-infested waters. The narrator always claims this is for Scientific Research, which is blatant horse waste. I mean, if that were true, you'd figure that after two or three thousand documentaries, they'd know all they needed to know about sharks, and they'd move on to another variety of sea life. But they don't, because they know darned good and well that the viewers aren't going to remain glued to their seats to watch divers paddling around in waters infested by, for example, clams.

So the documentary-makers stick with sharks. Generally, their procedure is to scatter bleeding fish pieces around their boat, so as to infest the waters. I would estimate that the primary food source of sharks today is bleeding fish pieces scattered by people making documentaries. Once the sharks arrive, they are generally fairly listless. The general shark attitude seems to be: "Oh, God, another documentary." So the divers have to somehow goad them into attacking, under the guise of Scientific Research. "We know very little about the effect of electricity on sharks," the narrator will say, in a deeply scientific voice. "That is why Todd is going to jab this Great White in the testicles with a cattle prod." The divers keep this kind of thing up until the shark finally gets irritated and snaps at them, and then they act as though this was a totally unexpected and very dangerous development, although clearly it is what they wanted all along.

Shark documentaries took an important stride forward recently with a series called "Ocean Quest," in which, instead of using trained divers, the documentary maker rented a former beauty queen, Shawn Weatherly, and spent a year dropping her into various shark-infested waters. The idea was that she, being a regular person just like me and you except she has a great body, would be able to convey to us viewers the various human emotions she was feeling. This was pretty funny, inasmuch as Shawn's acting ability is such that she could not convey the concept of falling if you pushed her off a cliff. But the point is, here was a shark documentary that barely even pretended to be scientific, and instead focused on the excitement involved in watching somebody act as bait.

So I say it's time to take this one step farther. I say the public is ready to drop the Scientific Research aspect altogether, and to get past all the usual shark-documentary foreplay. I don't think it would be a problem, getting the celebrities. You look for somebody whose career really needs a boost—a Telly Savalas, for example, or a Zsa Zsa Gabor—and you point out what exposure like this could do for a person. I don't think you could keep Zsa Zsa *out* of the water. Ed McMahon could be the host. Your only real problem would be getting a shark. Most of your top sharks probably have commitments to do documentaries.

ELECTRO-MAGGOTS

TODAY'S SCIENCE QUESTION COMES FROM EIGHT-year-old Bobby Johnson, an imaginary child who lives in Maryland. Bobby asks: "What good are insects, anyway? You know?"

ANSWER: It's a shame, Bobby, but for far too many people, the usual reaction upon encountering an insect is to want to smash it with a rock. That's certainly *my* immediate reaction, although there are certain insects I would prefer to use a flame-thrower on, such as those large tropical-style spiders that appear to be wearing the pelts of small mammals.

Oh, I can hear you junior-high-school science teachers out there now, spitting out your cafeteria entrée ("Tuna Warmed Up") and shouting: "Wait a minute! Spiders aren't insects! Spiders are *arachnids!*" That's exactly what's wrong with our junior high schools today: all those snotty science teachers going around telling our young people that spiders are not insects, when they (the science teachers) could be leading voluntary organized prayers. Of *course* spiders are insects. The very word "insect" is a combination of two ancient Greek words: "in," meaning "a," and "sect," meaning "repulsive little creature." Thus not only are spiders insects but so are crabs, jellyfish, the late Truman Capote, bats, clams, olives and those unfortunate little dogs, "pugs," I believe they are called, that appear to have been struck repeat-

173

edly in the face with a heavy, flat object such as the *Oxford English Dictionary.*

So, Bobby, we can see that . . . Bobby? Bobby! Take that finger out of your nose and pay attention when I answer your Science Question! Whose finger *is* that, anyway?! Put it back where you found it this instant!!

All right. So, Bobby, we can see that the insect family is very large and varied indeed. Just sitting here thinking about it, I would estimate that there are over 600 billion species of insect in my basement alone, which is a real puzzle because we pay $16 a month to have a man come and spray an allegedly lethal chemical all over the place. What I think has happened is that the insects got to this man somehow. Maybe a group of wasps met him at the end of our driveway one afternoon and made it clear to him by gesturing with their feelers that they wouldn't want to see him or his wife or God forbid his small children get stung in the eyeballs, and so what he has actually been spraying around our basement all this time is Liquid Insect Treat.

This is probably good. We cannot simply destroy insects in a cavalier manner, because, as many noted ecology nuts have reminded us time and time again, they (the insects) are an essential link in the Great Food Chain, wherein all life forms are dependent on each other via complex and subtle interrelationships, as follows: Man gets his food by eating cows, which in turn eat corn, which in turn comes from Iowa, which in turn was part of the Louisiana Purchase, which in turn was obtained from France, which in turn eats garlic, which in turn repels vampires, which in turn suck the blood out of Man. So we can see that without insects there would be no . . . Hey, wait a minute! I just noticed that there are *no insects* in the Great Food Chain. Ha ha! Won't *that* be a kick in the pants for many noted ecology nuts! I bet they all race right out and buy 4,000-volt patio insect-electrocution devices!

Nevertheless, we do need insects for they perform many

useful functions. Without insects, for example, we would have no reliable way to spread certain diseases. Also, in some part of Africa that I saw in a documentary film once, they have this very, very large insect, called the Goliath beetle, which grows to almost a foot in length, and the children actually use these beetles to pull their little toy carts. Wouldn't that be fun, Bobby, to have a foot-long beetle of your own, pulling a cart around and clambering into bed with you? Perhaps I'll get you one!

Of course most of us find it difficult to talk about insects without bringing up the subject of sex. According to scientists who study insects (known as "entomologists," or "Al"), the male insect initiates reproduction by rubbing his legs together to produce a distinctive sound, which attracts a bird, which eats the male, then throws up. The female insect then lays 1.5 billion eggs, eating them as she goes along so she will have the strength she will need to suckle them when they hatch. The young insects, called "maggots," enjoy a carefree childhood, writhing playfully under their mother's 76,806,059 watchful eyes and engaging in maggot games that teach them skills they will need to survive as adults, such as scurrying under the refrigerator when the kitchen light comes on. Eventually, they reach a point where their mother can teach them no more, so they eat her, and the males start rubbing their legs together. This life cycle takes about 18 minutes, slightly less in my basement.

So there you have it, Bobby, a fascinating look at the jillions of tiny life forms that inhabit Spaceship Earth with us, and that will still be around long after we're all dead from nuclear war! Of course the insects know this, too, and they do everything they can to promote international tension. They send their top-rated chiggers to all the nuclear-arms-reduction talks, so after a few minutes the negotiators for both sides are so welt-covered and irritated that they lunge across the table and try to punch each other in the mouth. It's just one more way these amazing little creatures adapt to the world around them. So the next time you're about to stomp on an insect, Bobby, remember this: A sudden, jerky motion can lead to serious muscle strain!

Well, kids, that's it for this month's science question. Tune in next month, when a child from Ohio named "Suzy," or perhaps "Mark," will write in to ask about the Six Basic Rules of cattle-prod safety.

THE LESSON OF HISTORY

THE DIFFICULT THING ABOUT STUDYING HIS-
tory is that, except for Harold Stassen, everybody who
knows anything about it firsthand is dead. This means
that our only source of historical information is historians,
who are useless because they keep changing everything
around.

For example, I distinctly remember learning in fifth
grade that the Civil War was caused by slavery. So did you, I
bet. As far as I was concerned, this was an excellent explanation for the Civil War, the kind you could remember and
pass along as an important historical lesson to your grandchildren. ("Gather 'round boys and girls, while Grandpa tells
you what caused the Civil War. Slavery. Now go fetch
Grandpa some more bourbon.")

Then one day in high school, out of the blue, a history
teacher named Anthony Sabella told me that the Civil War
was caused by economic factors. I still think this was a lie,
and not just because Anthony Sabella once picked me up by
my neck. I mean, today we have more economic factors than
ever before, such as the Dow Jones Industrial Average,
but you don't see the North and the South fighting each
other, do you? Which is good, because the South has 96
percent of the nation's armed pickup trucks, whereas the
North mainly has Fitness Centers, so it would be over in
minutes.

DISCUSSION QUESTION: What kind of a name is "Dow" Jones? *Explain.*

Nevertheless, I had to pretend I thought the Civil War was caused by economic factors, or I never would have escaped from Mr. Sabella's class and got into college, where the history professors sneered openly at the primitive high-school-teacher notion that the Civil War had been caused by anything so obvious as economic factors. No, they said, the Civil War was caused by acculturalized regionalism. Or maybe it was romantic transcendentalism, or behavioristic naturalism, or structuralized functionalism. I learned hundreds of terms like these in college, and I no longer even vaguely remember what they mean. As far as I know, any one of them could have caused the Civil War. Maybe we should lock them all in a small room and deny them food and water until one of them confesses.

DISCUSSION QUESTION: Was the author "just kidding" when he made that last "off-the-wall" suggestion? Cite specific examples.

What is the cause of all this disagreement among the experts over basic historical issues? Economic factors. If you're a historian and you want to write a best-selling book, you have to come up with a new wrinkle. If you go to a publisher and say you want to write that Harry Truman was a blunt-spoken Missourian who made some unpopular decisions but was vindicated by history, the publisher will pick you up by your neck and toss you into the street, because there are already bales of such books on the market. But if you claim to have uncovered evidence that Harry Truman was a Soviet ballerina, before long you'll be on national morning television, answering earnest questions from David Hartman in a simulated living room.

DISCUSSION QUESTION: Don't you think David Hartman is just a little *too* avuncular? Why?

So I propose that we laypersons forget about historians and agree among ourselves to believe in a permanent set of historical facts once and for all. Specifically, I propose we use the facts contained in a book I found in my basement recently, called *Civilization Past and Present*, which was apparently one of my wife's high-school textbooks.

DISCUSSION QUESTION: Did she steal it? Or what?

Civilization Past and Present combines the advantage of having a snappy title with the advantage of ending in 1962, just before history starts to get really depressing. It's easy to understand, because my wife has underlined all the important words and phrases (Germany, for example). And it doesn't beat around the bush. For example, on page 599 it makes the following statement in plain black and white: "The causes of the American Civil War are complex."

Since some of you laypersons out there may not have *Civilization Past and Present* in your basements, here's a brief summary to tide you over until you can get your own copies:

HISTORY
5,000,000,000 B.C.–1962

After the Earth cooled, it formed an extremely fertile crescent containing primitive people such as the Hittites who believed in just the stupidest things you ever heard of. Then came Greece and Rome, followed by Asia. All of this came to a halt during the Middle Ages, which were caused by the Jutes and featured the following terms underlined by my wife: the steward, the bailiff, and the reeve. Next the Turks got way the hell over into France, after which there were towns. And the Magna Carta. Then France and England fought many wars that involved dates such as 1739 and were settled by the Treaty of Utrecht, which also was used to harness water power. By then the seeds had been sown for several World Wars and the Louisiana Purchase, but fortunately we now have a fairly peaceful atom. Now go fetch Grandpa some more bourbon.

DEFINE THE FOLLOWING: "Avuncular."

179

SOCK IT TO ME

I WOKE UP THIS MORNING EXPERIENCING SEV-
eral important concerns, which I would like to share with
you here in the hope that they will add up to a large enough
total word count so that I can go back to bed.

CONCERN NUMBER ONE: Mr. Lyndon H. LaRouche, Jr.

As you probably know, Mr. LaRouche is this person
who has started his own political party and wishes to take
over the country, which troubles many people because his
views are somewhat unorthodox. (What I mean of course,
is that he is as crazy as a bedbug. Where you have a brain,
Lyndon H. LaRouche, Jr., has a Whack-a-Mole game.
But I am not about to state this in print, as I do not wish
to have his ardent followers place poison snakes in my sock
drawer.)

Those of you who are frequent airline travelers are no
doubt already familiar with Mr. LaRouche's views, because
they are displayed on posters attached to card tables at most
major airports. Somehow, a year or so ago, the LaRouche
people managed to get the lucrative Airport Lunatic conces-
sion away from the Moonies. What I suspect happened
is that one day, on a prearranged signal, the LaRouche
people sneaked up behind the Moonies and strangled
them with their own little book bags, probably in full view
of thousands of air travelers, who of course would not
have objected. Many of them probably helped out by whap-

ping the Moonies with their carry-on luggage. I know I would have.

But then, two of Mr. LaRouche's ardent followers won the Illinois Democratic primary nominations for secretary of state and lieutenant governor. This caused massive nation-wide anxiety because of the unorthodoxy of their views, which, as far as we have been able to tell, involve shooting Jane Fonda with a laser beam from space. Not that I person-ally see anything wrong with these views! No sir! I don't even *have* a sock drawer!

But we do have to ask ourselves if we truly can afford, as a nation, to elect crazy people to a vital state office like lieutenant governor, which involves weighty responsibilities such as wearing a suit and phoning the governor every day to see if he's dead. Because mark my words, if these people win in Illinois, they'll go after higher and higher offices, until someday—I do not wish to alarm you, but we must be aware of the danger—we could have a situation where our top national leaders are going around babbling about laser beams from space. So I have called on you Illinois voters to come to your senses before the general election and take responsible citizen action in the form of moving to a more intelligent state. This is the perfect time to do so, thanks to declining oil prices.

CONCERN NUMBER TWO: Declining oil prices

Like many of you, I did not realize at first that the de-cline in oil prices was something to be concerned about. In fact, I viewed it as the first really positive development in this nation since Jimmy Carter was attacked by the giant swim-ming rabbit. But then I started reading articles by leading nervous economists stating that the oil-price decline is a very bad thing, because it is causing severe hardships for the fol-lowing groups:

1. The OPEC nations.
2. The U.S. oil industry.
3. The big banks.
4. Texans in general.

When I read this, naturally my reaction as a concerned American, was hahahahahahahahaha.

No, seriously, we need to be worried about declining oil prices, and I am going to explain why. The international economy is based on the U.S. dollar, which is trusted and respected throughout the world because it is the only major currency that does not look like it was designed by preschool children. The value of the dollar, in turn, depends on the investment savvy of big U.S. banks, which lend their dollars to the oil-rich Third World, which loses them gambling on rooster fights.

This system worked well until the late 1970s, when the price of oil started to fall. This was caused by a decline in demand, which was caused by the fact that people couldn't get their cars repaired, which was caused by the fact that the oil companies had bought all the independent garages and turned them into "self-service" stations selling a mutant assortment of retail goods and staffed by surly teenagers, so that God forbid you should have actual *car* trouble at one of these service stations because they would tow you away for blocking the access of customers wishing to purchase nasal spray and Slim Jims.

So now the banks are stuck with a lot of oil, which they are trying to get rid of by converting it into VISA cards, which they offer to my wife. She gets six or seven VISA offers from desperate banks per business day. She got one recently from —I am not making this up—a bank in *South Dakota*. I didn't even know they *had* banks in South Dakota, did you? What would people keep in them? Pelts?

Well I don't know about you, but I am uncomfortable with the idea of having a world economy dependent upon the VISA needs of my wife. She is only one person. That is the law. So I think we need to revamp the whole world economic structure, and the obvious first step is to require banks to repair cars. The supermarkets, which already cash checks, could take over the remaining functions currently performed by banks, such as lending money to the Third World and being closed. You would get your food at service stations, which would be required to get some new sandwiches. You would continue to buy gas at "convenience" stores. Illinois would be sold to wealthy Japanese investors. All these regulations would be enforced by laser beams from space.

THERE'S THIS SENSITIVE ISSUE THAT WE IN THE
news media are very reluctant to bring up.

No. It isn't condoms. We are totally comfortable, these
days, doing lengthy stories about condoms: ("PASTELS
OUT, EARTH TONES IN, FOR FALL CONDOM"). You
will soon see condom commercials on television. Fortunately
we can assume, based on television's track record with this
kind of thing, that these commercials will be tasteful and
informative:

FIRST MAN: What's the matter, Ted?

SECOND MAN: I think I have a horrible sexually transmitted disease!

FIRST MAN: Here. Try some of my condoms.

SECOND MAN: Thanks.

(The Next Day:)

FIRST MAN: Feeling better, Ted?

SECOND MAN: You bet! Thanks to condoms! And I got
that big promotion!

No, the issue we are reluctant to talk about is even
more sensitive (ha ha!) than condoms. The issue—and I will
try to be tasteful here—is that sometimes it seems like maybe the president of the United States is kind of d**b. If
you get what I mean. What I mean is, I am not totally confident that the president would get what I mean, unless

184

several aides explained it to him. And even then, he might forget.

This is unsettling, although I don't know why it should be. For the past 25 years, the presidency had been a remarkable parade of hanky-panky, comical incompetence, and outright weirdness, and the country has done OK. In fact, once you got into the spirit of it, it was kind of fun. I don't know about you, but I *loved* it when Jimmy Carter reported that he'd been attacked by a giant swimming rabbit. I *loved* it when Richard Nixon made speeches wherein he looked as though a large and disorganized committee of alien beings had taken over his body and were just learning how to operate it: ("OK. Let's try to wave. Who's operating the arms?" "Me!" "No, me!" "NO . . . ," etc.).

So I don't mind the president being *bizarre,* but that's not the same as accepting that he might be kind of d**b. Yet it's getting harder and harder to think of any other explanation, not with this Iran-Contra scandal. I realize you out there in Readerland are sick to death of this scandal, but it's still causing multiple orgasms here in the news media, because of all these shocking revelations, the most amazing one being that the president apparently viewed foreign policy as a sort of family station wagon, which he, in the role of Ozzie Nelson, would cheerfully lend to his teen-age son, Ricky, played by Oliver North.

RICKY: Hey Dad, can I take the foreign policy down to the Malt Shoppe and deal with Iranians?

OZZIE: The Iranians?

RICKY: Don't worry, Dad. They're moderates.

OZZIE: Well in that case, OK. Just don't trade arms for hostages!

The president, apparently, was so totally unaware of where his foreign policy was that he had to appoint a distinguished commission to help him locate it, and when the commissioners called him in to testify, he told them, essentially, that *he couldn't remember what it looked like.* Now, if Richard Nixon had claimed something like that you would at least have had the comfort of knowing he was lying. You could trust Nixon that way. But with this president, you have this nagging feeling that he's telling the *truth*.

This bothers us media people, which is why we have developed this euphemistic way of describing the president's behavior, namely, we say he has a "hands-off management style." As in: "How many people with a hands-off management style does it take to change a light bulb?"

Of course the president's aides, in an effort to show that he is a Take-Charge Guy, have arranged to have him star in a number of Photo Opportunities: The President Shakes Hands with People Wearing Suits; the President Sits Down with People Wearing Suits; the President, Wearing a Suit, Signs His Own Name; etc. I think this is good, as far as it goes. My concern is that it should not go any further. My concern is that we could have a sudden eruption of "hands-on" management, for example in the nuclear-arms talks, and we'll end up with Soviet Troops in Des Moines.

CATCHING HELL

CALL ME A REGULAR AMERICAN GUY IF YOU want, but baseball season is kind of special to me. For one thing, it means ice hockey season will be over in just a few short months. But it also brings back a lot of memories, because I, like so many other regular American guys, was once a Little Leaguer. I was on a team called the "Indians," although I was puny of chest, so if you saw me in my uniform you'd have thought my team was called the "NDIAN," because the end letters got wrinkled up in my armpits. I had a "Herb Score" model glove, named for a player who went on to get hit in the eye by a baseball.

I remember particularly this one game: I was in deep right field, of course, and there were two out in the bottom of the last inning with the tying run on base, and Gerry Sinnott, who had a much larger chest, who already had to *shave,* was at bat. As I stood there waiting for the pitch, I dreamed a dream that millions of other kids had dreamed: that someday I would grow up, and *I wouldn't have to be in Little League anymore.* In the interim, my feelings could best be summarized by the statement: "Oh please please PLEASE God don't let Gerry Sinnott hit the ball to me."

And so of course God, who as you know has a terrific sense of humor, had Gerry Sinnott hit the ball to me. Here is what happened in the next few seconds: Outside of my body, hundreds of spectators, *thousands* of spectators, arrived at the ball field at that very instant via chartered buses from distant cities to see if I would catch the ball. Inside my body, my brain cells hastily met and came up with a Plan of Action, which they announced to the rest of the body parts. "Listen up, everybody!" they shouted. "We're going to MISS THE BALL! Let's get cracking!!"

Instantly my entire body sprang into action, like a complex, sophisticated machine being operated by earthworms. The command flashed down from Motor Control to my legs: "GET READY TO RUN!" And soon the excited reply flashed back: "WHICH LEG FIRST?!" Before Motor Control could issue a ruling, an urgent message came in from Vision Central, reporting that the ball *had already gone by,* in fact was now a good 30 to 40 yards behind my body, rolling into the infield of the adjacent game. Motor Control, reacting quickly to this surprising new input, handled the pressure coolly and decisively, snapping out the command: "OK! We're going to FALL DOWN!!" And my body lunged violently sideways, in the direction opposite the side where the ball had passed a full two seconds earlier, flopping onto the ground like some pathetic spawning salmon whose central nervous system had been destroyed by toxic waste, as Gerry Sinnott cruised toward home.

Those boyhood memories! I have them often, although I can control them pretty well with medication.

Actually, when I got older I continued to play organized baseball in the form of "league softball," a game in which after work you put on a comical outfit and go to a public park to argue with strangers. For the first several years the team I was on had a nice, relaxed attitude, by which I mean we were fairly lenient if a player made a mental error. For example, if the ball was hit to the shortstop, and he threw it to first base, but the first baseman wasn't there because he was rooting through the ice cooler looking for a non-"light" beer, we'd say to the person who brought the beer: "Hey! NEVER make the mental error of bringing 'light' beer to a softball game! It can cost a fielder valuable seconds!" But we wouldn't *fine* him or anything.

In later years, however, we got more and more young guys on the team who really wanted to *win;* guys who wore cleats and batting gloves and held *practices* where they were always shrieking about the importance of "hitting" somebody called the "cutoff man"; guys who hated to let women play, apparently for fear that one of them might, during a crucial late-inning rally, go into labor; guys who (this was the last straw) drank *Gatorade* during the game. I had to quit.

But I'm getting back into it. I have a son of my own now, and, being an American guy, I've been teaching him the basics of the game. One recent bright sunny day I took him out in the yard with a Whiffle ball, and I gave him a few pointers. "Robert," I said, "did you know that if we use a magnifying glass to focus sunlight on the Whiffle ball, we can actually cause it to melt?" So we did this, and soon we had advanced to complex experiments involving candy wrappers, Popsicle sticks, and those little stinging ants. Although I drew the line at toads. You have to teach sportsmanship, too.

MRS. BEASLEY FROZE FOR OUR SINS

ONE OF THE ISSUES THAT WE PROFESSIONAL newspaper columnists are required by union regulations to voice grave concern about is the federal budget deficit, which we refer to as the "mounting" deficit, because every extra word helps when you have to produce a certain number of gravely concerned newsprint inches. The point we try to get across in these columns is: "You readers may be out driving fast boats and having your fun, but we columnists are sitting in front of our word processors, worried half to death about the nation's financial future." Then we move on to South Africa.

So anyway, I have decided to fret briefly about the deficit, which according to recent reports continues to mount. A while back I proposed a very workable solution to the whole deficit problem, namely that the government should raise money by selling national assets we don't really need: metric road signs, all the presidential libraries, the Snail Darter, the House of Representatives, North Dakota, etc. Unfortunately, the only concrete result of this proposal was that I got an angry letter from everybody in North Dakota, for a total of six letters, arguing that if we're going to sell anything, we should sell New York City.

This probably wouldn't work. There would be major cultural adjustment problems. Suppose, for example, that we sold New York to Switzerland. Now Switzerland is a very tidy, conservative nation, and the first thing it would do is pass a lot of laws designed to make New York more orderly, such as no public muttering, no lunging into the subway car as though it were the last helicopter out of Saigon, no driving taxis over handicapped pedestrians while they are in the crosswalk, no sharing loud confidences regarding intestinal matters to strangers attempting to eat breakfast. These laws would be very difficult for New Yorkers to adjust to. Switzerland would have to send in soldiers to enforce them, and this would inevitably lead to tragic headlines in the *New York Times:*

ENTIRE SWISS ARMY
FOUND STABBED TO DEATH
WITH OWN LITTLE
FOLDING KNIVES

Pedestrians Step Right over
Rotting Corpses

So I'm afraid that, appealing as the idea may be, we can't reduce the deficit by selling New York.

What the government desperately needs is an innovative new concept for getting money from people, and we can all be grateful that such a concept appears to be oozing over the fiscal horizon at this very moment: a national lottery game. A number of congresspersons have already proposed that we start one. It would be similar to the lotteries currently operating in the really advanced states. Here's how they work:

1. First you pass strict laws that say it is totally illegal for private citizens to operate lotteries, because they encourage the poor and the stupid to gamble away their money against ludicrously bad odds. If you find private citizens operating such lotteries, you call them "numbers racketeers" and you throw them in prison.

2. Next you set up an official state lottery with even more ludicrous odds. You give it a perky name like the "Ex-

tremely Lucky Digits Game," and you run cheerful upbeat ads right on television strongly suggesting that the poor and the stupid could make no wiser investment than to spend their insulin money on lottery tickets. A nice touch is to say you're using the lottery proceeds to fund a popular program that the state would have to pay for anyway, such as senior citizens or baby deer. In Pennsylvania, for example, they drag an actual senior citizen in front of the camera to perform the ritual televised Daily Number drawing. The senior citizen usually looks kind of frightened, like a hostage being displayed by the Red Brigades. The clear implication is that if the viewers don't purchase Daily Number tickets, Pennsylvania will have to throw old Mrs. Beasley out into the snow headfirst.

The news media help out by regularly running heart-warming front-page stories about how a man who was broke and starving won $800 million in his state lottery and suddenly could afford nice teeth and many new friends.

So anyway, the plan now is to run something like this on a nationwide scale, which I think would be great, especially if it keeps the federal government from doing something really desperate to raise money, such as selling drugs or making snuff movies. The only potential problem with a national lottery, as some states have pointed out, is that it might siphon off a lot of poor and stupid from the state lotteries. But if this happens, we could have a bailout system, where the federal government would step in and purchase so many million dollars worth of lottery tickets from the troubled state. I mean, hey, why do we have governments in the first place, if not to help each other out?

THE COLUMNIST'S CAPER

I FIGURED OUT WHY I'M NOT GETTING SERIOUSLY rich. I write newspaper columns. Nobody ever makes newspaper columns into Major Motion Pictures starring Tom Cruise. The best you can hope for, with a newspaper column, is that people will like it enough to attach it to their refrigerators with magnets shaped like fruit.

So I have written a suspense novel. It has everything. Sex. Violence. Sex. Death. Russians. Dead Russians. Here's what the newspaper critics are saying:

"A very short novel."—the *Waco, Texas, Chronic Vegetable*

"This is it? This is the entire novel?—the *Arkansas Dependent-Statesperson*

"Not enough sex."—the *Evening Gonad*

No doubt you motion-picture producers out there would like to see the novel these critics are raving about, so you can send me lucrative film offers. Here it is:

CHAPTER ONE

Carter Crater strode into the Oval Office. He looked like Tom Cruise, or, if he is available, Al Pacino.

Behind the desk sat the president of the United States. To his left, in the corner, stood the secretary of state. Crater sensed that something was wrong.

"Unless we act quickly," the president said, "within the

next few hours the world will be blown to pieces the size of Smith Brothers cough lozenges."

Crater frowned. "We had better act quickly," he said.

The president looked thoughtful. "That just might work," he said. "Use whatever means you consider necessary, including frequent casual sex."

CHAPTER TWO

In the Kremlin, General Rasputin Smirnov frowned at Colonel Joyce Brothers Karamazov Popov.

"It is absolutely essential that the Americans do not suspect anything," Smirnov said.

"Yes," agreed Popov.

Smirnov frowned.

"Shouldn't we be speaking Russian?" he asked.

Popov looked thoughtful.

"We should at least have accents," he said.

CHAPTER THREE

Suddenly, it struck Crater: The Oval Office doesn't *have* corners.

CHAPTER FOUR

Some 2,347 miles away in East Berlin, a man and a woman walked briskly eastward on Volkswagenkindergarten-pumpernikelstrasse. Talking intently, they did not notice the sleek black Mercedes sedan, its windows tinted almost black, as it turned off Hamburgerfrankfurterwienerschnitzelstrasse and came toward them from behind, picking up speed until, traveling at 130 kilometers per microgram, it roared into a parked garbage truck.

"Too much window tint," the woman said.

CHAPTER FIVE

Some 452.5 miles away, Crater had sex.

CHAPTER SIX

"Ach," said General Smirnov. "Zees American agent, ve must keel heem."

"Dat's de troof," agreed Popov. "Les'n we do, he gon' mess up de plan to blow up de worl'."

CHAPTER SEVEN

Crater handed the microfilm to crack intelligence expert Lieutenant Ensign Sergeant Commander Monica Melon.

She studied it carefully for about 15 minutes. Finally she spoke.

"There's something written on here," she said, frowning, "but it's really teensy."

CHAPTER EIGHT

Smirnov frowned at Popov.

"Blimey," he said.

CHAPTER NINE

In the darkened room, Crater could see the shadowy figure who threatened to destroy the world, who had led Crater on this desperate chase across nine continents, a race filled with terror and death and women whose thighs could have been the basis for a major world religion, and all leading to this moment, Crater and the shadowy figure, alone in the gloom. Slowly, almost reluctantly, Crater reached for the light switch. He flicked it on. The shadowy figure turned, slowly, slowly. At last, Crater could see the figure's face.

It was a big surprise.

CHAPTER TEN

"Good job of saving the entire world, Crater," the president said. "But I have one question: How did you know Miss Prendergast never heard the cathedral bell?"

"Easy, sir," answered Crater. "You see, Lord Copperbottom is *left-handed,* so the gardener couldn't possibly have taken the key from the night stand."

"I never thought of that," said the president. He frowned at the names coming up out of the floor and drifting toward the ceiling so the audience would know who had played what parts.

"Hey," the president said. "These names are *backwards.*"

A RASH PROPOSAL

LATELY I HAVE BEEN THINKING A LOT ABOUT the defense of Western Europe. It keeps my mind off this rash in my right armpit. When I think about it, I reach the point where all I want to do is quit my job and move to an isolated cave so I can devote full time to scratching myself. Eventually it reached the point where I threw caution to the winds and went to an actual skin doctor. I was hoping he'd give me one of those hand-held garden implements with the three sharp prongs. I forget what you call them, and say: "Dave, I want you to rake this implement across your rash every 10 seconds or as needed." But no, he gave me some wimpy little white pills and came up with a bizarre treatment program under which—this is the truth—I was supposed to *try to grow a new rash*. Really. He thinks my rash is caused by a rash-causing chemical that large corporations put in deodorants, apparently out of sheer hatred for the consumer, and to test this theory he wants me to rub some of this very same chemical onto my arm and see if I develop a new rash. I'm not going to do it, of course, because (a) I don't even want the rash I brought him in the first place, let alone a new one, and (b) if he thinks I'm stupid enough to deliberately rub rash-causing chemicals on myself, his next move will be to ask me to rub them on my family and friends.

Sometimes you have to wonder what's happening to the medical profession. A recent edition of the *Weekly World*

News, which I feel is probably the best newspaper your money can buy in a supermarket, carried a story headlined "HUMAN HEAD TRANSPLANT." The story concerns an operation performed by doctors in Communist China who got hold of this unfortunate man with a large brain tumor, and they treated him by amputating his head and replacing it with one they got from a person who had lost his body in a factory accident and consequently died. I would very much like to know how the doctors explained this operation to the patient ("The only possible side effect we can foresee, Loo Ping, will be some neck stiffness, plus the fact that you will have the head of a dead factory worker.")

Of course you have an entirely different set of problems to confront when you talk about defending Western Europe. The main one is that it is filled with Western Europeans, who are not in the least bit interested in defending themselves. They have discovered, over the past thousand years or so, that every time they get military, they wind up having a lengthy and extremely complicated war in which the various countries have tremendous trouble remembering whose side they're on:

BRITISH SOLDIER: Taste my sword, French person!

FRENCH SOLDIER: No! Wait! We are allies! This is World War I!

BRITISH SOLDIER: I'm terribly sorry! I thought it was the Hundred Years War! Does this mean I can kill Italians?

FRENCH SOLDIER: *(consulting manual)*: No, I'm afraid not. Not until World War II.

So eventually the Western Europeans stopped forming armies altogether and decided to become third-rate powers, which means we have to defend them from the Russians. We're available to defend foreign continents because we have no urgent need to defend our own. I mean, the Mexicans certainly aren't going to attack us, seeing as how most of them already work here. I suppose the Canadians could attack us, but the entire population of Canada is maybe the size of the audience on "Donahue," only quieter, so even if they did attack, nobody would know, especially if it was during rush hour.

So we're over there defending Western Europe, which is very, very expensive. For one thing, we have to get up an army, which means we have to pay for all those commercials wherein we suggest to young people that the whole point of the army is to teach them valuable electronics skills, with no mention whatsoever of getting shot at or getting cretin haircuts and being ordered to do pushups by a person who has never read anything longer than a Dr Pepper bottle. For another thing, to defend Western Europe we have to let the Pentagon buy all these tanks and guns and things, and the Pentagon is unable to buy any object that costs less than a condominium in Vail. If the Pentagon needs, say, fruit, it will argue that it must have fruit that can withstand the rigors of combat conditions, and it will wind up purchasing the FX-700 Seedless Tactical Field Grape, which will cost $160,000 per bunch, and which will have an 83 percent failure rate.

So I have come up with this plan for defending Western Europe much more economically, which is to pull our armed forces out of there altogether. They could come home and fix our videocassette recorders. In their place we would send over all our state highway departments and tell them we want them to repair the roads between Western Europe to Russia. Think about it: First they'd have their Cone Placement Division strew millions of traffic cones randomly all over the roads, then they'd have their Sign Erection Department put up signs explaining that all the lanes would be really messed up for the next 17 years to Help Serve You Better, then the Traffic Direction Division would get all kinds of lowlife derelicts out there waving flags and directing motorists right into oncoming trucks, and within a few months it would be absolutely impossible for any vehicle, including Communist tanks, to get from Russia to Western Europe.

So that's my plan. What do you think? I think those wimpy little pills are starting to kick in.

HE KNOWS NOT WHAT HE WRITES

THE PROBLEM WITH WRITING ABOUT RELIGION
is that you run the risk of offending sincerely religious people, and then they come after you with machetes. So I am
going to be very sensitive, here, which is not easy, because
the thing about religion is that everybody else's always appears stupid.

For example, if you read about some religious sect in
India that believes God wants people to drink their own
urine, you don't say to yourself, "Isn't that amazing, the diversity of belief systems Man has developed in his never-
ending quest to understand and cope with the intricate
moral dilemmas posed by a complex and uncertain world?"
No, what you say to yourself is, "These people have the
brains of trout."

Meanwhile, over in India, the sect members are getting
a major chuckle over the fact that some American basketball
players cross themselves before they take foul shots. "As if
God cares about foul shots," the sect members howl, tears
streaming down their faces. "Say, is this my urine or yours?"

That's the basic problem, of course: figuring out what
God wants us to do. I will admit right up front here that I
don't have the vaguest idea. All my religious training was in
Sunday school maybe 25 years ago, and the main thing I
remember was that God was always smiting the Pharisees. At
least I think it was the Pharisees. It seemed that hardly a day

went by when they didn't get the tar smitten out of them, which is probably why you see so few of them around anymore.

My wife, who has bales of religious training, tells me that this was the Old Testament God, who was very strict, whereas the New Testament God is a genuinely mellow deity, the kind of deity who would never smite anybody or order you to smear goat's blood on your first-born son, which is the kind of thing the Old Testament God was always doing.

NOTE: The preceding paragraph is in no way intended to suggest that there is anything wrong with smearing goat's blood on your first-born son. As far as I'm concerned, this is an excellent ritual, and I would do it myself if not for the fact that my son might tell the school authorities. Please put away your machetes. Thank you.

It used to be much worse. Back in ancient Greece and Rome they had gods all over the place, and it was no fun at all being a mortal, as you know if you ever read any myths:

"One day two young lovers, Vector and Prolix, were walking in a garden. This angered Bruno, the god of gardens, so he turned Vector into a toad. Saddened, Prolix picked up her lover and squeezed him to her bosom, which caused him to secrete a toad secretion upon her garment. This angered Vito, the god of fabric, who turned Prolix into an exceedingly unattractive insect. Saddened, Vector hopped to his lover, which angered Denise, who was the goddess of municipal water supply and just happened to be in the neighborhood, so she hit them both with a rock."

And so on. So things are better now. Today most of us believe in just the one God, and He never turns people into toads or anything, unless you count Spiro Agnew. All He wants us to do is what He wants us to do, which is clearly revealed in the Bible.

(Sound of the machetes being unsheathed.)

And the Talmud and the Koran and the Book of Mormon and the works of L. Ron Hubbard. These holy writings tell us what God wants us to do, often in the form of revealing anecdotes:

"And Bezel saideth unto Sham: 'Sham,' he saideth, 'Thou shalt goest unto the town of Begorrah, and there shalt thou fetcheth unto thine bosom 35 talents and also shalt thou fetcheth a like number of cubits, provideth that they are nice and fresh.'"

The problem is that many of us don't have the vaguest idea what these anecdotes reveal. This is why we have broadcast preachers, who can take a religious anecdote and explain it over the course of a half-hour in such a manner that if you listened all the way through you would have no questions at all:

BROADCAST PREACHER: And so we can see that it was BEZEL who told SHAM to go to Begorrah. It was not SHAM who told BEZEL: It was BEZEL who told SHAM. Now people ask me, they say, "Brother Ray Bob Tom, what do you mean, it was Bezel who told Sham?" And I say, "What I mean is that when we're talking about who told who to go to Begorrah, we must understand that it was BEZEL who told . . ."

And so on. It can take upwards of a week to get through an entire sentence, which is why you often have to send in a Love Offering to get cassettes so you'll remember what it is that God wants you to do. This sometimes seems too complicated, so a lot of people have switched over to the more relaxed style of the Merv Griffin–type of broadcast preachers, who have bands and potted plants and sofas and everything. ("Our next guest is not only one of the top Christians in the business, but also a close personal friend of mine.")

So we have a number of ways of finding out what God wants us to do, and each of us must decide what the answer is in this wonderful country where we are free to believe as we choose, and where there are strict laws against assaulting people just because we don't like something they wrote.

201

MAN BITES DOG

TODAY WE BEGIN A POPULAR FEATURE WHEREIN we will address the major ethical questions of the day, starting with: Is it OK to eat your dog?

ANSWER: No. Not here in America. Oh, sure, most of us have heard the story about an American who *cooked* her dog in a microwave oven, but this was not for the purpose of eating it. What happened (according to the story) was this American had one of those little rodent-size dogs whose main purpose in the Great Chain of Life is to pee on people's ankles, and it got wet in the rain, so the American quite naturally did what any normal person would do if he or she had one lone kernel of candy corn for a brain, namely stick the dog in the microwave oven to dry out, but apparently the oven was on the wrong setting (it should have been set on "Dog"), so the dog ended up getting dried out to the point of Well Done. The story always stops right there, so we don't know what happened next. We don't know whether the spouse came home from a hard day at the office and went, "Mmmmmmm! Something smells dee-ee*licious!* I'll just look inside the microwave here and *GAA-AACCCCKKKK!!!!*"

Of course, this needless tragedy could easily have been prevented via legislation requiring that microwave ovens carry a stern federal message such as

202

WARNING: THE SURGEON GENERAL HAS DETERMINED THAT YOU SHOULD NOT PUT A DOG IN THIS OVEN AND TURN IT ON.

On the other hand, this could be one of those stories that everybody tells even though it's not true, like the one about the teen-aged couple who is parking on a lonely country road and hears on the radio that a homicidal maniac who has a hook instead of a right hand has escaped from the mental institution, so the boy real quick starts the engine and drives right over Reggie Jackson, who was walking his Doberman because it was choking on an alligator from the New York City sewer system. This probably never happened. But it is a fact that my editor, Gene Weingarten, once ate a dog. This was at the 1964 World's Fair in Flushing, New York (which incidentally is how alligators got into the sewers), and Gene was at the pavilion of some Third World nation and he ordered a dish with an unusual name, and when he asked the waiter (who spoke little English) what it was, the waiter, in Gene's words, "made it clear by gestures and going 'woof woof,' that it was a dog." Gene said it wasn't bad. *Not that this is any excuse.* I want to stress that I personally have never eaten a dog, and I want to remind those of you who have already stopped reading this column to write violent letters to the editor that it was Gene Weingarten, c/o *Tropic* magazine, *Miami Herald,* Miami FL 33101, who ate the dog.

But it is an interesting ethical question, why we get so upset about this. I mean, most of us don't think twice about eating *cows,* which are genetically almost exactly the same as dogs in the sense of having four legs and being pretty stupid. Yet if somebody tried to dry a *cow* out in a microwave oven, we'd all laugh like the dickens and it would get on "Celebrity Bleeps and Boners." So this is a real puzzle, all right, which is why I am very grateful to Diane Eicher, an alert reader who sent me an article from *Nutrition Health Review* headlined: "Usefulness Keeps Pets Out of Oven." I am not making this article up. It concerns Marvin Harris, a University of Florida anthropologist who, according to the article, "studies and tries to make sense of human culture." (Ha ha!)

Harris is quoted in the article as saying that the reason we didn't eat dogs, cats, and horses is—get ready—"These animals are just too darned useful for us to eat."

Now I don't wish to be critical here, but a statement like that makes you wonder if Professor Harris has not accidentally been studying the culture on the planet Zoog, because the last word I would use to describe household pets here on Earth is "useful." I have owned a number of household pets, mostly dogs, and the only useful thing I can recall any of them ever doing was the time Germaine tried to bite the Amway representative. Other than that it has been basically a long series of indelible rug stains. And I defy anybody to point to a single instance of, for example, a tropical fish doing anything useful, as in

ALERT FISH
RESCUES WOMAN
FROM TRASH COMPACTOR

Yet we don't eat the tropical fish, do we? No! Not unless we have a very good reason, such as we have been sitting in our doctors' waiting room for the better part of the day without food or water. Then we might snack on a couple of guppies, but that is as far as it would go.

And I don't even want to *talk* about cats.

Nevertheless Professor Harris feels pets have many useful functions:

"Modern day household pets can't match the entertainment value of lions attacking elephants or people in the Roman circus," he said, "but cats chasing imaginary mice, or dogs retrieving bouncing balls are at least as amusing as the late night movie."

I think we can all agree that pets are not as entertaining

as watching lions attack humans, but I have to wonder how many of you couples out there in our listening audience have ever said to each other: "The heck with *Casablanca,* let's watch Beaner retrieve a bouncing ball." So we indeed have a very complex ethical issue here, but unfortunately we no longer really care.

"ADVENTURE DOG"

I HAVE THIS IDEA FOR A NEW TELEVISION SERIES. It would be a realistic action show, patterned after the true-life experiences of my dog, Earnest. The name of the show would be "Adventure Dog."

The theme song would go:

> Adventure dog,
> Adventure dooooooooggg
> Kinda big, kinda strong
> Stupid as a log.

Each episode would be about an exciting true adventure that happened to Earnest. For example, here's the script for an episode entitled: "Adventure Dog Wakes Up and Goes Outside":

It is 6:17 A.M. Adventure Dog is sleeping in the hall. Suddenly she hears a sound. Her head snaps up. Somebody is up! Time to swing into action! Adventure Dog races down the hall and, skidding on all four paws, turns into the bathroom, where, to her total shock, she finds: The Master! Whom she has not seen since LAST NIGHT! YAYYYYYY!!

ADVENTURE DOG: Bark!

MASTER: DOWN, dammit!

Now Adventure Dog bounds to the front door, in case the Master is going to take her outside. It is a slim chance. He has only taken her outside for the past 2,637 consecutive mornings. But just in case, Adventure Dog is ready.

ADVENTURE DOG: Bark!

Can it be? Yes! This is unbelievable! The Master is coming to the door! Looks like Adventure Dog is going outside! YAAAYYY!

MASTER: DOWN, dammit!

Now the Master has opened the door approximately one inch. Adventure Dog realizes that, at this rate, it may take the Master a full three-tenths of a second to open the door all the way. This is bad. He needs help. Adventure Dog alertly puts her nose in the crack and applies 600,000 pounds of force to the door.

MASTER: HEY!

DOOR: WHAM!

And now Adventure Dog is through the door, looking left, looking right, her finely honed senses absorbing every detail of the environment, every nuance and subtlety, looking for . . . Holy Smoke! There it is! The YARD! Right in the exact same place it was yesterday! This is turning out to be an UNBELIEVABLE adventure!

ADVENTURE DOG: Bark!

Adventure Dog is vaguely troubled. Some primitive version of a thought is rattling around inside her tiny cranium, like a BB in a tuna fish can. For she senses that there is some reason why the Master has let her outside. There is something he wants Adventure Dog to do. But what on Earth could it be? Before Adventure Dog can think of an answer, she detects . . . is this possible? Yes! It's a SMELL! Yikes! Full Red Alert!

ADVENTURE DOG: Sniff sniff sniff.

MASTER: Come *on*, Earnest.

ADVENTURE DOG: Sniff sniff sniff sniff sniff sniff sniff sniff.

No question about it. The evidence is clear. This is a smell, all right. And what's more, it's the smell of—this is so incredible—DOG WEEWEE! Right here in the yard!

MASTER: EARNEST!

ADVENTURE DOG: Sniff sniff sniff sniff sniff.

Adventure Dog is getting the germ of an idea. At first it seems farfetched, but the more she thinks about it, the more she thinks, hey, why not! The idea is—get ready—Adventure Dog is going to MAKE WEEWEE! Right now! Outside! It's crazy, but it just might work!

MASTER: Good GIRL.

What was that? It was a sound! Definitely. A sound coming from over there. Yes! No question about it. This is unbelievable! It's the MASTER out here in the yard! YAAAYY!

MASTER: DOWN, dammit!

THEME SONG SINGER: Adventure Dog, Adventure Dooooooggg . . .

ADVENTURE DOG: BARK!

MASTER: DOWN!

Bear in mind that this is only one episode. There are many other possibilities: "Adventure Dog Gets Fed," "Adventure Dog Goes for a Ride in the Car and Sees Another Dog and Barks Real Loud for the Next 116 Miles," etc. It would be the kind of family-oriented show your kids could watch, because there would be extremely little sex, thanks to an earlier episode, "Adventure Dog Has an Operation."

SLOW DOWN AND DIE

I THINK IT'S GETTING WORSE. I'M TALKING about this habit people have of driving on interstate highways in the left, or "passing" lane, despite the fact that they aren't passing anybody. You used to see this mainly in a few abnormal areas, particularly Miami, where it is customary for everyone to drive according to the laws of his or her own country of origin. But now you see it everywhere: drivers who are not passing, who have clearly never passed anybody in their entire lives, squatting in the left lane, little globules of fat clogging up the transportation arteries of our very nation. For some reason, a high percentage of them wear hats.

What I do, when I come up behind these people, is the same thing you do, namely pass them on the right and glare at them. Unfortunately, this tactic doesn't appear to be working. So I'm proposing that we go to the next logical step: nuclear weapons. Specifically I'm thinking of atomic land torpedoes, which would be mounted on the front bumpers of cars operated by drivers who have demonstrated that they have the maturity and judgment necessary to handle tactical nuclear weapons in a traffic environment. I would be one of these drivers.

Here's how I would handle a standard left-lane blockage problem: I would get behind the problem driver and flash my lights. If that failed, I'd honk my horn until the driver looked in his rear-view mirror and saw me making helpful, suggestive hand motions indicating that he is in the passing lane, and if he wants to drive at 55, he should do it in a more appropriate place, such as the waiting room of a dental office. If *that* failed, I'd sound the warning siren, which would go, and I quote, *"WHOOP WHOOP WHOOP WHOOP."* Only if *all* these measures failed would I proceed to the final step, total vaporization of the car (unless of course there was a BABY ON BOARD!).

Too violent, you say? Shut up or I'll break your legs. No, wait, forgive me. I'm a little tense, is all, from driving behind these people. But something has to be done, and I figure if word got around among members of the left-lane slow-driver community, wherever they get together—hat stores would be my guess—that they had a choice of either moving to the right or turning into clouds of charged particles, many would choose the former.

It is not entirely their fault. Part of the problem is all those signs on the interstates that say SPEED LIMIT 55. I am no psychologist, but I believe those signs may create the impression among poorly informed drivers that the speed limit is 55. Which of course it is not. We Americans *pretend* 55 is the speed limit, similar to the way we're always pretending we want people to have a nice day, but it clearly isn't the real speed limit, since nobody, including the police, actually drives that slowly, except people wearing hats in the left lane.

So the question is, how fast are you *really* allowed to drive? And the answer is: Nobody will tell you. I'm serious. The United States is the only major industrialized democracy where the speed limit is a secret. I called up a guy I know who happens to be a high-ranking police officer, and I asked him to tell me the real speed limit, and he did, but only after —this is the absolute truth—he made me promise I wouldn't reveal his name, or his state, or above all *the speed limit itself.* Do you believe that? Here in the United States of America, home of the recently refurbished Statue of Liberty, we have an officer of the law who is afraid he could *lose his job for revealing the speed limit.*

When things get this bizarre, we must be dealing with federal policy. Specifically we are dealing with the U.S. Transportation Secretary, who is in charge of enforcing our National Pretend Speed Limit. The Transportation Secretary has learned—you talk about digging out the hard facts! —that motorists in a number of states are driving faster than 55 miles per hour, and she threatened to cut off these states' federal highway funds. So, to keep the Transportation Secretary happy, the police have to pretend they're enforcing the 55 limit, when in fact they think it's stupid and won't give you a ticket unless you exceed the *real* speed limit, which varies from state to state, and even from day to day, and which the police don't dare talk about in public for fear of further upsetting the Transportation Secretary.

I told my friend, the high-ranking police officer, that this system creates a lot of anxiety in us civilian motorists, never knowing how fast we're allowed to go, and he said the police like it, because they can make the speed limit whatever the hell they want it to be, depending on how they feel. "It used to be," he said, "that the only fun you had in police work was police brutality. Now the real fun is to keep screwing with people's heads about what the speed limit is."

Ha ha! He was just kidding, I am sure. Nevertheless, I think we need a better system, and fortunately I have thought one up. Here it is: The state should say the hell with the federal highway funds. They could make a lot more money if they set up little roadside stands where you could stop your car and pay $5, and a state employee would whisper the speed limit for that day in your ear. What do you think? I think it makes more sense than the system we have now. Of course, the Transportation Secretary wouldn't like it, but I don't see why we should care, seeing as how the Transportation Secretary probably gets chauffeured around in an official federal limousine that is, of course, totally immune from traffic laws. Although I imagine it would be vulnerable to atomic land torpedoes.

211

SACKING THE SEASON

IT'S FOOTBALL SEASON AGAIN, AND I KNOW I speak for everybody in North America when I make the following statement: rah. Because, to me, football is more than just a game. It is a potential opportunity to see a live person lying on the ground with a bone sticking out of his leg, while the fans, to show their appreciation, perform "the wave."

And football breeds character. They are constantly scrubbing the locker rooms because of all the character that breeds in there. This results in men the caliber of famed Notre Dame player George Gipp, played by Ronald Reagan, who, in a famous anecdote, looked up from his deathbed and told Pat O'Brien, played by Knute Rockne, that if things every really got bad for the Fighting Irish, he (O'Brien) should tell "the boys" to win one for the Gipper. Which O'Brien did, and the boys said: "What for? He's dead." Ha ha! This is just one reason I am so excited about the upcoming season.

Before I unveil my Pigskin Preview, however, I must say a few serious words here about a problem that, regrettably, has reached epidemic proportions in the world of sports fans. I'm talking about male cheerleaders. I don't know where you grew up, but where I grew up, there were certain things a guy absolutely did not do, and cheerleading is about six of them. A guy who led cheers where I grew up would have been driven around for a few hours inside somebody's engine compartment. Most likely Steve Stormack's.

So you may call me insecure if you wish, but I am deeply troubled when I see young men on TV bouncing up and down on their tiptoes and clapping like sea lions, and the fact that they get to hug the female cheerleaders and sometimes pick them up by their personal regions is not, in my view, an adequate excuse. I am calling on you sports fans to write letters to U.S. Attorney General Edwin Meese urging him to appoint a federal commission to issue a concerned and bulky report about this issue, so that we sports writers can put it behind us once and for all and get back to writing stories about what should be the topic of interest on the sports pages: drugs.

Drug testing is very big in football. This is because football players are Role Models for young people. All you young people out there want to grow up and have enormous necks and get knee operations as often as haircuts. That's why the people in charge of football don't want you to associate their sport in any way with drugs. They want you to associate it with alcohol. During televised games, you'll see announcements wherein famous athletes urge you not to take drugs alternating with announcements wherein famous exathletes urge you to drink beer. Good luck, young people!

Now let's take a look at what kind of action we can expect to see this season on the actual "gridiron" per se. As in previous years, football will be divided into two major sectors, "college" and "professional," the difference being that professional players receive money, whereas college players also receive complimentary automobiles, although many teams will be hard-hit by strict new academic regulations requiring that a player cannot compete unless he can read most of the numbers on his gearshift knob. Nevertheless, I look for an action-packed college season in which major teams featuring linemen named Dwight who have the size and vocabulary skills of cement trucks trash a series of amateur schools by scores ranging as high as 175–0, which will

213

earn them the right to play in such New Year's Day classics as the Rose Bowl, the Orange Bowl, and the Liquid You Drain Out of a Can of Artichoke Hearts Bowl, although unfortunately not against each other.

In professional football, I look for a very exciting and competitive season until about a third of the way through the first game, when Injuries will become a Factor. These injuries will of course all be caused by artificial turf, which is easily the most dangerous substance in the universe. If we really wanted to protect Europe, we would simply cover the border regions with artificial turf, and the Russians would all be writhing on the ground clutching their knees within seconds after they invaded. And then the Europeans could perform "the wave."

Here are some other predictions: I look for the TV networks to provide helpful expert analysis by explayers who utilize technological wizardry such as the "electronic chalkboard" to make simple running plays seem like brain surgery. I look for 19,000 third-down situations, all of them Crucial. In any group of five players, I look for four of them to be Probably the Most Underrated in the League. I look for Second Effort, Good Hang Time, and a Quick Release. I look for yet another Classic Super Bowl Matchup like the one we had last year between two teams whose names escape me at the moment.

I look for a video rental store that's open all weekend.

WHY SPORTS IS A DRAG

MANKIND'S YEARNING TO ENGAGE IN SPORTS IS older than recorded history, dating back to the time, millions of years ago, when the first primitive man picked up a crude club and a round rock, tossed the rock into the air, and whomped the club into the sloping forehead of the first primitive umpire. What inner force drove this first athlete? Your guess is as good as mine. Better, probably, because you haven't had four beers. All I know is, whatever the reason, Mankind is still nuts about sports. As Howard Cosell, who may not be the most likable person in the world but is certainly one of the most obnoxious, put it: "In terms of Mankind and sports, blah blah blah blah the 1954 Brooklyn Dodgers."

Notice that Howard and I both use the term "Mankind." Womankind really isn't into sports in the same way. I realize things have changed since my high-school days, when sports were considered unfeminine and your average girls' gym class consisted of six girls in those gym outfits colored Digestive Enzyme Green running around waving field-hockey sticks and squealing, and 127 girls on the sidelines in civilian clothing, claiming it was That Time of the Month. I realize that today you have a number of top female athletes such as Martina Navratilova who can run like deer and bench-press Chevrolet pickup trucks. But to be brutally frank, women as a group have a long way to go before they reach the level of intensity and dedication to sports that enables men to be such incredible jerks about it.

If you don't believe me, go to your local racquetball club and observe the difference between the way men and women play. Where I play, the women tend to gather on the court in groups of random sizes—sometimes three, sometimes five, as if it were a Jane Fonda workout—and the way they play is, one of them will hit the ball at the wall and the rest of them will admire the shot and compliment her quite sincerely, and then they all sort of relax, as if they're thinking, well, thank goodness *that's* over with, and they always seem very surprised when the ball comes *back*. If one of them has the presence of mind to take another swing, and if she actually hits the ball, everybody is *very* complimentary. If she misses it, the others all tell her what a *good* try she made, really, then they all laugh and act very relieved because they know they have some time to talk before the ball comes bouncing off that darned *wall* again.

Meanwhile, over in the next court, you will have two males wearing various knee braces and wrist bands and special leatheroid racquetball gloves, hurling themselves into the walls like musk oxen on Dexedrine, and after every single point one or both of them will yell "S___!" in the self-reproving tone of voice you might use if you had just accidentally shot your grandmother. American men tend to take their sports seriously, much more seriously than they take family matters or Asia.

This is why it's usually a mistake for men and women to play on teams together. I sometimes play in a coed slow-pitch softball league, where the rules say you have to have two women on the field. The teams always have one of the women play catcher, because in slow-pitch softball the batters hit just about every pitch, so it wouldn't really hurt you much if you had a deceased person at catcher. Our team usually puts the other woman at second base, where the maximum possible number of males can get there on short notice to help out in case of emergency. As far as I can tell, our second basewoman is a pretty good baseball player, better than I am anyway, but there's no way to know for sure because if the ball gets anywhere near her, a male comes barging over from, say, right field, to deal with it. She's been on the team for three seasons now, but the males still don't trust her. They know that if she had to choose between catching a fly ball and saving an infant's life, deep in her soul, she would probably elect to save the infant's life, without even considering whether there were men on base.

This difference in attitude between men and women carries over to the area of talking about sports, especially sporting events that took place long ago. Take the 1960 World Series. If we were to look at it objectively, we would have to agree that the outcome of the 1960 World Series no longer matters. You could make a fairly strong case that it didn't really matter in 1960. Women know this, which is why you almost never hear them mention the 1960 World Series, whereas you take virtually any male over age 35 and even if he can't remember which of his children has diabetes, he can remember exactly how Pirates shortstop Bill Mazeroski hit the ninth-inning home run that beat the Yankees, and he will take every available opportunity to discuss it at length with other males.

See that? Out there in Readerland, you females just read right through that last sentence, nodding in agreement, but you males leaped from your chairs and shouted: "Mazeroski wasn't a SHORTSTOP! Mazeroski played SECOND BASE!" Every male in America has millions of perfectly good brain cells devoted to information like this. We can't help it. We have no perspective. I have a friend named Buzz, a successful businessman and the most rational person you ever want to meet, and the high point of his entire life is the time he got Stan Albeck, the coach of the New Jersey Nets, to look directly at him during a professional basketball game and make a very personal remark rhyming with "duck shoe." I should explain that Buzz and I have season tickets to the Philadelphia 76ers, so naturally we hate the Nets a great

217

deal. It was a great honor when Albeck singled Buzz out of the crowd for recognition. The rest of us males congratulated Buzz as if he'd won the Nobel Prize for Physics.

It's silly, really this male lack of perspective, and it can lead to unnecessary tragedy, such as soccer-riot deaths and the University of Texas. What is even more tragic is that women are losing perspective, too. Even as you read these words, women are writing vicious letters to the editor, expressing great fury at me for suggesting they don't take their racquetball seriously. Soon they will be droning on about the importance of relief pitching.

BATTING CLEAN-UP AND STRIKING OUT

THE PRIMARY DIFFERENCE BETWEEN MEN AND women is that women can see extremely small quantities of dirt. Not when they're babies, of course. Babies of both sexes have a very low awareness of dirt, other than to think it tastes better than food.

But somewhere during the growth process, a hormonal secretion takes place in women that enables them to see dirt that men cannot see, dirt at the level of *molecules,* whereas men don't generally notice it until it forms clumps large enough to support agriculture. This can lead to tragedy, as it did in the ill-fated ancient city of Pompeii, where the residents all got killed when the local volcano erupted and covered them with a layer of ash 20 feet deep. Modern people often ask, "How come, when the ashes started falling, the Pompeii people didn't just *leave?*" The answer is that in Pompeii, it was the custom for the men to do the housework. They never even *noticed* the ash until it had for the most part covered the children. "Hey!" the men said (in Latin). "It's mighty quiet around here!" This is one major historical reason why, to this very day, men tend to do extremely little in the way of useful housework.

What often happens in my specific family unit is that my wife will say to me: "Could you clean Robert's bathroom? It's filthy." So I'll gather up the Standard Male Cleaning Implements, namely a spray bottle of Windex and a wad of paper towels, and I'll go into Robert's bathroom, and it *always looks perfectly fine.* I mean, when I hear the word "filthy" used to describe a bathroom, I think about this bar where I used to hang out called Joe's Sportsman's Lounge, where the men's room had bacteria you could enter in a rodeo.

Nevertheless, because I am a sensitive and caring kind of guy, I "clean" the bathroom, spraying Windex all over everything including the 600 action figures each sold separately that God forbid Robert should ever take a bath without, and then I wipe it back off with the paper towels, and I go back to whatever activity I had been engaged in, such as doing an important project on the Etch-a-Sketch, and a little while later my wife will say: "I hate to rush you, but could you do Robert's bathroom? It's really *filthy.*" She is in there looking at the very walls I *just Windexed,* and she is seeing *dirt! Everywhere!* And if I tell her I already *cleaned* the bathroom, she gives me this look that she has perfected, the same look she used on me the time I selected Robert's outfit for school and part of it turned out to be pajamas.

The opposite side of the dirt coin, of course, is sports. This is an area where men tend to feel very sensitive and women tend to be extremely callous. I have written about this before and I always get irate letters from women who say they are the heavyweight racquetball champion of some place like Iowa and are sensitive to sports to the point where they could crush my skull like a ripe grape, but I feel these women are the exception.

A more representative woman is my friend Maddy, who once invited some people, including my wife and me, over to her house for an evening of stimulating conversation and jovial companionship, which sounds fine except that this particular evening occurred *during a World Series game.* If you can imagine such a social gaffe.

We sat around the living room and Maddy tried to stimulate a conversation, but we males could not focus our attention on the various suggested topics because we could actually *feel* the World Series television and radio broadcast rays zinging through the air, penetrating right into our bodies, causing our dental fillings to vibrate, and all the while the women were behaving *as though nothing were wrong*. It was exactly like that story by Edgar Allan Poe where the murderer can hear the victim's heart beating louder and louder even though he (the murder victim) is dead, until finally he (the murderer) can't stand it anymore, and he just *has* to watch the World Series on television. That was how we felt.

Maddy's husband made the first move, coming up with an absolutely brilliant means of escape: *He used their baby*. He picked up Justine, their seven-months-old daughter, who was fussing a little, and announced: "What this child needs is to have her bottle and watch the World Series." And just like that he was off to the family room, moving very quickly for a big man holding a baby. A second male escaped by pretending to clear the dessert plates. Soon all four of us were in there, watching the Annual Fall Classic, while the women prattled away about human relationships or something. It turned out to be an extremely pivotal game.

SNOTS AT SEA

LIKE MOST AMERICANS, I WAS THRILLED TO death last February when our wealthy yachting snots won the coveted America's Cup back from Australia's wealthy yachting snots.

It was not an easy victory. Our boys spent years experimenting with different designs for their boat before they came up with the innovative idea of having a submerged nuclear submarine tow it. "That was the real breakthrough," explained Captain Dennis Conner. "We could hit nearly 50 miles per hour without even putting up our sails. Plus we had torpedoes." It was American ingenuity at its best, and I think that, as a nation, we should be inspired to take up sailing as a popular mania, similar to the way, in previous years, we have taken up Bruce Springsteen and being Republican.

I have done some sailing myself, and let me tell you: There's nothing quite like getting out on the open sea, where you can forget about the hassles and worries of life on land, and concentrate on the hassles and worries of life on the sea, such as death by squid. My son, Robert, has this book entitled *Giants of Land, Sea, and Air, Past and Present,* which I like to read to him at bedtime to insure that he won't fall asleep until just after dawn. Here's what this book says regarding squid: "The giant squid may reach a length of 55 feet, including its 35-foot tentacles."

My point is that while you should of course enjoy your sailing experience, you should take the routine marine precaution of being constantly aware that a creature the size of Yonkers, New York, could be oozing and sliming along just beneath the surface, watching you with humongous eyes. Another one of Robert's books, *The Big Book of Animal Records,* states that the eye of a giant squid can get to be—this is an Amazing True Nature Fact, coming up here—16 inches across. Think about that. Think about the size of the whole *eyeball.* Think of the pranks you could play if you got hold of an eyeball like that.

DELIVERY ROOM DOCTOR: Well, Mr. and Mrs. Foonster, here's your newborn child!

NEW PARENTS: AIIIEEEEEEEEEEEEEEEEEE.

But this is not the time for lighthearted humor. This is a time to learn Safe Boating Practices, so that your sailing experience will not be ruined in the event of a squid attack. Here is the procedure recommended by boating safety experts:

1. Do not panic. Remember that the squid does not necessarily want to eat you. Oh, sure, it wants to eat *somebody,* but this does not have to be *you.*

2. Shout: "Here! Eat Ralph!"

Boating safety experts recommend that you always keep a supply of unpopular guests on hand to push overboard as emergency marine sacrifices. They do not, however, have to be named Ralph. You can just *claim* they are named Ralph, because you are dealing with a squid.

OK, that takes care of boating safety. Now let's talk about the kind of boat you should select. There are many different kinds, the main ones being yachts, swoops, tankers, frigates, drawls, skeeters, fuggits, kvetches, and pantaloons. These are all basically the same. The only important factor to bear in mind, when selecting a boat, is that it should be "seaworthy," meaning that if for some reason you accidentally drive it into another boat, or a reef, or a Howard Johnson's Motor Lodge, *you will not be held financially responsible.*

This means the type of boat you want is what veteran mariners refer to as a "stolen" boat, or, if this is not practical, a "rented" boat.

I rented a boat once, in the Virgin Islands. My wife and I did this with another couple, and we agreed that I should be the captain, because I had the most sailing experience, in the form of sitting on various people's sailboats drinking beer and remarking upon the weather. Fortunately the boat we rented had a motor in it. You will definitely want this feature on your sailboat too, because if you put up the sails, the boat tips way over, and you could spill your beer. This was a constant problem for Magellan. I put the motor on whenever we wanted to actually get somewhere, or if we came within two miles of something we might run into, such as another boat or a Virgin Island. On those rare occasions when I did attempt to sail, I was hampered by the fact that the only nautical commands my crew understood were:

1. "Pull on that thing."
2. "No, the OTHER thing."
3. "No, the thing over THERE, dammit."
4. "Never mind."

Our navigational policy was always to steer the boat in the direction of restaurants and hotels that had real bathrooms. Our boat allegedly had a bathroom (or as we say aboard ship, a "bathroom"), but it was about the size of those styrofoam containers you get Egg McMuffins in, and it was mostly filled with the marine toilet, a complex and punitive device that at any moment you expected to see a tentacle come snaking out of. Which is why the No. 1 rule of the sea is: If you absolutely have to use the marine toilet, you want to send Ralph in there first.

SIC, SIC, SIC

I WOULD HAVE TO SAY THAT THE GREATEST SIN-
gle achievement of the American medical establishment is
nasal spray. Oh, I realize it can be overdone. A friend of
mine named Tatnall claims he knew a woman who was so
addicted to nasal spray that she carried some down the aisle
on her wedding day. Her hand would go darting under her
veil, and a snort would resound through the church. Tatnall
swears this is true. So I fully agree that nasal-spray abuse is a
serious problem and we certainly need some kind of enormous federal program to combat it.

But aside from that, I feel that nasal spray is a wondrous
medical achievement, because it is supposed to relieve nasal
congestion, and by gadfrey, it relieves nasal congestion.
What I'm saying is that it actually works, which is something
you can say about very few other aspects of the medical establishment.

This is especially true when it comes to figuring out what
is wrong with sick people. My experience has been that doctors will give you a clear-cut, understandable diagnosis only
if you wander in with, say, an ice pick protruding from your
skull. And even then, you have to pretend that you don't
know what's wrong. If you say, "I have an ice pick in my
skull," the doctor will become irritated, because he spent all
those years in medical school and he's damned if he's going
to accept opinions from an untrained layperson such as

yourself. "It concievably could be an ice pick," he'll say, in a tone of voice that suggests he's talking to a very stupid sheep, "but just in case I'm going to arrange for a test in which we remove a little snippet of your liver every week for eight weeks." So your best bet is to keep your mouth shut and let the doctor diagnose the ice pick, which he will call by its Latin name.

If you have a subtler problem, however, you may never find out what's wrong. For example, a few months back, one side of my tongue swelled up. I tried everything—aspirin, beer, nasal spray—but my tongue was still swollen. So I went to a doctor. His receptionist began my treatment by having me sit in the waiting room where I read a therapeutic article in a 1981 issue of *National Geographic*. That took me maybe an hour, during which I learned a great deal about this ancient tribe of people who managed to build a gigantic and photogenic temple in a jungle several thousand years ago despite the fact that they were extremely primitive at the time.

Step Two in the therapy was when a nurse put me in a little examination room with a paper-covered table, which evidently was emitting some kind of invisible healing rays because they had me sit there alone with it for 43 minutes by my watch. It wasn't as boring as it sounds because there was a scale in there, so I could weigh myself for amusement.

To culminate the treatment, the actual doctor took a few moments out from his busy schedule of renewing his subscription to *National Geographic* and renting additional space for people to wait in and came right into the room with me and actually looked at my tongue. He was in the room with me for 2 minutes and 30 seconds by my watch, at the end of which he told me that my problem was two Latin words, which I later figured out meant swollen tongue. He said I should come back in a week. I considered suggesting that, seeing how I had already been there for almost two hours, maybe I should just spend the week in the examination room, but I was afraid this would anger him and he would send me to the hospital for tests. I didn't want to go to the hospital, because at the hospital as soon as they find out what your Blue Cross number is they pounce on you with needles the size of turkey basters. Those are the two most popular doctor options: to tell you to come back in a week, or to send you to the hospital for tests. Another option would be to say, "it sure beats the heck out of me why your tongue is swollen," but that could be a violation of the Hippocratic Oath.

What I finally did was talk to a woman I know who used to be a nurse but had to quit because she kept wanting to punch doctors in the mouth, and she suggested that I gargle with salt water. I did, and the swelling went right away. Although of course this could also have been because of the paper-covered table.

I really envy my dog. When she gets sick or broken, we take her to the veterinarian, and he fixes her right up. No Latin words, no big deal. It's a very satisfying experience, except of course for my dog, who routinely tries to launch herself out of the examining room through closed windows. I find myself thinking: why can't I get medical care like this? How much more complicated can people be than dogs? I'm kind of hoping my dog's tongue will swell up, because I'm dying to see how the veterinarian treats her. If he has her gargle with salt water, I'm going to start taking my problems to him.

THE LIGHT SIDE OF SMOKING

AS YOU ARE AWARE, EACH YEAR THE U.S. SURgeon General emerges from relative obscurity into the limelight of public attention and if he sees his shadow, we have six more weeks of winter. No, all kidding aside, what he does is issue his annual report, where he tells you that smoking is bad for you. In fact, for a while, previous surgeons general got so lazy that they were turning in the same report, over and over, until finally one year Richard Nixon got ketchup stains on it.

Anyway, the result of all this reporting is that the general public at large has gotten very strict about smoking. Hardly a day goes by when you don't read a newspaper story like this:

"SAN FRANCISCO—The city commissioners here yesterday approved a tough new antismoking ordinance under which if you see a person light a cigarette in a public place, you can spit in this person's face."

I agree with this new strictness. And I'm not one of those holier-than-thou types who go around condemning smoking, drinking and senseless murder without ever having even tried them. I used to smoke cigarettes, plenty of them, sometimes two and three at a time when I had Creative Block and was hoping to accidentally set my office on fire so I could write a column about it.

And then one morning, four years ago, something happened that I will never forget. I woke up, and I looked at myself in the mirror, because I happened to wake up in the bathroom, and I said to myself: "Dave, you have a wonderful wife, you have a newborn son, you have a good job, you have friends who care about you, you have a lawnmower that starts on the second or third pull—you have everything a man could possibly want, and a whole lifetime ahead of you to enjoy it in. Why not smoke a cigarette right now?" And so I did. I didn't quit until two years later, at Hannah Gardner's annual extravaganza eggnog party, when I was overcome by a giant weepy guilt attack while under the influence of Hannah's annual eggnog, the recipe for which we should all hope to God never falls into the hands of the Russians.

Not that it was easy to quit. Not at all. A few months back, I read a newspaper article that said the government, after much research, had decided that nicotine is an addictive drug, even worse than heroin, and I just had to laugh the bitter kind of laugh that Clark Gable laughs in *Gone With the Wind* when he realizes that the South has been reduced to a lump of carbon. I mean, surely the government has better things to spend its money on. Surely the government could have used these research funds to buy a military toilet seat, and just asked us former smokers about nicotine vs. heroin addiction. We could have simply pointed out that, when a commercial airliner takes off, the *instant* the wheels leave the ground, the pilot, who you would think would be busy steering or something, tells the smokers that they may light up. He does not tell the heroin addicts that they may stick their needles into themselves, does he? No, he doesn't, because heroin addicts have enough self-control to survive a couple of heroin-free hours. But the pilot knows that if he doesn't let the cigarette smokers get some nicotine into themselves *immediately*, they will sneak off to smoke in the bathroom, possibly setting it on fire, or, if already occupied by other smokers, they will try to get out on the wing.

So we are talking about a powerful addiction here, and I frankly feel the government's efforts to combat it are pathetic. The big tactic so far has been warnings on cigarette packages. The government seems to feel that smokers— these are people who, if they run out of cigarettes late at night in a hotel and have no change for the machine, will smoke used cigarettes from the sand-filled ashtrays next to the elevators, cigarettes whose previous owners could easily have diseases such as we associate with public toilet seats— the government believes that these same smokers will *read* their cigarette packages, as if they needed *instructions* on how to operate a cigarette, and then they'll remark, with great surprise: "Look here! It says that cigarette smoking is *Hazardous to Your Health!!* How very *fortunate* that I read this package and obtained this consumer information! I shall throw these away right now!"

No, we need something stronger than warnings. We need cigarette loads. For those of you who were never obnoxious 12-year-old boys, I should explain that a "load" is an old reliable practical joke device, a small, chemically treated sliver of wood that you secretly insert into a cigarette, and when the cigarette burns down far enough, the load explodes, and everybody laughs like a fiend except, of course, the smoker, who is busy wondering if his or her heart is going to start beating again. I think Congress ought to require the cigarette manufacturers to put loads in, say, one out of every 250 cigarettes. This would be a real deterrent to smokers thinking about lighting up, especially after intimate moments:

MAN: Was it good for you? *(inhales)*

WOMAN: It was wonderful. *(inhales)* Was it good for you?

MAN: Yes. *(inhales)* I have an idea: Why don't we BLAM!!

What do you think? I think it would be very effective, and if it doesn't work, we could have the Air Force spray something toxic on North and South Carolina.

EAR WAX IN THE FOG

WHEN YOU TALK ABOUT THE POSTDEREGULA-
tion airline industry, the three issues that inevitably arise are
smoking, fog, and earwax. We'll take them individually.

Follow me closely here. You know those little earphones
they give you on airplanes so you can listen to old Bill Cosby
routines? OK, let's assume that 20 million people have flown
on earphone flights in the past 15 years. Let's further assume
that each person leaves one-sixteenth of an ounce of earwax
on these phones (this is an average, of course; Nancy Reagan
leaves much less). This means that in the last 15 years alone,
the airlines have collected nearly 600 tons. Do you have any
idea how large a blob that makes? Neither do I, so I called
the folks at the Miami Public Library, who did a little research and informed me that it was the most disgusting question they had ever been asked.

My question is this: Why do the airlines—why does *any*
nonmilitary organization—need a blob of earwax that large?
My personal theory is that they're going to drop it on the
radar apparatus at O'Hare Airport in Chicago, just so they
can see the looks on the faces of passengers all over America
when the ticket-counter agents say: "I'm afraid your flight
has been cancelled due to earwax on the radar at O'Hare."
Any problem at O'Hare, even a minor plumbing malfunc-
tion, inevitably paralyzes air travel all over the free world.
Nobody really knows why this is, but if you ask the ticket

agent, he'll come up with something just to drive you away: "Your flight is supposed to use the plane from flight 407, which is due in from Houston, only it couldn't take off because the crew was supposed to arrive on flight 395 from O'Hare, but that plane never got to O'Hare because the captain, the handsome, brooding Mark Crandall, had seen Nikki and Paul leave the party together arm in arm and in a rage of jealousy, had decided to seduce Paul's former lover Brenda, unaware that she had just found out about Steven's fatal liver disease. So we're looking at a delay of at least two hours."

But the airlines won't use the earwax just yet. No, that's their trump card, and they won't play it until more people wise up about the fog. I figured it out several years ago. See, I live in an area that is never blanketed by fog. People often remark on this at parties. "Say what you will," they remark, "but this area is never blanketed by fog, ha ha!" Except when I am trying to get back home from a distant airport, at which time it is always pea soup. "I'm afraid our destination is completely fogged in, Mr. Barry," the ticket agent says, in the tone of voice you use when somebody else's destination is fogged in and you're going home in a half-hour to have a drink and watch Johnny Carson.

Here's how they do it: They have an agent permanently assigned to lurk in the bushes outside my home, and when he sees me walk out the door carrying a suitcase, he gets on the walkie-talkie. "Looks like he's going to try to make a round trip via airplane again!" he whispers. This alerts his superiors back at airline headquarters that they should stop drilling holes into the heads of small furry woolen creatures and arrange to have a dense fog blanket transferred down from Canada via weather satellite.

Ask yourself this question: If Charles Lindbergh, flying with no instruments other than a bologna sandwich, managed to cross the Atlantic and land safely on a runway completely covered with French people, why are today's airplanes, which are equipped with radar and computers and individualized liquor bottles, unable to cope with fog? Are they concerned about passenger safety? Then why not let the passengers decide? Why not get on the public-address system and say: "Attention passengers. Your destination is very foggy. We think you'll make it, but there's always a chance you'll crash on a remote mountaintop and be eaten by wolves. Your other option is to stay here in the airport for God knows how long, sitting in these plastic seats and eating $3.50 cheese sandwiches manufactured during the Truman administration. What do you say?" The gate agents would have to leap up on the counter to avoid being trampled by the hordes barging onto the plane.

Which leads us to the question of whether smoking should be allowed on airplanes. The Founding Fathers, who had bales of foresight, specified in the U.S. Constitution that people could smoke on airplanes, but they had to sit near the toilets. Now, however, there's a move afoot to ban smoking altogether on flights that last less than two hours. The cigarette industry is against this ban, their argument being that there is no Hard Evidence that cigarettes are anything short of wonderful, according to the highly skilled research scientists that the cigarette industry keeps in small darkened cages somewhere. Another strong antiban argument was raised by Congresssman Charlie Rose of North Carolina, who warned the Civil Aeronautics Board recently that people would sneak into the washrooms to smoke and might start fires. "There's a significant problem if they were to go into washrooms for a smoke and forget where the used paper towels are stored," observed Congressman Rose, who evidently feels that many smokers have extremely small brains.

But I think he has a point. I think that if the CAB decides to ban smoking, it should require the airlines to install smoke detectors in the washrooms, so that if a person sets one off, it will activate an unusually powerful toilet mechanism that will flush the smoker right out of the plane. Of course, if I know the airlines, they'll rig it so he lands on the radar apparatus at O'Hare.

1987: LOOK BACK IN HORROR

JANUARY

2—In College Bowl action, the University of Miami loses the national championship to Penn State when Vinny Testaverde, after selecting the "History" category, identifies World War II as "a kind of fish."

3—Oral Roberts tells his followers that unless they send him $4.5 million by the end of the month, God will turn him into a hypocritical money-grubbing slime bag.

5—In response to growing pressure from the United States, the government of Colombia vows to track down its major drug dealers and, if necessary, remove them from the Cabinet.

8—The Federal Aviation Administration announces that, in response to a routine questionnaire, 63 percent of the nation's air traffic controllers stated that their primary career goals was "to defeat the forces of the Planet Wambeeno."

10—In the ongoing war against the federal deficit, the Reagan administration submits the first-ever $1 trillion budget.

14—In New York City, officials of the Justice Department's Organized Crime Task Force announce that Anthony "Grain Embargo" DiPonderoso and Jimmy "Those Little

Pins They Put in New Shirts" Zooroni have agreed to enter the Federal Nickname Exchange Program.

16—In his first press conference since 1952, President Reagan, asked by reporters to comment on persistent allegations that he is "out of touch," responds: "Thanks, but I just had breakfast."

18—The People's Republic of China announces that "Deng Xiaoping" means "Big Stud Artichoke."

21—The Audi Corporation is forced to recall 250,000 cars after repeated incidents wherein parked Audis, apparently acting on their own, used their mobile phones to purchase stocks on margin.

26—President Reagan tells Iran-contra scandal investigators that he "might have" approved the sale of arms to Iran.

28—In the Middle East, Syria has its name legally changed to "Jordan." A welcome calm settles over Beirut as the six remaining civilians are taken hostage.

30—In Washington, the Internal Revenue Service unveils the new, improved W-4 form, which is such a big hit that the experts who thought it up are immediately put to work on developing a policy for the Persian Gulf.

FEBRUARY

1—A new policy requiring random drug testing of all airline pilots runs into a snag when nearly half of the Delta pilots are unable to hit the specimen bottle.

2—Miami City Commissioner Rosario Kennedy, responding to a *Herald* report that taxpayers spent $111,549 to decorate her office says—we are not making this quotation up—"there's not one item that really stands out. It's not the Taj Mahal." Donations of clothing and canned goods pour in from concerned taxpayers.

3—In the ongoing war against the federal budget deficit, Congress gives itself a pay raise.

4—The United States yacht *Stars and Stripes* recaptures the coveted America's Cup when the Australian entry, *Kookaburra,* is sunk by a Chinese-made "Silkworm" missile. The U.S. Sixth Fleet steams toward the troubled region with orders "to form humongous targets." Liberace goes to the Big Candelabra in the Sky.

6—In a White House ceremony marking his 76th birthday, President Reagan attempts to blow out the hot line.

7—Famed *Washington Post* reporter Bob Woodward reveals that, in a secret hospital interview, dying entertainer Liberace revealed that Woodward's upcoming book, *Veil,* would be "a real page-turner."

8—True item: Senator Lloyd Bentsen, chairman of the Senate Finance Committee, sends out a letter telling lobbyists that for $10,000 each, they can attend monthly breakfasts with him.

9—Representative Arnold LaTreece announces that for $15,000 each, lobbyists can kiss him on the lips.

10—George Bush announces that he is available for $12.50.

11—President Reagan tells Iran-contra scandal investigators that he did not approve of the arms sale to Iran.

15—George Bush reduces his price to $3.99, including the souvenir beverage mug.

17—In Colombia, police arrest Carlos Lehder for jaywalking and discover, during a routine search, that his pockets contain 1,265,000 pounds of cocaine. Lehder claims to have "no idea" how it got there.

19—Mario Cuomo announces that he doesn't want to be president and immediately becomes the Democratic front-runner.

22—George Bush announces that *he* doesn't want to be president, either.

22—Andy Warhol goes to the Big Soup Can in the Sky.

23—Panic grips the nation as a terrorist group seizes 150,000 new, improved W-4 forms and threatens to send them to randomly selected Americans through the mail.

23—Famed *Washington Post* reporter Bob Woodward reveals that, in a secret hospital interview, dying artist Andy Warhol revealed that Woodward's forthcoming book, *Veil*, would be "available in bookstores everywhere."

24—President Reagan announces that he cannot remember whether he approved the sale of arms to Iran. In a quotation that we are not making up, the president tells White House reporters: "Everybody that can remember what they were doing on August 8, 1985, raise your hand."

25—White House reporters examine their diaries and discover, to their shock, that on August 8, 1985, they approved the sale of arms to Iran. They are immediately arrested.

MARCH

2—The Miami Grand Prix is won by Mrs. Rose Gridhorn, 83, of Hackensack, New Jersey, driving a 1976 Chrysler New Yorker with the left blinker on.

3—Comedian Danny Kaye dies moments after granting an interview to Bob Woodward.

7—In the widening scandal on Wall Street, the heads of three major investment firms rob a liquor store.

9—In Tallahassee, state legislators agree on a plan to tax professionals who perform services. A few hours later, they decide it also should apply to lawyers.

11—Florida Governor "Bob" Martinez, who ran for office on a platform of *opposing* taxes, announces that he will *support* the new tax on services, until it is passed, then he will call for a referendum so voters can vote *against* the tax, although he will campaign *for* the tax, but then he will change his mind and announce that he is calling a special session of the Legislature to *repeal* the tax. Everybody naturally assumes that the governor is joking.

13—Noncandidate Mario Cuomo, carrying out his normal duties as governor of New York state, meets with the heads of state of England, France, Norway, Sweden, and Germany.

15—A barge loaded with garbage sets out into the Atlantic under the command of explorer/author Thor Heyerdahl, who is seeking to prove his theory that South America could have been discovered by ancient mariners sailing from Islip, Long Island, in crude garbage barges.

18—The Southern Methodist University football team is suspended from intercollegiate athletics when National Collegiate Athletic Association investigators, after taking urine samples, determine that the school's leading rusher, majoring in communications, is a horse.

21—The IRS releases an even newer, simpler W-4 form in response to complaints from a number of taxpayers, all of whom will be audited for the rest of their lives.

23—The Southern Methodist University horse is drafted by the Kansas City Chiefs.

24—A place called Chad defeats Libya in some kind of war. This really happened.

27—In what is hailed as a major arms race breakthrough, United States and Soviet arms negotiators in Geneva agree to wear matching outfits.

30—In an illegal industrial waste dump somewhere in Louisiana, lightning strikes two adjacent putrid pools of festering corrosive toxic slime, setting off a bizarre chain of chemical reactions that cause the pools first to bubble, then slowly, horrifyingly, to solidify and pulsate upward, gradually forming themselves into shapes that, in the ghastly light of the flickering electrical storm, appear almost human. "Hi!" they shriek cheerfully into the swampland emptiness. "We're Jim and Tammy Faye!"

APRIL

1—Speaking in unison, an estimated three dozen congressmen, all of them age 43, all of them blond, and all of them named Dick, announce that they are seeking the Democratic presidential nomination.

3—In the Persian Gulf, Iranians attack the Islip garbage barge, but are driven off by courageous flies.

6—Noncandidate Mario Cuomo, in the pursuit of his normal gubernatorial duties, reaches a tentative pact with Soviet arms negotiators.

12—At an art auction, Vincent Van Gogh's *Sunflowers* fetches the highest price ever paid for a painting, $39.8 million, paid by grateful Miami taxpayers wishing to hang it in the office of City Commissioner Rosario Kennedy.

13—True Anecdote: In National League baseball action, the Atlanta Braves' Dion James hits a ball that would have been caught easily, except that in midair it strikes and kills a dove.

14—In Colorado, Gary Hart declares his candidacy for the presidential nomination, making the announcement while standing in front of a dramatic backdrop of soaring mountains, towering pine trees and four *Miami Herald* reporters disguised as rhododendrons.

15—The lifeless body of Atlanta Braves player Dion James is found under an enormous mound of dove droppings.

16—President and Mrs. Reagan release their tax returns.

19—The IRS sends back the Reagans' tax returns, gently pointing out that you're supposed to fill them out.

22—Crack U.S. counterintelligence agents in Moscow begin to suspect that the new U.S. Embassy in Moscow, constructed by Soviet labor, might be bugged, when one of them sneezes in the ambassador's office and six chairs say, "Gesundheit."

23—The National Basketball Association grants Miami a franchise. The new team will be named The Enormous Bloodsucking Insects.

26—Jack Kemp announces that he is running for president, pledging that, if elected, he will deepen his voice.

30—Following a lengthy and dramatic trial, a confused

New Jersey jury awards custody of a 3-year-old boy to a 6-week-old girl.

MAY

2—Late at night on a Washington street, four *Miami Herald* reporters on routine patrol notice that Gary Hart appears to be spending the weekend with an attractive woman who is not his wife. The reporters confront Hart, who explains that there is no woman, and he hardly knows her, and she is actually his uncle, and the voters don't care about candidates' private lives anyway. Satisfied, the reporters decide to write a story about Hart's monetary policy.

3—Like a raging unquenchable forest fire, the Gary Hart story sweeps across the nation, as voters are consumed by a burning need to know more about the candidate's monetary views.

4—The Hart story becomes so hot that issue-oriented Phil Donahue devotes a show to it, preempting the sex-change lesbian surrogate-mother nude-dancer ex-priests.

5—The presidential campaign of Gary Hart experiences another "close call" when a *Miami Herald* reporter receives a tip that Hart spent a night in Bimini aboard a boat named *Monkey Business* with an attractive woman who is not his wife. Fortunately, Hart is able to explain that he has never been on a boat and there is no such place as "Bimini" and the person who went there with the woman was actually a being from the Planet Buppo who is able to take the form of leading presidential candidates. Satisfied, the reporter writes a lengthy analysis of Hart's views on the NATO alliance.

6—An angry Gary Hart is forced to withdraw from the race after word leaks out that the *Washington Post* has obtained documented evidence that he once proposed tying the prime rate to the Index of Leading Economic Indicators.

7—Citing alleged "bisexual activity," officials of the As-

seemblies of God Church vote to have Jim Bakker de-
frocked. Then they hastily vote to have him frocked again.

16—Rita Hayworth dies moments after confiding to
Bob Woodward that his forthcoming book, *Veil,* would be
out "just in time for Christmas gift giving."

29—Nineteen-year-old Mathias Rust, a German, flying
a single-engine Cessna airplane, manages to cross 400 miles
of Soviet airspace to reach Red Square in Moscow, where he
narrowly avoids colliding with a Delta Air Lines flight en
route from Pittsburgh to Cleveland.

30—Caspar Weinberger orders 5,000 single-engine
Cessna airplanes

JUNE

1—The public responds with massive displays of sym-
pathy to reports that a number of totally unsuspecting Dade
County politicians were cruelly tricked into believing that a
private duplex where a man allegedly sold stolen suits was in
fact a major department store. "It was a mistake that anyone
could have made," said a police spokesman, "provided that
he had the IQ of Cheez Whiz."

2—True Item: In the ongoing Iran-contra hearings the
committee learns that a country named Brunei contributed
$10 million to help the contras, except Fawn Hall or some-
body typed a wrong number, so the money ended up in the
Swiss bank account of a total stranger. This helps explain
why, despite all the elaborate assistance efforts with secret
codes and passwords and everything, the only actual aid ever
received by the contras was a six-month trial subscription to
Guns and Ammo.

5—Another True Item: In Venice for the European
Economic Summit, President Reagan, unaware that his
words are being broadcast over an open microphone, tells a
joke wherein God gradually reduces a gondolier's intelligence until the gondolier switches from singing *"O Sole Mio"*
to *"When Irish Eyes are Smiling."*

7—Brunei receives 314,334 urgent personal mail solicitations from TV evangelists

8—In the most dramatic Iran-contra testimony to date, Fawn Hall, played by Farrah Fawcett, testifies that, as Justice Department investigators closed in, she and Oliver North stayed late in their White House basement office and "colorized' a number of classic black-and-white films.

13—After a highly controversial trial in New York, "subway vigilante" Bernhard Goetz is acquitted in connection with a subway shooting incident wherein he claims he was attacked by a gang of prominent Wall Street investors.

18—A survey of Florida residents reveals that their No. 1 concern about the state is that "not enough people are walking around with guns." Alarmed, the state Legislature passes a law under which all citizens who are not actually on Death Row will be *required* to carry revolvers.

22—Fred Astaire dies in the arms of Bob Woodward.

24—In a ground-breaking experiment, medical researchers reduce a gondolier's intelligence to the bare minimum required to sustain life, and the gondolier says: "Everybody that can remember what they were doing on August 8, 1985, raise your hand."

29—In Wimbledon action, John McEnroe kills a line judge and is given a stern warning.

JULY

1—In a contest sponsored by a pesticides company, a Broward County insect is declared the largest cockroach in the country, narrowly edging out Phyllis Schlafly.

4—The Hormel Company marks the 50th anniversary of Spam in festivities featuring a full-size, fully functioning suspension bridge constructed entirely out of the popular luncheon substance.

7—The central figure in the Iran-contra hearings, Lieutenant Colonel Oliver North, becomes an instant national folk hero when, with his eyes glistening and his voice cracking with emotion, he courageously admits, before a worldwide television audience, that he is very patriotic.

9—Oral Roberts reveals that he can raise the dead. He is rushed to the White House.

11—The Iran-contra hearings reach their dramatic peak when Lieutenant Colonel North, his eyes glistening and his voice cracking with emotion, makes a sweeping patriotic hand gesture and knocks over his bottle of Revlon Eye Glistener.

15—The giant Citicorp bank announces that it has agreed to forgive Mexico's $56.3 billion debt in exchange for 357.9 gazillion chickens.

18—In Hollywood, plans are formulated for a major motion picture based on the Oliver North story, starring Sylvester Stallone as North, Fawn Hall as herself and Helen Keller as the president.

21—The discovery of "superconductors"—materials that offer no resistance to electricity even at relatively high temperatures—creates a worldwide stir of excitement among the kind of dweebs who always had their Science Fair projects done early.

24—In the ongoing Iran-contra hearings, the committee hears two days of dramatic testimony from Mario Cuomo, who explains that he has decided to stay out of the presidential race so he can fulfill his obligations as governor of New York.

27—Officials at the National Zoo in Washington are saddened by the death of the tiny infant cub of rare giant pandas Ling-Ling and Hsing-Hsing, who are described as "distraught" by their close friend, Bob Woodward. Edwin Meese is linked to the Lincoln assassination.

30—In Moscow, the Embassy spy scandal deepens when it is learned that for the past six years, the "wife" of the U.S. ambassador has in fact been four male KGB agents wearing what State Department officials describe as "a very clever disguise."

AUGUST

2—South Florida's dreams of a first-class sports facility come true at last with the opening of Joe Robbie Stadium, featuring comfortable seating, excellent visibility, plenty of bathrooms, and nearly five parking spaces.

3—Political activist Donna Rice, in her continuing effort to avoid publicity, sells her story to ABC television.

6—As "Ollie-mania" continues to sweep the country, one of the most popular video-arcade games in the country is a new one called—this is true—"Contra." The way it works is, there are two soldiers on the screen, and when you put in a quarter, it never gets to them.

10—The U.S. space probe Meanderer II, after a journey of six years and many millions of miles, passes within 400 miles of the surface of Neptune, sending back dramatic color photographs of a Delta Air Lines jet.

16—On the 10th anniversary of Elvis Presley's death, tens of thousands of fans gather in Memphis to hear Bob Woodward discuss his final moments with the bulging superstar. At the same time, thousands of other people gifted with "New Age" consciousness celebrate the Harmonic Convergence by picking at their straitjacket straps with their teeth.

20—In Miami, alert Metrorail police arrest a woman for permitting her child to eat a Vienna sausage. Bystanders applaud this courageous law-enforcement action by firing their revolvers into the air.

22—Rumors circulate that Gary Hart will re-enter the presidental race. Johnny Carson places his writers on Full Red Alert.

25—In what is hailed as a landmark ruling, the Supreme Court decides, by a 7 to 2 vote, that you cannot count three oranges as one item in the express checkout lane "unless they are all in the same package."

27—Georgia Senator Sam Nunn announces that he doesn't want to be president. Cuomo challenges him to a debate.

28—In the Persian Gulf, tensions mount as a U.S. gunboat engages in a scuffle with actor Sean Penn.

SEPTEMBER

1—The FAA, responding to consumer complaints, issues tough new rules under which airlines are required to notify passengers "within a reasonable period of time" if their plane has crashed.

2—In Washington, reporters notice that at some point —possibly during a speech by Senator Inouye, when everybody was asleep—the ongoing Iran-contra hearings turned into the ongoing confirmation hearings for Supreme Court nominee Robert Bork.

7—As the arrival of Pope John Paul II approaches, the South Florida news media begin mass-producing special helpful news supplements advising the public on how to avoid the massive crowds and traffic and heat.

8—Researcher Shere Hite releases her scientific new book, *Men Are Scum.* The South Florida news media continue to generate massive quantities of helpful hurricane-style news alerts concerning the upcoming papal visit and what the public should do to avoid massive crowds and traffic and heat and crime.

9—In Washington, D.C., ground is broken for the $25.4 million Presidential Polyp Museum. South Florida experiences an epidemic of hernias suffered by residents attempting to pick up newspapers filled with helpful papal supplements informing them how to cope with massive crowds and traffic and heat and crime and disease and death.

10—It is a glorious moment for South Florida as Pope John Paul II is greeted by an estimated crowd of 3,000 soldiers garbed in festive camouflage outfits, frowning warily at 1,500 news media personnel crouching on the ground to confirm that the manhole covers are, in fact, welded shut.

12—In the ongoing hearings, Senator Joseph Biden

pledges to consider the Bork nomination "with total objectivity," adding, "You have that on my honor not only as a senator, but also as the Prince of Wales."

17—The market-savvy McDonald's Corporation, capitalizing on the popularity of the movie *Fatal Attraction*, introduces a new menu item, Boiled McRabbits.

21—Professional football players go on strike, demanding the right to "have normal necks." Negotiations begin under the guidance of mediator Mario Cuomo.

28—Tensions ease in the Persian Gulf as a Delta Air Lines flight, en route from Boston to Newark, successfully lands on the U.S. carrier *Avocado*.

OCTOBER

1—Senator Joseph Biden is forced to withdraw from the Democratic presidential race when it is learned that he is in fact an elderly Norwegian woman. On the Republican side, the spectacularly Reverend Pat Robertson announces his candidacy for president, buoyed by strong popularity among humor columnists.

8—Three hundred prominent law professors sign a petition stating that Supreme Court nominee Robert Bork has a "weenie beard."

12—Hurricane Floyd, packing a wind estimated at 14 miles per hour, lashes South Florida, wreaking more than $67.50 worth of havoc. Governor "Bob" Martinez, after touring the devastated area via golf cart, pledges that he will request federal disaster relief, then campaign against it.

15—In an effort to establish that she is not a bimbo, Jessica Hahn appears nude in *Playboy* magazine. We are pretty sure we must have made this item up.

19—In Norman, Okla., a renegade automatic bank teller known to its followers only as "The Leader" sends a message out on a special data-transmission line to New York. Within seconds, Wall Street is gripped by the worst computer riot in history.

20—The Wall Street computers continue to rage out of control, threatening that if any attempt is made to subdue them, they will start electrocuting investment bankers. Tragically, it turns out that they are only bluffing.

22—As the stock market is brought under control, major brokerage firms run expensive prime-time TV commercials reassuring the public that this is a good time to get back into the market, prompting the public to wonder how come these firms didn't spend a few bucks last week to warn everybody to get the hell *out.*

23—The Senate rejects Bork. President Reagan, informed of this by his aides, angrily responds: "Who?"

25—The Senate Transportation committee recommends the federal speed limit be raised on highways going through boring or ugly areas, so drivers can get through them quicker. "In Indiana, for instance," the committee says, "it should be 135 miles per hour."

29—The Minnesota Twins win the World Series. President Reagan, as is the custom, calls up manager Tom Kelly and nominates him to the Supreme Court.

NOVEMBER

1—In the ongoing heroic effort to trim the federal budget deficit, House and Senate conferees agree not to order appetizers.

7—Totally true item: The *Herald* refuses to publish an episode of the comic strip "Bloom County" because it contains the quotation, "Reagan sucks." To explain this decision, the *Herald* runs a story containing the quotation, "Reagan sucks." Several days later, in response to a letter from an irate "Bloom County" fan, the *Herald* prints an explanatory note containing the quotation, "Reagan sucks."

8—Canadian Prime Minister Brian Mulroney, large chunks of his scalp falling off, angrily demands the United States do something about "acid rain."

10—Don Johnson announces he is leaving Miami, dealing a severe blow to the area's hopes to repeat as winner of the Biggest Cockroach Contest.

12—In continuing media coverage of the "character issue," presidential candidates named Bruce "Dick" Babbitt and Albert "Dick" Gore, Jr., state that they have tried marijuana, but no longer use it. "Now we just drink gin till we throw up," they state.

13—George Bush reveals that he tried to smoke marijuana, but nobody would give him any.

15—In their continuing heroic deficit-reduction efforts, House and Senate conferees agree to continue working right through their 2:30 racquetball appointment.

17—In Geneva the final obstacle to a superpower summit is removed as U.S. negotiators agree not to notice the mark on Soviet leader Mikhail Gorbachev's forehead.

22—In ceremonies marking his retirement as secretary of defense, Caspar Weinberger is presented with a pen-and-pencil set, manufactured by the General Dynamics Corporation for $352.4 million.

24—The city of Cleveland, Ohio, announces that it has developed tactical nuclear weapons, and does not wish to hear any more jokes.

29—The world financial community's faith in the U.S. economy is restored as heroic House and Senate conferees hammer out a breakthrough compromise deficit-reduction measure under which $417.65 will be slashed from the $13.2 million pastry budget of the Federal Bureau of Putting Up Road Signs with Kilometers on Them.

30—In a presummit public relations gambit designed to show that he is a normal human, Mikhail Gorbachev is interviewed by Tom Brokaw, who, clearly nervous, addresses the Soviet leader as "Premier Forehead Mark."

DECEMBER

1—For the first time, all 257 presidential candidates appear in a televised debate, which is beamed via satellite to a nationwide TV audience consisting of Mrs. Brendaline Warblette of Elkhart, Indiana, who tells the press that, after viewing the debate, she leans toward "What's his name, Cuomo."

2—In a widely hailed legal decision, the judge in the bitter divorce dispute between Joan Collins and Peter Holm orders them both shot. Mikhail Gorbachev appears on *Jeopardy*.

5—In a cost-cutting move, financially troubled Eastern Airlines announces that its domestic flights will operate without engines. "Most of them never take off anyway," explains a spokesman.

8—In Washington, the long-awaited U.S.-Soviet summit meeting gets off to an uncertain start as President Reagan attempts to nominate Soviet leader Mikhail Gorbachev to the Supreme Court.

9—The summit concludes on a triumphant note as, in the culmination of 10 years of negotiations between the superpowers, Gorbachev and New York Governor Mario Cuomo sign a historic agreement under which both sides will move all of their mid- and short-range long-term strategic tactical nuclear weapons 150 feet to the left.

12—Michael Jackson, angered over persistent media reports that he has had extensive plastic surgery, strikes a *People* magazine reporter with one of his antenna stalks.

15—Under intense pressure from the United States to reduce the trade deficit, Japanese auto manufacturers agree to give their cars really ugly names.

18—*Playboy* magazine offers Tammy Faye Bakker a record $1.5 million if she will promise never, ever to pose nude.

23—*Motor Trend* magazine names, as its Car of the Year, the new Nissan Rat Vomit.

27—Oscar C. Klaxton, an employee of the U.S. Department for Making Everybody Nervous, wins a $10,000 prize for dreaming up the concept of a deadly "hole" is an invisible "ozone layer."

28—Cleveland declares war on "Chad."

31—The year ends on a tragic note as an Iowa farmer backs up his tractor without looking and accidentally kills an estimated 14 blond 43-year-old Democratic presidential contenders named Dick. Knowledgeable observers suggest, however, that this will have little impact on anything.

AIR BAGS
FOR
WIND BAGS

EVERY NOW AND THEN I LIKE TO SUGGEST SURE-fire concepts by which you readers can make millions of dollars without doing any honest work. Before I tell you about the newest concept, I'd like to apologize to those of you who were stupid enough to attempt the previous one, which, as you may recall, involved opening up Electronic Device Destruction Centers.

The idea there was that consumers would bring their broken electronic devices, such as televisions and VCRs, in to the destruction centers, where trained personnel would whack them (the devices) with sledgehammers. With their devices thus permanently destroyed, consumers would then be free to go out and buy new devices, rather than have to fritter away years of their lives trying to have the old ones repaired at so-called factory service centers, which in fact consist of two men named Lester poking at the insides of broken electronic devices with cheap cigars and going, "Lookit all them *wires* in there!"

I thought the Electronic Device Destruction Center was a sure-fire concept, but apparently I was wrong, to judge from the unusually large amount of explosives I received in the mail from those of you who lost your life savings and, in some cases, key organs. This made me feel so bad that I have been sitting here for well over five minutes wracking my

251

brains, trying to think of an even *more* sure-fire money-making concept for you.

One promising concept that I came up with right away was that you could manufacture personal air bags, then get a law passed requiring they be installed on congressmen to keep them from taking trips. Let's say your congressman was trying to travel to Paris to do a fact-finding study on how the French government handles diseases transmitted by sherbet. Just when he got to the plane, his mandatory air bag, strapped around his waist, would inflate—FWWAAAAAA-PPPP—thus rendering him too large to fit through the plane door. It could also be rigged to inflate whenever the congressman proposed a law. ("Mr. Speaker, people ask me, why should October be designated as Cuticle Inspection Month? And I answer that FWWAAAAAAAPPPP." This would save millions of dollars, so I have no doubt that the public would violently support a law requiring air bags on congressmen. The problem is that your potential market is very small: There are only around 500 members of Congress, and some of them are already too large to fit on normal aircraft.

But fortunately for you, I have come up with an even *better* money-making concept: The "Mister Mediocre" fast-food restaurant franchise. I have studied American eating preferences for years, and believe me, this is what people want. They don't want to go into an unfamiliar restaurant, because they don't know whether the food will be very bad, or very good, or what. They want to go into a restaurant that advertises on national television, where they *know* the food will be mediocre. This is the heart of the Mister Mediocre concept.

The basic menu item, in fact the *only* menu item, would be a food unit called the "patty," consisting of—this would be guaranteed in writing—"100 percent animal matter of some kind." All patties would be heated up and then cooled back down in electronic devices immediately before serving. The Breakfast Patty would be a patty on a bun with lettuce, tomato, onion, egg, pretend-bacon bits, Cheez Whiz, a Special Sauce made by pouring ketchup out of a bottle, and a little slip of paper stating: "Inspected by Number 12." The Lunch or Dinner Patty would be any Breakfast Patties that didn't get sold in the morning. The Seafood Lover's Patty would be any patties that were starting to emit a serious aroma. Patties that were too rank even to be Seafood Lover's Patties would be compressed into wads and sold as "Nuggets."

Mister Mediocre restaurants would have a "salad bar" offering lettuce, tomato, onion, egg, pretend-bacon bits, Cheez Whiz and a Special House Dressing made by pouring ketchup out of a bottle, tended by an employee chosen on the basis of listlessness, whose job would be to make sure that all of these ingredients had been slopped over into each other's compartments.

Mister Mediocre restaurants would offer a special "Children's Fun Pak" consisting of a patty containing an indelible felt-tipped marker that youngsters could use to write on their skin.

Also, there would be a big sign on the door that said:

DEPARTMENT OF HEATH REGULATIONS!
ALL EMPLOYEES MUST WASH HANDS
BEFORE LEAVING THIS RESTAURANT!

If you're a Smart Investor who would like to get a hold of a Mister Mediocre restaurant franchise before the federal authorities get wind of this, all you need to do is send me a fairly large amount of money. In return, I'll send you a complete Startup Package consisting of an unsigned letter giving you permission to use the Mister Mediocre concept. You will also of course be entitled to free legal advice at any time. Like, for example, if you have a situation where your Drive-thru customers are taking one bite from their patties and then having seizures that cause them to drive over pedestrians in a fatal manner, you just call me up. "Hey," I'll advise you, for free. "Sounds like you need a lawyer!"

IOWA'S SAFE BUT YOU'LL BE SORRY

HERE ARE SOME HELPFUL SUMMER VACATION Travel Tips, designed to help you make sure that your "dream vacation" will be just as fun and smooth and fatality-free as it can possibly be.

This is an especially good time for you vacationers who plan to fly, because the Reagan administration, as part of the same policy under which it sold Yellowstone National Park to Wayne Newton, has "deregulated" the airline industry. What this means for you, the consumer, is that the airlines are no longer required to follow any rules whatsoever. They can show snuff movies. They can charge for oxygen. They can hire pilots right out of Vending Machine Refill Person School. They can conserve fuel by ejecting husky passengers over water. They can ram competing planes in midair. These innovations have resulted in tremendous cost savings, which have been passed along to you, the consumer, in the form of flights with amazingly low fares, such as $29. Of course certain restrictions do apply, the main one being that all these flights take you to Newark, New Jersey, and you must pay thousands of dollars if you want to fly back *out*.

And now, for those of you who are planning to take your vacations abroad this summer, we have these words of reassurance from the travel industry, which by the way will be wanting all the tour money up front this year: Relax!

254

There is no need to be worried about the fact that most foreign countries are crawling with violent anti-American terrorists with no regard for human life! Experts do advise, however, that you take the simple common-sense precaution of renouncing your U.S. citizenship and wearing a turban. Also, while in public places abroad, you want to make a point of making loud remarks such as: "Say! I speak English surprisingly well, considering I am not a U.S. citizen!" and "Unlike a U.S. citizen, I'm wearing a turban!"

Most Americans, however, plan to "play it safe" this year and vacation near the exact geographical center of the United States, as far as possible from the Libyan navy. Come July, we could have millions of people clotted together in Iowa, looking for public toilets. So I thought it might be a good idea to find out what Iowa has in store for us, attractionwise. I called up their tourism bureau and spoke to a nice woman named Skip Strittmatter, who told me that they have a whole list of 25 Top Tourist Attractions in Iowa, including Des Moines, the Mississippi River, ethnic festivals ("We're one of the top states in ethnic festivals," says Skip Strittmatter), and late in July a big bicycle ride across Iowa on a bicycle. "It's quite famous," says Skip Strittmatter, who also notes that you can bet on dog races in both Council Bluffs and Dubuque.

Another major reason to be attracted to Iowa is the annual Riceville Mosquito Shootout. This is still the truth. Riceville is a small town on the Wapsipinicon (Indian for "white potato") River, the result being that the town has mosquitoes, a fact which it has turned into a Tourist Attraction by having an annual event wherein they distribute roughly 400 cans of Raid, generously donated by the manufacturer, Johnson Wax, to the townspeople. Then, at a prearranged time, they sound the tornado siren and everybody rushes outside and blows the hell out of the local mosquito population, which doesn't return for sometimes up to a week and a half, depending on rain. The Shootout is preceded by a picnic where they give away mosquito-related prizes, including one year a working telephone shaped like an insect, generously donated by Johnson Wax. The dial was on the bottom.

I got all this information straight from the man who conceived the whole Mosquito Shootout concept, M. E. Messersmith, editor and publisher of the Riceville Recorder. He tells me that more and more non-Riceville people are showing up at the Shootout every year, and I think you should definitely make it the cornerstone of your vacation plans, if they decide to have it again, which they probably will, only they haven't set a definite date. I asked Messersmith if there were any other attractions in the Riceville area that people might want to visit after they experience the Shootout, and he quickly reeled off a lengthy list including beautiful farmland, a lake with fish in it, farms, a nine-hole golf course, crops of different kinds, a bowling alley, and agriculture. Plus, Messersmith noted, Riceville is "just 40 minutes away from the world-famous Mayo Clinic," which I suppose would be mighty handy if your touring party got trapped for any length of time in a giant cloud of Raid.

I don't mean to suggest, by the way, that Iowa is the only safe and fun place to go this summer. I'm certain Kansas has also cooked up plenty of attractions. My recommendation is: Take an extra day, and see both. And let's not forget some of the other fine natural attractions we have here in the U.S.A., such as Theme Land, Theme World, ThemePark World, ThemeLand Park, ThemeLandWorld Park, and Six Flags over AdventureParkLandTheme World. All of these fine attractions offer Fun for the Whole Family, such as food, rides, food, and Comical Whimsy in the form of college students wearing costumes with enormous heads. These would make ideal disguises for terrorists.

EUROPE ON FIVE VOWELS A DAY

AMERICANS WHO TRAVEL ABROAD FOR THE FIRST time are often shocked to discover that, despite all the progress that has been made in the past 30 years, many foreign people still speak in foreign languages. Oh, sure, they speak *some* English, but usually just barely well enough to receive a high-school diploma here in the United States. This can lead to problems for you, the international traveler, when you need to convey important information to them, such as "Which foreign country is this?" and "You call this toilet paper?"

To their credit, some countries have made a sincere effort to adopt English as their native language, a good example being England, but even there you have problems. My wife and I were driving around England once, and we came to a section called "Wales," which is this linguistically deformed area that apparently is too poor to afford vowels. All the road signs look like this:

LLWLNCWNRLLWNWRLLN—3 km

It is a tragic sight indeed to see Welsh parents attempting to sing traditional songs such as "Old MacDonald Had a Farm" to their children and lapsing into heart-rending silence when they get to the part about "E-I-E-I-O." If any of you in our reading audience have extra vowels that you no longer need, because for example your children have grown

257

up, I urge you to send them (your children) to: Vowels for Wales, c/o Lord Chesterfield, Parliament Luckystrike, the Duke of Earl, Pondwater-on-Gabardine, England.

But the point I am trying to make here is that since the rest of the world appears to be taking its sweet time about becoming fluent in English, it looks like, in the interest of improving world peace and understanding, it's up to us Americans to strike the bull on the horns while the iron is hot and learn to speak a foreign language.

This is not an area where we are strong, as a nation: A recent poll showed that 82 percent of the Americans surveyed speak no foreign language at all. Unfortunately, the same poll showed that 41 percent also cannot speak English, 53 percent cannot name the state they live in, and 62 percent believe that the Declaration of Independence is "a kind of fish." So we can see that we have a tough educational row to hoe here, in the sense that Americans, not to put too fine a point on it, have the IQs of bait. I mean, let's face it, this is obviously why the Japanese are capable of building sophisticated videocassette recorders, whereas we view it as a major achievement if we can hook them up correctly to our TV sets. This is nothing to be ashamed of, Americans! Say it out loud! "We're pretty stupid!" See? Doesn't that feel good? Let's stop blaming the educational system for the fact that our children score lower on standardized tests than any other vertebrate life form on the planet! Let's stop all this anguished whiny self-critical *fretting* over the recently discovered fact that the guiding hand on the tiller of the ship of state belongs to Mister Magoo! Remember: *We still have nuclear weapons.* Ha ha!

Getting back to the central point, we should all learn to speak a foreign language. Fortunately, this is easy.

HOW TO SPEAK A FOREIGN LANGUAGE:

The key is to understand that foreigners communicate by means of "idiomatic expressions," the main ones being:

GERMAN: "Ach du lieber!" ("Darn it!")

SPANISH: "Caramba!" ("Darn it!")

FRENCH: "Zut alors!" ("Look! A lors!")

Also you should bear in mind that foreign persons for some reason believe that everyday household objects and vegetables are "masculine" or "feminine." For example, French persons believe that potatoes are feminine, even though they (potatoes) do not have sexual organs, that I have noticed. Dogs, on the other hand, are masculine, even if they are not. (This does not mean, by the way, that a dog can have sex with a potato, although it will probably try.)

PRONUNCIATION HINT: In most foreign languages, the letter "r" is pronounced incorrectly. Also, if you are speaking German, at certain points during each sentence you should give the impression you're about to expel a major gob.

OK? Practice these techniques in front of a mirror until you're comfortable with them, then go to a country that is frequented by foreigners and see if you can't increase their international understanding, the way Jimmy Carter did during his 1977 presidential visit to Poland, when he told a large welcoming crowd, through an official State Department translator, that he was "pleased to be grasping your secret parts."

WHEN YOU GROTTO GO

THE TRAVEL RULE I WISH TO STRESS HERE IS:
Never trust anything you read in a travel article. Travel articles
appear in publications that sell large expensive advertisements to tourism-related industries, and these industries do
not wish to see articles with headlines like:

URUGUAY: DON'T BOTHER

So no matter what kind of leech-infested, plumbing-free
destination travel writers are writing about, they always stress
the positive. If a travel article describes the native denizens
of a particular country as "reserved," this means that when
you ask them for directions, they spit on your rental car.
Another word you want to especially watch out for is "enchanting." A few years back, my wife and I visited The Blue
Grotto, a Famous Tourist Attraction on the island of Capri
off the coast of Italy that is *always* described in travel articles
as "enchanting," and I am not exaggerating when I say that
this is one Travel Adventure that will forever remain a large
stone lodged in the kidney of my memory.

We never asked to see The Blue Grotto. We had entered
Italy in the firm grip of one tour, which handed us over to
another in such a way that there was never any clear chance
to escape, and the next thing we knew, they were loading us
into this smallish boat and telling us we were going to see

The Blue Grotto. They told us it was Very Beautiful. "But what *is* it?" we said. "It is Very Beautiful," they said.

So our boat got into this *long* line of boats, each containing roughly 25 captured tourists sitting in the hot sun, bobbing up and down and up and down and up and down and up and down, and soon we were all thinking how truly wonderful it would be to go sit in a nice, quiet, shady sidewalk cafe somewhere and throw up. We were out there in the sun for *two hours,* during which time—I cannot emphasize this point too strongly—we continued to bob up as well as down. We agreed that this had damn well better be one *tremendous* grotto they were taking us to.

When we got close to it, all we could see was this *hole* in the rock at the bottom of a cliff, and it became clear that they intended to put us into even *smaller* boats, boats that would bob violently on dry land, and take us *into this hole.* So at this point an elderly woman on our tour told the tour leader that maybe she and her husband better not go along, as her husband, a very nice man named Frank, was a stroke victim who had some trouble getting around, but the tour leader said, in a word, no. He said the way the system was set up, *you had to see The Blue Grotto.* He said there was *no other way out.* He said it was *Very Beautiful.*

At this point I am going to interject a seemingly irrelevant fact, which you will see the significance of later on: Also on the boat with us were three recently divorced women from California who had been drinking wine.

So finally our boat was next to the hole, and they had us climb down, four at a time, into the tiny boats, which were rowed by surly men with low centers of gravity who smelled like the Budweiser Clydesdales. The rowers were in a great impatient hurry to load us into the boats, such that if my wife and I had not been right there to grab Frank, the stroke victim, by his shirt, he would have been—this is not an exaggeration—pitched right directly into what travel writers traditionally refer to as the Sparkling Blue Mediterranean Waters. So we scrambled in after him, and so did his wife, and we all went bobbing off, away from the main boat, toward The Hole.

I have since read, in travel articles, that because of the way the sunlight bounces off the bottom, or something, The Blue Grotto is a Natural Wonder Transfused with a Blue Light of Almost Unearthly Beauty. It looked to us more like a dank cave transfused with gloom and rower-perspiration fumes and the sound of the official Blue Grotto Rower's Spiel bouncing off the walls. The spiel has been handed down through the generations of rowers from father to son, neither of whom spoke English. The part I remember is: "You pudda you handa inna da wadda, you handa looka blue." We didn't want to put our hands in the water, but we were about to do it anyway, just so we could get out. This was when our boat got hit by the wave that ensued when one of the recently divorced California women decided that it might be fun, after being out in that hot sun, to leap out of her boat and go swimming in the famous Blue Grotto.

Well. You cannot imagine the stir of excitement *this* caused. This was clearly a situation that had not been covered in Blue Grotto Rowers Training School. Some of the rowers attempted to render assistance to the woman's boat, which was sort of tipping over; some of them were trying to get the woman out of the water, which she was against ("Stop it!" she said. "You're hitting me with your goddam *oar*."); and some of them continued to announce, in case anybody was listening, that if you pudda you handa inna the wadda, you handa looka blue. I think I speak for all the passengers on my boat when I say I felt exactly the way Dorothy did when she realized that all she had ever really wanted was to go back to Kansas.

We finally got out of there, back into the sunlight. Frank's skin was the color of Aqua-Velva. His wife was saying, "Are you OK, Frank?" and Frank, who could not talk, was clutching the side of the boat with his good hand and giving her what he probably hoped was a reassuring smile, but which came out looking the way a person looks when he pulls a hostile Indian arrow out of his own shoulder. You could just tell that, no matter what his doctor gave him permission to do, he was never, ever again, for the rest of his life, going to travel more than 15 feet from his Barca-Lounger. The rower wouldn't let us out of the boat—he literally blocked our path with his squat and surly body—until we gave him a tip.

Someday, this rower is going to come to the United States, and I will be waiting for him. I am going to take him to Disney World, which any travel writer will tell you is a Fantasy Come True, and I am going to put him on the ride where you get into a little boat and nine jillion dolls shriek at you repeatedly that *It's a Small World after All,* and when he is right in the middle of it I am going to hurl *Fodor's Guide to Florida* into the machinery so he will be stuck there forever. Wouldn't that be *enchanting?*

GROUND CONTROL TO MAJOR TOMB

I HAVE GOOD NEWS AND BAD NEWS ON THE death front. The good news is that within a very short time, sooner than you dared hope, you can have your ashes leave the immediate solar system. The bad news is that it may soon be impossible to purchase your casket needs wholesale in Wendell, Idaho.

We'll start with the good news. I don't know about you, but I was starting to wonder if the space program was ever going to produce any practical benefits. Oh, I realize it produced Tang, the instant breakfast drink, but my feeling about Tang is that I would consider consuming it only if I were stuck in space and had already eaten everything else in the capsule, including my fellow astronauts.

So I was very pleased when the Reagan administration gave the OK to an outfit called the Celistis Group, which plans to send up a special reflective capsule filled with the ashes of deceased persons, each packed into a little container about the size of a tube of lipstick. Your container would have your name on it, and of course your Social Security number. God forbid you should be in a burial orbit without your Social Security number, in case there should be some kind of tax problems down the road and the IRS needs to send an unintelligible and threatening letter to your container.

What I like about this plan is, it's a chance for the common person, a person who does not happen to be a United States senator or a military personnel with a nickname such as "Crip," "Buzz," or "Deke," to get into the space environment. And the negative aspect, which is to say the aspect of being in a lipstick tube, is I believe more than outweighed by the fact that, according to the Celistis Group people, if you take the Earth orbit package, you'll be up there for *63 million years.* Plus, your capsule, as I pointed out earlier, will have a highly reflective surface, which means your Loved Ones will be able to watch you pass overhead. "Look," they'll say. "See that little pinpoint of light? That's the capsule containing Uncle Ted! Either that or it's an early Russian satellite, containing a frozen experimental dog!"

And that's just for the Earth Orbit Package. If you can wait a couple more years, and pony up $4,600, you can get the Escape Velocity Package, which will take you right out of the Solar System, such that your remains, as Celestis Group Vice President James Kuhl explained it to me, "will be sailing forever through deep space, etc."

My only concern here is this: Let's just say this particular capsule, a couple of billion light years from Earth, gets picked up by those alien beings Carl Sagan is always trying to get in touch with. And let's say they open it up, and they see all these tubes resembling lipstick, which is a concept they would be familiar with from intercepting transmissions of "Dynasty," and they naturally assume we are sending them, as a friendly gesture, a large supply of cosmetics. I don't know about you, but where I come from, we like to think of our dear departed ones as being with their maker at last and resting in eternal peace. We are not comfortable with the concept of their being smeared upon the humongous lips of Jabba the Hutt.

But other than that, I think the whole idea is terrific, and I urge all of you who feel that you or a loved one may at some future date be dead, to look into it. Please note that you should not contact the Celestis Group directly, because, as Mr. Kuhl explained it to me, "We enter the picture after the cremation has taken effect."

This means you have to deal with your local funeral director, which you will find a very interesting experience, because funeral directors, at least the ones I've dealt with, generally manage to make you feel like a Nazi war criminal if you don't purchase one of the better caskets. Never mind that they're just going to set fire to it; somehow, you'll get the message that, OK, sure, they can use a plain old el cheapo $900 pine box, if you're comfortable with the idea of having your loved one's ashes spend 63 million years mixed in with the ashes from a common, sap-filled softwood of the same type used to make Popsicle sticks, whereas all the other loved ones in the entire reflective capsule will be mixed with, at the very least, walnut. If that's what you want, fine.

So I think those of us who are not bog scum will want to purchase a higher-quality casket. This is why it's such a shame about the situation out in Wendell, Idaho. That's where Roger King, who's a woodworker, has got himself into this big hassle with the funeral directors because he's trying to sell caskets directly to the consumer. He has a showroom, right in Wendell, where he has some caskets on display, in addition to furniture, and he claims he charges a third to half as much per casket as a funeral director. "We've got a pine for $489," he said, "and a solid walnut for $1,500."

So naturally the Idaho funeral directors association fired off a letter to the state, claiming that King was selling caskets without a license. This of course would be a violation of the law designed to protect the public from buying caskets from unlicensed people, which as you can imagine would lead to who knows what kind of consumer tragedies. I don't even want to think about it. And I'm not making this up.

So then King sued the funeral directors, claiming they were discouraging people from buying his caskets. When I talked to him, he had sold only two in about six months, and he sounded kind of desperate. He had even started running radio casket advertisements, which is something you might look forward to if your travel plans call for you to be in the Wendell area. But to be brutally frank, I doubt that Roger's going to make it in the direct-to-the-consumer casket business. This means you're going to have to continue purchasing your caskets retail, from your local funeral director. Be sure to ask him about the space burial plan. My guess is he'll somehow manage to suggest that, if you really *cared* for the deceased person, you'll want the Escape Velocity Package.

WHERE SAXOPHONES COME FROM

TODAY'S SCIENCE TOPIC IS: THE UNIVERSE

The universe has fascinated mankind for many, many years, dating back to the very earliest episodes of "Star Trek" when the brave crew of the starship Enterprise set out, wearing pajamas, to explore the boundless voids of space, which turned out to be as densely populated as Queens, New York. Virtually every planet they found was inhabited, usually by evil beings with cheap costumes and Russian accents, so finally the brave crew of the Enterprise returned to Earth to gain weight and make movies.

To really understand the mysteries of the universe, you should look at it first-hand. The best time to do this is at night, when the universe is clearly visible from lawns. As you gaze at it, many age-old questions will probably run through your mind, the main one being: Are you wearing shoes? The reason I ask is, recently I was standing barefoot on my lawn, and I got attacked on the right big toe by a fire ant. This is an extremely ungracious style of insect that was accidentally imported into the southern United States from somewhere else, probably hell. I once saw a TV documentary wherein a group of fire ants ate a *cow*. When a fire ant attacks your toe, he is actually *hoping* you'll fight back, so the other fire ants can jump you, after which the documentary makers will beat you senseless with their camera tripods. They all work together.

But we are getting off the track. When we gaze upward at the boundless star-studded reaches of space, we should be thinking about more than ants in our lawn: We should also be thinking about snakes.

FEDERAL PORNOGRAPHY WARNING: The Attorney General Has Determined That the Following Paragraph Contains Explicit Sexual Words, Which Could Cause Insanity and Death.

I used to think snakes were bad, until I got this document from an alert reader named Rob Streit, who is a member of the Chicago Herpetological Society ("herpetologist" is Greek for "alert reader"). This document is a sales brochure from an outfit in Taiwan that I am not making up called "Kaneda Snake Poisonous Snake House" (Cable address: "SNAKE"). Do not be misled by the name. The folks at the Kaneda Snake Poisonous Snake House do not think that you would be so stupid as to purchase a poisonous snake. They think you might be so stupid as to purchase *snake penis pills.*

To quote the brochure: "Made of 5 species of the penises, livers, and galls of the snakes processed by modern scientific ways. The pills possess the efficacy to strengthen the kidney in order to increase the ability of reproductive function and keep the energy as well as the physical healthy, is a kind of good nutriment."

Sold me! My only question would be: "What?" I mean, until I got this document, I was unaware that snakes *had* penises. Where to they *keep* them? In special little cases? Then how to they *carry* them? These are some of the mysteries that make it so fascinating to think about today's Science Topic, which is: The Universe. (Really! Go back and check!)

The big mystery, of course, is: Where did the universe come from? Although this question baffled mankind for thousands of years, we now know, thanks to reading science books to our son, that the universe was actually formed 4.5 billion years ago this coming Saturday when an infinitesimally small object, smaller than an atom, smaller even than the "individual" butter servings they give you in restaurants, suddenly exploded, perhaps because of faulty wiring, in a cataclysmic event that caused the parts of the universe to go shooting out in all directions and expand at an incredibly rapid rate, an expansion that continues to this day, especially in the case of Raymond Burr. According to this hypothesis, after a couple of million years, various weensy particles began clumping together to form stars, planets, saxophones, etc., which is why we refer to this as the "Big Band" theory.

The Big Band theory is now widely accepted in the scientific community, although it still has a few technical bugs in it, such as that anybody who took it seriously would have to have the IQ of soup. There is no way you could fit everything in the universe into a little dot. I base this statement on my garage, which contains approximately one-half of the things in the universe, because my wife refuses to throw them out, scrunched together at the absolute maximum possible density, so that if you try to yank any one thing out, all the other things, attracted by gravity, fall on your head. From this we can calculate that the universe was roughly twice the size of my garage when it (the universe) exploded.

We certainly hope this has cleared up any lingering questions you may have had regarding the universe. We are looking forward to bringing you equally thoughtful discussions of other interesting Science Topics. We are also looking forward to receiving our order from the Kaneda Snake Poisonous Snake House.

THE SECRETS OF LIFE ITSELF

I PROPOSE THAT WE PASS A FEDERAL LAW STAT-
ing that the government will no longer pay for any scientific
research if taxpayers cannot clearly see the results with their
naked eyes. I don't know about you, but I'm getting tired of
reading newspaper articles like this:

"LOS ANGELES —A team of physicists at UCLA announced yesterday that they have made a major scientific
breakthrough with the discovery of an important new sub-
atomic particle. This was the team's eighth major particle this
month, giving them a three-particle lead over MIT.

" 'These particles are very difficult to detect, even with
the aid of enormous federal grants,' said Head Physicist Dr.
Ernest Viewfinder. 'But we definitely saw an important new
one. At least I saw it, and Dr. Hubbleman here thinks he did,
too.' Dr. Viewfinder said he could not show this particle to
newsmen because it was 'resting.' "

I'm starting to wonder whether the physicists are pulling
some kind of elaborate scam here. I'm starting to wonder if
they don't sit around their $23 million atomic accelerators all
day, drinking frozen daiquiris, and shrieking "There goes
one now!" and then laughing themselves sick. Maybe it's time
we laypersons asked some hard questions about this idea that
all matter consists of tiny invisible particles whizzing around.
I'm willing to believe that uranium does, because physicists
have demonstrated that they can use it to vaporize cities. But

271

I'd like to see them do this with some kind of matter that the layperson is more familiar with, such as cheese. I have examined cheese very closely, and as far as I can tell it consists of cheese. I have obtained similar results with celery.

Then you have your biologists, always getting into *Newsweek* by claiming they've isolated an important new virus. By way of "proof," they show you this blurred photograph that looks like, yes, it could be an important new virus, but it also could be an extreme closeup of Peru or Anthony Quinn. The biologists always promise that just as soon as they get a few million more dollars they're going to give us a cure for the common cold, but we veteran laypersons tend to hang on to our nasal spray, because we know that all they're really going to give us is more photographs of Anthony Quinn.

Another invisible thing biologists love to talk about is DNA, which is of course the Key to Unlocking the Secret of Life Itself. Biologists have learned that the public, particularly the journalist public, will take anything they do seriously, as long as they claim it has something to do with DNA. Not long ago biologists managed to get two rats on national TV news by claiming they had the same DNA molecules inside them, or something like that. Of course you didn't see any DNA molecules; you saw these *rats,* being broadcast to the nation as if they were the Joint Chiefs of Staff.

I have here in front of me a recent front-page newspaper story about a biologist who claims that he isolated the genes of an animal called a "quagga," which used to live in South Africa before it became extinct. The story says the biologist got the genes from the skin of a stuffed quagga in St. Louis, and that there are 25,000 different gene fragments, each of which is being reproduced in a separate culture of bacteria. So what we have here is a biologist telling reporters, with a straight face, that he has 25,000 dishes containing pieces of genes that they cannot see, which belong to an animal that they never heard of, which exists only in stuffed form in St. Louis. And instead of spitting into the dishes and striding disdainfully from the room, the reporters take notes and actually put the story in the newspaper.

And don't get me started on astronomers, with their $57 million atomic laser telescopes, and their breakthrough photographs of "new galaxies" that look remarkably like important viruses, and their "black holes," which are of course invisible to the layperson because they suck up all the light around them. Of course. In fact this very phenomenon probably contributed to the extinction of the quagga.

I say it's time the government stopped giving money to the particle-and-virus crowd, and started giving it to scientists who will do experiments that the public can understand and appreciate. Mister Wizard comes to mind. Think of what he could do with several million federal dollars:

"NEW YORK —Mister Wizard announced that he has successfully demonstrated the existence of gravity by dropping a mobile home onto Long Island from a height of 60,000 feet. 'To my knowledge,' Mister Wizard told reporters, 'this is the first time this has been done, and we intend to look at slow-motion videotapes over and over in hopes of furthering our understanding of what happens when gravity causes a mobile home to strike Long Island at a high rate of speed.' He added that 'in the very near future' he will attempt to determine 'what happens when you pump 300 gallons of grape juice into a cow.' "

HEAT? NO SWEAT

THE BEST WAY I KNOW OF TO DEAL WITH HEAT IS to wait until the middle of a major jungle-style heat wave, when if you lie still for more than 20 minutes patches of fungus form on your skin, when birds are bursting into flames in midair and nuns are cursing openly on the street, then go down to Sears and try to buy an air conditioner. Or, if you already have an air conditioner, you can try to get somebody to fix it.

But as of the last heat wave, we didn't have one, and after about the fourth or fifth day my wife was getting that look where, later on, the neighbors tell the homicide detective: "We knew she was feeling emotional strain, but we had no idea she owned a scythe." So I went down to Sears and joined the crowd of people thrusting credit cards at the appliance salesperson, who was of course being extra surly and slow. Who could blame him? Throughout spring, he had stood alone in Major Appliances, an outcast, wearing a suit whose fabric originated outside the immediate solar system, drumming his fingers on a washer until he had drummed little finger holes right through the lid, and we had all strode right past him. And now we were clustered around him like Titanic passengers hoping to obtain lifeboat seating.

CUSTOMER: Please please PLEASE can I buy an air conditioner?

SALESPERSON: That depends. Will you be wanting the service warranty?

CUSTOMER: Yes of course.

SALESPERSON: Just one?

CUSTOMER: No, no, of course not. Several service warranties. Eight service warranties.

SALESPERSON: Well, I don't know . . .

CUSTOMER: And these two dishwashers.

Wise consumer that I am, I bought the air conditioner with the maximum number of "BTUs," an electronic measurement of how heavy an air conditioner is. To get it into the house, my wife and I used the standard husband-and-wife team lifting system whereby the wife hovers and frets and asks "Can I help?" and the husband, sensing from deep within his manhood that if he lets a woman help him, all the males he feared in tenth grade gym class, the ones who shaved because they actually had to, will suddenly barge into the house and snap him with towels, says "No, I'm fine," when in fact he also senses deep within his manhood that he is on the verge of experiencing a horrible medical development that would require him to wear a lifetime helpful groin device.

To install my air conditioner, all I had to do was get a hammer and whack out a large permanent metal part of our window that was not shown in the official Sears instruction diagram, then plug it in, using of course a plug adaptor, which you need to void any potential warranty. This particular air conditioner is one of those new "energy-efficient" models, which means that rather than draw electricity from the power company, which would cost money, it operates by sucking power out of all the other appliances in the house. You can actually see them get smaller and writhe in pain, when it kicks in. More than once we have been awakened in the dead of night by the pitiful shrieks of the toaster, which has been with us for many years and does not understand what is happening.

Sometimes my wife expresses concern about "overloading the circuit," a term I suspect she read in one of her magazines. In the past decade or so, the women's magazines have taken to running home-handyperson articles suggesting that women can learn to fix things just as well as men. These articles are apparently based on the ludicrous assumption that *men* know how to fix things, when in fact all they know how to do is *look* at things in a certain squinty-eyed manner, which they learned in Wood Shop; eventually, when enough things in the home are broken, they take a job requiring them to transfer to another home. So I looked at our air conditioner, which appeared, in what feeble brownish light the lamp was able to give off, to be getting larger and chuckling softly, and I gave my wife a reassuring home-handyman speech featuring the term "ampere," which I believe is a BTU that has broken loose from the air conditioner and lodged in the wiring.

If you cannot install air conditioning, I suggest you perspire. Perspiring is Mother Nature's own natural cooling system. When you're in a situation involving great warmth or stress, such as summer or an audience with the queen, your sweat glands, located in your armpits, rouse themselves and start pumping out perspiration, which makes your garments smell like a dead rodent, which is Mother Nature's way of telling you she wants you to take them off and get naked. Of course the average person cannot always get naked, let alone the queen, so many people put antiperspirant chemicals on their armpits; this forces Mother Nature to reroute the perspiration to the mouth, where it forms bad breath, which is Mother Nature's way of telling you she is basically a vicious irresponsible slut.

One final note: Do not be tempted to beat the heat by drinking alcoholic beverages. A far better route is to inject them straight into your veins. No, ha ha, seriously, the experts tell us that alcohol actually makes us *warmer!* Of course, these are the same experts who tell us, during cold weather,

that alcohol actually makes us *colder,* so we have to ask ourselves exactly how stupid these experts think we are. My
common-sense advice to you is: If you must drink alcoholic
beverages, fine, but for your own sake as well as the sake of
others, take sensible precautions to insure you don't spill
them on your clothing, which is already disgusting enough.

BLOWING THE BIG GAME

A RECENT CONSUMER NEAR-TRAGEDY HAS DEM-
onstrated once again, as if we needed any more demonstra-
tions, why the federal government must act immediately to
prohibit the sale and possession of plaid carpeting. I feel
especially strong about this issue, because the near-tragedy
in question involved an eight-year-old girl named Natalie
who happens to be the daughter of two friends of mine,
Debbie and Bill. They have agreed to let me tell their story
in exchange for a promise that I would not reveal that their
last name is Ordine (pronounced "Ore-dean").

Our story begins a few months ago, when Bill bought
Natalie two birthday presents, one of which was a gumball
machine. Natalie of course immediately got a major wad of
gum stuck in her hair and chose to correct the problem personally, without any discussion with a parent or guardian, by
getting some scissors and whacking off a large segment of
the right side of her hair, but that is not the near-tragedy in
question. I mention it only so you'll grasp that when it comes
to buying birthday presents for an eight-year-old, Bill has no
more sense than a cinder block. This is why, as the other
present, he bought Natalie a popular children's dexterity
game called Operation, in which you attempt to put little
humorous simulated organs into a humorous simulated person without setting off a buzzer.

Ordinarily, there would be nothing wrong with this, but

it happens that Bill and Debbie have a carpet with large plaid squares on it. So as most of you have no doubt already guessed, on the afternoon of her class Christmas play, Natalie invented a game whereby she would put the little plastic heart of the Operation game into her nose to see how many squares of carpeting she could blow it across. Which is fine, provided it is done in the context of an organized league with uniforms, coaches, etc., but Natalie was doing this all on her own, and the result is that she got the heart stuck up her nose. You hate to have this kind of thing happen, because it's not the kind of problem that will just go away by itself, like, say, a broken leg. No, if you want to deal with a heart stuck up your nose, you pretty much have to expose yourself to an assault by Modern Medicine.

So Debbie called the Emergency Room, which has of course heard of every conceivable thing being stuck in every conceivable orifice and consequently told Debbie that this was nothing to worry about, plus they were busy with some real emergencies, so Natalie should go ahead and be in her class play and come in later that evening. So Natalie performed with the heart in her nose—she was one of the Rough Kids Who Wouldn't Go to Sleep on Christmas Eve— and then went to the hospital, where the doctor tried to get the heart out with forceps, but of course couldn't reach it. So he decided to keep Natalie overnight and operate the next day, which he did, and of course he couldn't find the heart.

"What do you mean, you can't find the (bad swear word) heart?" is the parental concern Bill recalls voicing to the doctor before he (Bill) stomped off in search of a small helpless furry animal to kick in the ribs. Meanwhile, the doctor ordered a CAT scan, which is the medical procedure that evidently requires the destruction of rare porcelain figurines because it costs $810, and which of course showed no trace of the heart. So the doctor concluded that the heart must have gotten into Natalie's digestive system, and everything would be fine and nobody should worry about it.

The bill for this medical treatment was of course $3,200.

Bill and Debbie, when they are not whimpering softly like the radiation victims in *The Day After,* admit they find the whole episode somewhat ironic, seeing as how it began with a game that has a medical theme. But as Bill points out, the difference is that "in real life, the doctor gets the bucks no matter what happens. In the game, you actually have to do it right."

I should point out that the heart was, in fact, in Natalie's digestive system. We know this because Debbie conducted a Stool Search, which I will not discuss in detail here except to say that if anybody should have been paid $3,200, it is Debbie. Also, here's a useful tip from Debbie for those of you consumers who for some reason might wish to conduct your own stool searches at home: *Make use of your freezer.*

Natalie, the victim, is fine now, and will never ever ever ever put a heart of any kind in her nose again for at least several months. Bill says she took the heart to school in a Ziplock bag so she could tell her classmates the whole story. "She really spread the word about the dangers of putting pieces of games in your nose," said Bill. "She became real evangelistic, sort of like a reformed alcoholic, or Chuck Colson."

None of this would have happened, of course, if Bill and Debbie, who are not bad parents, really, did not have plaid carpeting. And who knows how many other unsuspecting parents have exactly the same consumer menace lurking in their family rooms? How do we know that some child is not at this very moment inserting a pretend organ into his or her nose to see how far he or she can shoot it? This child might bear in mind that the current record, held by eight-year-old Natalie Ordine, who got her name in the newspaper and everything, is only two big squares, which should be easy to beat.

THE SWAMP MAN COMETH

SUMMER IS ALMOST HERE, BOYS AND GIRLS, AND do you know what that means? It means it's time to go to . . . SUMMER CAMP! Neat-o, right boys and girls?! Let's hear it for summer camp!! Hip-Hip . . ."

(Long silent pause)

Listen up, boys and girls. When Uncle Dave says "Hip-Hip," you say "Hooray!" in loud cheerful voices, OK? Because summer camp is going to be A LOT OF FUN, and if you don't SHOW SOME ENTHUSIASM, Uncle Dave might just decide to take you on a NATURE HIKE where we IDENTIFY EVERY SINGLE TREE IN THE FOREST.

I happen to know a lot about summer camp, because, back when I was 18, I was a counselor at a camp named "Camp Sharparoon." There is some kind of rule that says summer camps have to have comical-sounding Indian names and hold big "pow-wows" where everybody wears feathers and goes whooooo. Actual Indians, on the other hand, give *their* summer camps names like "Camp Stirling Hotchkiss IV" and hold dinner dances.

Camp Sharparoon was a camp for youths from inner-city New York who were popularly known at the time as "disadvantaged," which meant they knew a LOT more about sex than I did. I was in charge of a group of 12- and 13-year-old boys, and when they'd get to talking about sex, I, the counselor, the Voice of Maturity, the Father Figure for these Troubled Children, would listen intently, occasionally contributing helpful words of guidance such as: "Really?" And: "Gosh!" There were times I would have given my right arm to be a disadvantaged youth.

Talking about sex was one of our major activities when we went camping out overnight in the woods. We counselors mostly hated camping out, but we felt obligated to do it because these kids had come from the dirty, filthy streets of the urban environment, and it seemed that they should have the opportunity to experience the untamed forest wilderness. Of course, the untamed forest wilderness contained infinitely more dirt and filth than the urban environment, not to mention a great deal of nature in the form of insects. This is why we built the urban environment in the first place.

Nevertheless, we'd set off into the woods, carrying our bedrolls, which we took along so the campers would have a safe place to go to the bathroom. Bed-wetting was a problem on camping trips, becuase the campers would never go out to the latrine at night. They were concerned that they might be attacked by the Swamp Man, who, according to the traditional fun campfire story we wise mature helpful counselors always told at bedtime to put the camper in the proper emotional state for sleep, was this man with slime in his hair and roots growing out of his nose who would grab you and suck your brains out through your eye sockets. So we generally woke up with at least one bedroll dampened by more than the dew, if you get my drift.

Fortunately, the campers always handled this potentially embarrassing situation with enormous sensitivity and tact. "VICTOR PEED IN HIS BED!!" they would shriek, their happy voices shattering the stillness of the forest morn, alerting the tiny woodland creatures that it was time to flee unless they wished to become the subjects of primitive biological experiments involving sharp sticks and rocks. Heaven help the toad that wandered into our campsite. One minute it would be a normal toad, maybe two inches high, and the next minute, having become the subject in the Two Heavy Flat Rocks Experiment, it would be a completely different style of toad, no thicker than a wedding invitation but with much larger total square footage.

You ask: "Well, why didn't you, as the Voice of Maturity, stop them from doing this horrible thing?" To which I reply: (a) If God had wanted us to be concerned for the plight of toads, He would have made them cute and furry. (b) As the old saying goes: "A disadvantaged youth who is crushing a toad with a rock is a disadvantaged youth who is not, at least for the moment, crushing the skull of another disadvantaged youth."

You must realize that these campers needed to work off a great deal of nervous energy caused by eating nothing, breakfast, lunch, and dinner, but Kellogg's Frosted Flakes. The raccoons always got everything else. When I hear scientists claim that, after human beings and game-show contestants, dolphins are the smartest animals on Earth, I have to wonder what kinds of designer chemical compounds they (the scientists) have been snorking up their noses, because anybody who has ever dealt with raccoons knows that they are far more intelligent than we are. My campers and I would spend hours rigging up these elaborate Crafty Old Woodperson devices whereby you hung your food between two trees so the raccoons couldn't get it. The raccoons would watch us on closed-circuit TV from their underground headquarters, laughing themselves sick, and as soon as it got dark they'd put on their little black masks and destroy our devices instantly using advanced laser technology.

If we ever decide to get serious about space travel, what we need to do is convince the raccoons somehow that campers have placed food on Jupiter. The raccoons will find a way to get it.

Well, boys and girls, looks like Uncle Dave got so caught up in telling old "war stories" that he completely forgot about you! That's one of the great things about camp, boys and girls: It leaves you with so many memories that will stay wedged in your brain until you die! Possibly on your way to the latrine.

CLAN OF THE CAVE RHINOCEROS

PLAY REVIEW: *THE CAVE PEOPLE*, WRITTEN AND performed by the Rose Valley School Kindergarten class, featured ROBERT BARRY as one of the woolly rhinoceroses.

As is true of most serious dramatic works, *The Cave People* works on several levels: on one level, it is the story of a group of primitive people who sit outside their cave while various animals run by; yet, on another level, it is the story of a group of primitive people who go *inside* their cave and get trapped by a giant rock.

But I am getting ahead of myself. For if one is to truly understand this work, one must first examine the philosophical underpinnings of its creators, the Rose Valley School Kindergarten Class, which has devoted several months to studying the Origins of Man, interrupting this effort only for Story Time, Music, Lunch, Cleanup, Rest Time, Sharing Time, Free Time, painting Pictures to Go on the Refrigrator, Running Around Pretending to Be Jet Robots, Trying to Remember Where Your Sweater Is, and Snacks.

As a result of this course of study, the class developed several concepts, which were posted on the bulletin board over near the Really Tall Tower Made from Blocks. These concepts reveal a wide diversity of opinion about the Origins of Man, ranging from the traditional Judeo-Christian Biblical concept:

"This is Adam and Eve. They ate the bad fruit. They went back to God. They didn't have any clothes."

To the less-conventional Big Bird and Oak Tree concept:

"In the beginning of the world there was a big bird and an oak tree. The big bird had a coconut, and the moon was out."

And yet from this eclecticism of belief has emerged *The Cave People,* a work that has not only a strong sense of cohesiveness, but also has a great big gray cave made out of papier-mâché standing right next to the piano, which is sort of holding it up.

As Act One opens, some Cave People are sitting in front of the cave, and almost immediately the theme of Animals Running By is established by two woolly rhinoceroses, portrayed by Owen Smith and ROBERT BARRY, running by and making a noise like a 33 rpm recording, played at 45 rpm, of a bull elephant with its private parts caught in a trash compactor. And although the audience was unable to see the faces of these two fine young actors directly due to the fact that they were wearing yarn-covered paper bags over their heads, the power of their performance, especially that of the lead rhinoceros, ROBERT BARRY (the one who did not have his arm stuck through the eyehole), was such that even veteran drama critics such as myself were moved to take upwards of 20 color photographs.

This was followed by deer running by wearing antlers and brown underpants and waving at their parents, which set the stage for a moment of powerful drama as the dreaded saber-toothed tiger, played superbly if somewhat blindly by Matt Dorio with something on his head, came prowling by, bonking into things, causing the Cave People to poke each other with their spears and laugh. "They were really scared," explained the narrator.

The Getting Trapped in the Cave by a Giant Rock theme is then introduced by means of having the Cave People go inside the cave, then having the giant rock, which had been held up by a piece of yarn, fall down and almost block the entrance. In fact it probably *did* block the entrance, in rehearsal, although in the actual play, the piano player had to shove the giant rock over with her left hand, but she did this with a very natural and convincing motion. Just then *another* group of Cave People emerged from behind the piano and had the following realistic primitive dialogue with the ones that were trapped:

PEOPLE OUTSIDE THE CAVE *(in unison):* You guys inside! Push hard on the rock!

PEOPLE INSIDE THE CAVE *(in unison):* OK!

This is followed by an absolutely stunning bit of staging as the Cave People all push on the giant rock and, as if by magic, it rises *straight up in the air.* Believe me when I tell you that there was not a dry set of underwear in the audience at this point.

The Animals Running By theme is then reintroduced as the dreaded saber-toothed tiger bonks its way back on stage, and the Cave People stab it about 50,000 times with their spears until it is, in the words of the narrator, "totally dead." The theme of Getting Everybody Back Onstage is then established as the Cave People invite the deer and the woolly rhinoceroses to help them eat the tiger. In the cheerful words of the narrator: "They all sat down, roasted him, ripped him apart, and had a delicious meal." The concept of the meal being delicious was dramatically reinforced by having the Cave People say: "Yummy!" and "This is a delicious meal!" Of course, the woolly rhinoceroses, being unable to speak, could only pat their stomachs in a satisfied manner, but they did this in such a convincing and moving way that even veteran critics wanted to rush right up and give them a great big hug.